Cumb
Within Living Memory

WITHIN LIVING MEMORY SERIES

Other Counties in this series include:

Bedfordshire
Buckinghamshire
Cheshire
Devon
Hampshire
Herefordshire
Hertfordshire
Isle of Wight
East Kent
Leicestershire & Rutland
Northamptonshire
Oxfordshire
Shropshire
Somerset
Staffordshire
Suffolk
Surrey
West Sussex
Warwickshire
Wiltshire

Cumbria Within Living Memory

Compiled by the Cumbria Federations of Women's Institutes from notes sent by Institutes in the County

Published jointly by
Countryside Books, Newbury
and
CCFWI, Kendal
CWFWI, Carlisle

First Published 1994

COUNTRYSIDE BOOKS
3 Catherine Road
Newbury, Berkshire

ISBN 1 85306 301 0

The cover photograph shows Jim Benson with his wife and daughter in the farmyard at Knott Houses, Grasmere in 1902, supplied by Hawkshead WI

Designed by Mon Mohan
Produced through MRM Associates Ltd, Reading
Printed in England by J.W. Arrowsmith Ltd, Bristol.

Contents

Acknowledgements

Cumbria Cumberland and Cumbria Westmorland Federations of Women's Institutes would like to acknowledge with thanks the contributions made to this book by so many members and friends. All have given much time and thought to this joint project.

Sadly, we were not able to include extracts from every submission as to do so would have meant some duplication of content and of course, we had to take into account the total amount of space available in the book. However, all have been extremely valuable in deciding the shape and content of the finished book and we are grateful for each and every one.

Mrs Marjorie Morris (Cumberland)
Mrs Edna Hodgson (Westmorland)
Joint Co-ordinators

Foreword

Cumberland and Westmorland, the most north-westerly counties of England, and the Furness area of Lancashire, were moulded into Cumbria with the national boundary changes in 1975.

Cumbria is predominantly rural. We have England's highest mountain, Scafell Pike, although Helvellyn and Great Gable are most popular with climbers. Wastwater is England's deepest lake with its forbidding screes. To the north is Hadrian's Wall on the border with Scotland. To the east the Settle railway (Carlisle–Leeds), with its magnificent viaducts, cuts across the fells; wild beautiful countryside concealing remote villages, where the local dialects are still preserved in this modern age.

Tourists come to the Lakes in search of Wordsworth's daffodils, Beatrix Potter's Peter Rabbit or the islands of Arthur Ransome's Swallows and Amazons.

This century is disappearing all too quickly. Let us recapture the period 1900–1960, not as the historians will record it, but told first hand by ordinary people going about their day to day lives in this beautiful county. The kind of reminiscences, sometimes happy, sometimes sad, which our members enjoy sharing with their grandchildren or remembering with a friend, are all part of life's pattern.

Doreen Galbraith
Eileen Wilson
Federation Chairmen

CUMBRIA

SCOTLAND
NORTHUMBERLAND
Brampton
Carlisle
Wigton
Alston
Aspatria
Maryport
Cockermouth
Workington
Penrith
Keswick
DURHAM
Whitehaven
Appleby
Brough
Kirkby Stephen
Ambleside
Ravenglass
Windermere
NORTH
YORKSHIRE
Kendal
Sedbergh
Kirkby Lonsdale
Ulverston
Barrow
LANCASHIRE

TOWN & COUNTRY LIFE

Snow Ploughing

SOME TOWNS AND VILLAGES REMEMBERED

'Standing the market' in Kendal, life on the shores of Windermere during the First World War, the communal bakehouse in Wigton in the 1920s, the bustling seaside resort of St Bees in the 1930s – how long ago it seems, but all within living memory. Here is just a flavour of Cumbria's towns and villages as they used to be.

LIVING ON WINDERMERE

'In 1871, my grandfather, James Richardson, a leather manufacturer from Newcastle, hearing that Mr St George Curwen of Belle Island, Windermere, was offering for sale two plots of land with water rights on the west shore of Windermere Lake, purchased one opposite White Cross Bay. On this land he built a house as a holiday home for his increasing family and a boat house and pier on the lake. This made Balla Wray, the name he called the house, in Furness, while the boathouse (which jutted out into the lake) was in Westmorland. For some years until their death, he arranged for his wife's parents, Jeremiah Dixon and his wife, who had suffered badly from a bank failure in Newcastle, to live in the house. About this time, following the great shipping and cotton boom in Lancashire, large houses were built on the east side of the lake, with beautiful gardens, many designed by Thomas Mawson.

Until my grandmother died in 1914, my two sisters and I, my mother, father, governess, cook and housemaid, came for a few glorious weeks in the summer, by train from Newcastle to Carlisle, changing at Oxenholme, travelling past the Shap Fells, where we sometimes saw wild horses. At Oxenholme, a cart and horse took the mountains of luggage and we travelled in an open waggonette drawn by two horses, the ten miles to Balla Wray. The only public transport to Ambleside and Grasmere was an open yellow-painted charabanc, known to us as the "yellow peril".

In 1914 the house became our permanent home. During the war, Father was working in Newcastle, coming over by train for the weekend. Mother used to row across the lake to Millerground, where there was a ruined chapel built by the monks from Furness Abbey.

It might sound as though life, in what is still a fairly remote place, was difficult, but once a month the grocer, Gibson, called from Ambleside, to take grocery orders and these were delivered the following week. A butcher's cart came from Ambleside each week and the meat had to be cooked at once as there was no refrigeration. We grew our own vegetables, and the gardener's wife kept our hens and did the laundry in the gardener's cottage behind the house. The post office was at High Wray, a quarter of a mile away. Mr Weedon, the postmaster, drove in his trap to Wray Road End, where he met up with our gardener to exchange mail – he collected the post from our gardener and the gardener brought back our post in a locked leather bag. Telegrams were delivered from Ambleside by a boy on a bicycle. Milk was delivered from Beyond The Fields Farm, owned during the First World War by a family called Bennet, whose 13 children included three sets of twins. Large quantities of goods such as coal came in on the cargo steamer, the *Raven*, from the station at Lakeside. Four pleasure steamers, the *Swan*, the *Tern*, the *Teal* and the *Cygnet* plied up and down the lake in the summer, with a brass band on board for entertainment.

We had a rowing boat so we could row up to Waterhead and walk into Ambleside to shop. I well remember rowing up with our gardener to visit Hayes Nursery Garden, then only recently opened and full of all sorts of horticultural goodies.

The story of life at Balla Wray continued through the next war. My mother died very suddenly in 1942 and my father retired. My sister, whose husband was working in India, came back with her three children.

Woolton pies were delivered to High Wray each week and my sister would deliver these. The school had closed and Miss Taylor, the excellent headmistress retired and the children walked the two miles into Hawkshead. A telephone had been installed in the post office, but no electricity as yet.

The scientists at the Fresh Water Biology Research Station, then at Wray Castle, added greatly to the social amenities. Amongst other research, the scientists inaugurated a scheme for improving the fishing in Lake Windermere by culling the over-large population of perch. Traps were laid in suitable places during the spawning season. My father volunteered to help and was allocated ten traps. The traps were lifted once a week. The fish were then collected by the scientists at the castle, weighed and measured, and then sold to the fish canners. Some people may remember buying tinned perch instead of sardines. Father received an honorarium from the fish sales money. The scheme lasted for about three years.

One day, arriving home from picking up her youngest from school in Hawkshead, my sister heard faint shouts from the lake and could see in the middle an upturned boat and two heads in the water. My father had also heard, so we both rushed down, got out the boat and rowed as fast as possible to the heads. Two Canadians were hanging on to an upturned canoe. The men were "salvaged" and shortly rescued by men in an outboard motor boat who had seen the accident and promised to find transport for the soldiers.

By 1946 passages to India were beginning to be available and so my sister was anxious to return to her husband. However, postal strikes and the war had made communications difficult and she had children to look after. One day, a young man on a motorbike arrived at Balla Wray. He explained that he was a radio operator recently demobbed, and being licensed he was occupying himself on the HAM band and made contacts all over the world – one of his contacts turned out to be the radio officer working for her husband in the remote Himalayan state of Sikkin. He suggested taking my sister to his home in Troutbeck if he could arrange a time for her to have a conversation with her husband. It seemed miraculous and a day or two later she was whisked up to Troutbeck on the motorbike and had a ten minute conversation with her husband half a world away. A few months later she was able to join him, leaving her family, my father and the house in my tender care. By this time we had both electricity and telephone and slightly more public transport.

All the large houses on the east side of Windermere Lake have become hotels. The steamers are still running in the summer but very few rowing boats. Despite the cars, the tourists, the noise and the pollution, the area is still incredibly beautiful at all times of the year.'

'I remember Windermere being frozen several times, but one time especially. It would be about 1935, and the ice was so thick that cars were being driven onto and over the lake. A brazier was set up and baked potatoes and chestnuts were in great demand. Being a venturesome child, it had been instilled in me that I must treat frozen ponds and lakes with respect – the idea of the brazier melting the ice and the people crowding round it, resulted in me giving it a wide berth!

In contrast, I was on Windermere in a motor launch when Sir Henry Seagrave attempted to break the world water speed record. Imagine our horror when his boat, apparently after hitting a log, went head over heels, resulting in the death of Sir Henry. I still have a piece of his boat that we picked up as it floated by. Sadly, on Coniston Water much more recently, the quest for the water speed record resulted in Donald Campbell's death.'

LIFE IN WATER STREET

'We lived in a one up, one down in Water Street, Wigton in the 1920s. There were six of us then, but nine before we got a council house. There was a communal bakehouse where you could get your bread and cakes baked. We had to borrow their tins and Mother made the bread. Everybody had a special mark to put on top, then they were baked in the big oven: it cost threepence for six loaves. You borrowed a tray for teacakes, which cost threepence a dozen. People took tatie pots, meat pies and cakes; they cost a penny or twopence. There was a special day for Christmas cakes.

On Thursdays Sara Jane Thurlow made a big pan of broth. Neighbours went with bowls or jugs; she charged a penny or twopence. There was a fish and chip shop in the street; it was threepence for fish and a penn'orth of scrams were free. For milk you went with a jug to the horse and cart where they ladled it out of big churns.

There were certain old women who went to the back door of the pubs for a jug of ale; some of them smoked clay pipes. It is said they could make a tatie pot with only an Oxo. On Saturday night after ten o'clock we were sent to the butcher's to get a "wrap up" for a shilling. There were no fridges in those days. We were lucky at Christmas – we always had a goose as Dad helped to pluck poultry for Dick Pooley. We used to hunt mushrooms and sell them for a penny a pound, and brambles for a halfpenny. We had to give the money to Mother. There was a sweet shop in the street. He used to loan money – you could borrow £1 and you had to pay back £1 1s.

Washing days Mother had to take the clothes down the lonnings near the gasworks and hang them on the fence. One of us had to stay off school to stay with the washing to keep the cows off it. I can never remember having to take them home because it rained. Those days we never had anything on our feet all the summer holidays. We could play marbles on the street as there was no traffic, only horses and carts. When it was the horse sales we would stand holding a horse for a farmer for threepence a day.

At Whitsun time the fair came to Wigton. We used to go out on the Carlisle road to meet them. We used to put our ears to the road listening, then there would be a shout, "They're coming they're coming", and off we'd run to meet them. Most of the roundabouts cost a penny or twopence a ride. They used to be on Market Hill. There were stalls up the streets and young lads stood at the fountain waiting for farmers to ask them "Are you for hire, me lad?" They used to hire them for six months for £4 or £5. That was a good wage.

A peaceful scene in the village square at Dalston in 1920, before the motor car took over the roads.

When Dad had a boiled egg for breakfast we took turns getting the top of his egg. It was a great treat as we only had bread and jam. If we wanted our clogs "corkered" we went to Jimmy Johnston; it was a penny for a front caulker and a halfpenny for a heel, and we sat and watched him doing them. When we went to pay our weekly bill at Maggie Ann's grocer's shop, which was always between £1 and £1 3s, she gave us a bag of mixed sweets. There were two other shops where we could get goods and pay it off at sixpence a week. John Studholme and Willie Park were kind shopkeepers. We could take our hoops to Bob Nixon, a blacksmith, to be mended. If he was in a bad mood he made us wait an hour or more, but he didn't charge.

On Sunday we had to go to church in the morning, Sunday school in the afternoon and Benediction at night. We didn't like Sundays, and Dad was a member of the Salvation Army so we had to go and listen to them singing on the street. The family, except Mam and Dad, are all still living around Wigton but it is a different world nowadays.'

MORESBY MEMORIES

'As a result of conditions laid down by Lord Lonsdale, the previous owner of the land on which Moresby Parks is built, no public houses were allowed in the village itself. The nearest was at Scilly Banks, a 15 minute walk via the steep Scool Brow, and another, slightly further away, was at Quality Corner. Neither possessed a bar, the beer being served straight from barrels in the cellar.

The butcher, fish man and fruit man came round the village three times a week. During the war the butcher used to come round, and because of rationing the meat was already wrapped up – it could even include a sheep's head. Mum made pig's foot pie with lights, hearts and pig's foot. Also during the war, there were soup kitchens for the children.

I can remember living at Grandma's. We had the front room where we cooked, ate and lived. We also had a bedroom. Mostly Mum cooked on a little fire, but on a Sunday she used to put her meat in the oven in Grandma's kitchen. There was a deal table in the kitchen which we used for everything including ironing – "a long wallop" was an expression Mum used when she was just going to give something a quick rub over with the iron.

There was no water in the miners' cottages, except for the pit manager's house. He and the pit deputies had the "better houses", i.e. the ones at the ends of the rows. Occupants of the other cottages shared three outside taps to a row. There were outside washhouses with dolly tubs and dolly sticks. The washing was put to soak on a Sunday, but in the early days of Moresby Parks, the pit manager had very strict rules – no washing was to be hung out on Sunday, or tenants would be put out of their houses. It seems, on recollection, that somehow everything was washed, dried and ironed all in one day. Where there was a communal washhouse, each person had their own set day for washing – heaven help you if it rained on that day.

The same strict rules decreed that steps must be washed and roads swept, and a policeman and two roadmen enforced those rules. The outside steps were smartened up using "Red Raddle-Ironstone" which was wetted and rubbed over the step. The steps were then edged with white using a local type of pumice stone. Knives were sharpened on the sandstone side of the front door.

Homes were heated by coal fires and lit by oil lamps. The local joiner, who was also the undertaker, carpenter and churchwarden, sold paraffin. The drum with the tap still exists. Electric lights were only put in in 1934. Everyone burnt as much of their rubbish as they could on the fire. In Parton, the rest was thrown through the arches onto the shore. People would take a bucket of rubbish, dump it, and then fill the bucket with coal collected from the shore. Washed sea coal burned bright. The locals knew that, after a high tide, there would be plenty of coal for the picking.

We would sometimes take our tea down to the beach – jam sandwiches and a bottle of water. We played for hours. When we got a bit peckish we would go and find an old tin can and boil "covins" (cockles). They made a lovely snack, as did "flithers" (limpets) which we could fry on a tin lid.

There was a very good train service locally, and trains ran regularly. A special memory is of going to Keswick on the train to see the fireworks. We also went down to see Grandma at Drigg on the train. Grandad used to man the crossing at Saltcoats. During the war there were trains carrying armaments passing through Saltcoats, running at different times in case they were sabotaged. Grandad would never know when he would have to close the gates until the phone call came, sometimes in the middle of the night. The railway line through Moresby Parks became a goods only line after the war, and then, in common with many other small branch lines, closed down altogether in the 1960s.'

BORN IN BORROWDALE

'I was born in Borrowdale but came to live in Little Langdale when I was nine years old. How very different my childhood was to that of today's children – no cars, no radio or television but I am sure we were more contented than children are today.

Four-horse coaches came up the valley each day from Keswick in the summer, taking visitors over Honister Pass to Buttermere and back to Keswick. Passengers had to walk up the steepest parts of the old road to make the going easier for the horses. One of my earliest memories is of a journey from Keswick to Ambleside by horse coach and then by horse and trap to Little Langdale to visit my grandparents; I was four years old.

I started school in Borrowdale when I was five and I hated it. Our cottage was in a block of four; oil lamps and candles were used for lighting, water was carried in buckets from the nearby beck. The weekly washing was done in the back kitchen where there was a large boiler; dolly tub and dolly legs were used and a large mangle with wooden rollers – not the easiest thing to use.

Flooding was a real hazard in the valley which could be cut off for some time in very wet weather; there was a big flood in 1895 when the front of my grandparents' house in Rosthwaite was washed away. I have a pewter pint mug which my father picked up from the beck edge, obviously from one of the hotels.

Slate quarries provided employment for many of the local men, who had to walk each morning to the top of Honister to work and back at night. Wages were paid monthly and varied greatly depending on how much saleable slate was produced. Men who worked on the valley farms were hired at the half yearly hirings, as were girls who worked in the farmhouses. All the farmers' wives would make butter and take it to Keswick market to sell along with eggs and perhaps fruit and flowers. Most girls in the Lakeland valleys went into private service, as I did on leaving school. The work was hard and days long. There was usually a large cooking range to be blackleaded each morning if one was a kitchenmaid. My first wage was seven shillings a week and when I married in 1940 I was earning 18 shillings a week. We were allowed one half day off and half a day every other Sunday and had to be back in the house at 10 pm.

There were many more children attending the village school in the early days of the century; I was told that 50 children came to school from the ten cottages at Lingmore View. Now these houses are all holiday cottages as are many others in the valley. At Eastertime when I was at school I remember it was customary for many children to have a new dress or coat to wear at Sunday school or church on Easter Sunday. At Sunday school we were given the Collect for the appropriate Sunday to learn and to be able to repeat it. On Easter Monday we rolled our pasche eggs which were dyed by being wrapped in onion skins and a piece of cloth, each egg turned out with a different pattern. I have two that are about 40 years old.

The annual outing to Morecambe was a great treat when we were children in Little Langdale. We had to walk down to Colwith Farm to board the bus, an old fashioned open-topped one with a canvas hood. We left at 7.30 am, stopped at Strickland Arms and again at Carnforth, arriving at Morecambe about 10.10 am. It was a wonderful day for everybody.

The slate quarries provided employment for a hundred men at one time but at present only seven or eight here in Langdale; others are at the Kirkstone quarries. How times have changed, but not always for the better.'

KENDAL

'Until I was 13 we lived on a small farm about three miles north of Kendal on the Appleby road. We had a "lot" (allotment) on Benson Knott where we gathered bracken for bedding. This was loaded onto a big, low sledge pulled by a horse, and it always seemed to be my job to go on the sledge to load the bracken as my father forked it to me. I shall never forget the painful scratched legs I had (no jeans then).

We used to "stand the market" (have a stall) in Kendal on Saturdays, selling butter, eggs, poultry and sometimes flowers and plants. At Easter we sold pasche eggs and at Christmas, holly wreaths. These were made on a base of hazel decorated with holly sprigs (some variegated if possible) fastened on with raffia. After the market finished we would go to the shops for essentials like wicks and glasses for oil lamps from Baillie and Hargreaves in Finkle Street, or tea and sugar from the Co-op (also in Finkle Street) or Daish's or the Maypole. All these shops had wooden floors and lovely polished wooden counters. Brunskill's, on the corner of the Market Place, was a special favourite which sold haberdashery, materials, household linens and clothes. We also had travelling salesmen who came round once a fortnight for a grocery order. Shopping done, we would go to Thackeray's on the Market Place for fish and chips, or the Cocoa Rooms in Stramongate for pie and peas. The Cocoa Rooms belonged to my Auntie's parents and her father and brother made the pies at their bakehouse at the bottom of Kent Street and carried them along the New Road in big wooden trays covered with tea-towels, on their heads!'

'Monday mornings in the early 1920s would find me waiting on the shop doorstep to watch the farmers guiding their flocks of sheep along Stricklandgate on their way to the Auction Mart, which is still on Appleby Road.

On Saturday afternoons I would hear the roar of voices and loud cheers and a passer-by say, "Someone has scored a goal." These sounds came from the nearby rugby field at the top of Maude Street.

Then, in 1929, I remember, with the rest of the scholars from Castle Street school, going over the Stramongate Bridge, through Stramongate up Finkle Street, down Stricklandgate and up Maude Street into Maude Meadow, once the rugby field and now a beautiful park to be renamed "Nobles Rest" in memory of Dr Noble, a well respected physician in Kendal.

His widow, Mrs Noble, had had the field transformed into a beautiful garden with a large shelter, a sandpit for the children, paths and a lawn for the children to play with their balls, two more shelters and plenty of seats for the older people to chat as they enjoyed the colourful flower beds and sunshine and kept their eyes on the tiny tots at play. On warm days Mrs Noble would come into the park with her maid Ada and enjoy hearing what we had learnt at school that day.

The garden is now mature and well cared for, very popular with people who enjoy a picnic lunch there. It is still well used after over 60 years.'

'Yard 50 Stramongate was once the servants' quarters, and stable block, of a Young Ladies Academy. The school building is Georgian in style, and has an elegant frontage. It was divided up long ago into separate housing.

My best friend lived with her godparents in the old servants' quarters down the cobbled yard. I first went there in 1945, and have never forgotten those happy days, and the surprise of stepping back in time.

Fay's godparents were in their sixties when they offered to adopt her. She was the last of a very large family. Fay called them "Alf and Liz", and loved them dearly. Alf kept pigs in the old stable block, and the little house, which was a wing of the old school, was a living museum of Victorian days.

Liz had been a housemaid to Lord Ashton of Lancaster. The stories she told could fill a book. Alf helped his father deliver milk by horse and cart to the big house. They met, married and moved to Yard 50, in a horse and cart, of course.

The house had two rooms and a small kitchen and a pantry downstairs. From each room, a door concealed a staircase which led to two bedrooms. They had no gas or electricity. Tilley lamps, candles and a huge black range provided lighting and heating. The kitchen had a stone sink underneath, and a pump. I understand the old well was still in use.

The floor in the kitchen was stone-flagged with rag rugs. The ceiling was studded with hooks for hanging hams and flitches which Alf cured. A huge black kettle always steamed away over the fire on a ratchet. The walls in the kitchen and the sitting room or parlour were a picture gallery. Liz had gone to Lancaster and bought up pictures and bric-a-brac from the sale, when Lord Ashton's mansion and estate were sold. I remember titles like "Bridal Morn", "Two Strings To Her Bow" etc. The parlour held treasures which we did not recognize then. Every flat surface was covered with china figures, china plant holders, lovely photograph frames in ornate wood and brass, and a mahogany china cabinet half filled the room, packed to the hinges.

I lived in a terraced house, and although we had "mod cons", I thought Yard 50 was fabulous even then.

Fay and I were typical young girls, not too interested in past history. However, we were intrigued with the idea of the school ghost. Liz told us the story. She was a "Miss Blackdrop". This was her nickname. She had been the head teacher. Her father had made his fortune by manufacturing the opium-based medicine locally named Kendal Black Drops. I have a feeling that they were extremely addictive, and no doubt were used with ill effect.

Poor Miss Blackdrop, so we were assured, was the victim of a violent death. The story spread that she kept her father's fortune in the garden buried in a strong box. Her ghost haunted the garden, still guarding the spot.

Fay and I often sat in the garden. It was full of old apple trees, and old rambling roses. Needless to say we never saw Miss Blackdrop. I sometimes wonder if we had had the use of a metal detector, maybe we might have found her fortune. Now, alas, it must lie, if it ever existed, under tons of concrete. Yard 50 was the victim of so called modernisation. The Georgian facade of the school is still there, and all my lovely memories remain.'

ST BEES IN THE 1930s

'In the 1930s St Bees was a popular seaside resort. People mostly had no transport and did not go on continental holidays. During the holidays long trains from Whitehaven pulled into the station, every carriage bursting with people, especially families with buckets and spades going to the beach. Even from Seamill Lane at the top end of the village swarms of people could be seen walking along the road to the beach. Buses also dropped people at the station. Holiday makers from the Lancashire mill towns used to come up and have bed, breakfast and evening meal in the guest houses, those on the Crescent being nearest the beach, although any house which could take visitors did.

Quite a lot of the well-to-do people from Whitehaven and Cockermouth, mothers and their children, would come to stay in the guest houses for the whole summer; the fathers joined them either each evening or at weekends.

The promenade at St Bees was not built until about 1960. Before that grass led onto the shingle with the sand and rocks beyond. Mr Tyson had the concession to sell from his ice cream barrow on the grass. There was a small car park for about twelve cars. An old bus was parked from which snacks and pots of tea were sold and deck-chairs rented out.

Outings to the beach for the village children involved a walk or ride on a bike to the beach, taking sandwiches and pop, which was sherbet put into bottles of water. They could not always afford lemonade, which came in bottles with marbles at the top.

In 1935 a swimming pool was opened; it had been blasted out of solid rock by the unemployed men of the village under the direction of Capt Spedding (retired). It had a deep end, with a diving board made out of scaffolding and also a spring board, and a shallow end. There were chains around the pool. High tides came over and filled it (sometimes bringing in crabs and jellyfish); when the tide went out it stayed filled. At one end was an old car; the engine was used to pump the pool clean.

Popular St Bees beach in the 1930s.

On payment of twopence children received an ordinary elastic band to wear around the wrist and to hand in at night. This allowed them to go in the swimming pool. They used to make house-like changing places in the crevices in the rocks, putting towels across the top. Some used bathing-robes, made from a towel with a string around the neck.

Parents gave very strict instructions, but were not afraid of the children going out and playing all day. They had to be home by six o'clock. They were not to go round the rocks alone, in case they slipped and fell, but they were allowed to go in groups. They were not allowed to climb the cliffs, although some of the boys did. They knew not to swim at high tide or when the rocks around the pool were too slippery. Frank Lewis generally sat near the pool with a book. When they were not swimming the children went onto the sand to play ball games, build sand castles decorated with shells and seaweed, make tunnels in the sand for the sea water to come in or they played around the rocks catching crabs.

The swimming pool had been built by men with expertise gained through working in the pits (mainly the iron-ore mines at Egremont). It closed because of the war; men found work in the pits again and the pool gradually silted up as there was no one to maintain it.

A shop in Finkle Street sold sweets, groceries, home-made ice cream, "Monster" lemonade and mineral waters; its sign was a giant tin "Monster" bottle. There was an electric shock machine outside, a penny a go.

Across the road was a bakery selling bread and cakes. Across

Lonsdale Terrace, Miss Walker's needlework and haberdashery shop ("Outfitter's for the Public School") was famous for the shilling bundles of oddments in the sales about three times a year. Miss Walker painted on china, sending goods away to be fired, before putting them on sale in the shop.

Next door was a high class grocer's, smelling of freshly ground coffee. Mr Goss always had a lovely white coat on.

The Gas Office was upstairs on the corner opposite. Next door on Cross Hill was the butcher's shop. Up above by some stairs outside was the clogger and shoe repairer. The paint and wallpaper shop was across the road. Next to this was the blacksmith's shop. Children could watch the horses being shod by peering through some knot holes low down on the big double doors. Carts were also mended there. Next door (on Main Street) was The Royal Oak.

Near the bottom of Main Street were a sweet shop, a hardware store and a plumber's and a very small shop selling high class chocolate and sweets, jewellery and fancy goods. "You went around the tiny counter to have your hair cut."

There were three banks, all near "The Queen's". Next door to "The Queen's" was another bakehouse, then the Co-op. The greengrocer's was next to the Co-op and two doors farther up next door to the post office was The Queen's Arms, a jerry pub, just selling ale and beer.

A coal merchant and haulier's was across the road and the newsagent's with a chocolate machine outside like the post office. A market gardener lived next to the newsagent's. Across the road were the stonemason's office in a little old cottage and another grocer's. A bike shop where cycles were repaired was opposite School Lane next but one to another plumber's. The joiner and undertaker was farther up Main Street.

The middle cottage opposite Outrigg was a shoe shop and repairer's. Up Outrigg was the slaughterhouse. Animals were bought at the Monday auction in Whitehaven. Boys wishing to play football used to go to the slaughterhouse for pigs' bladders. Lower down Outrigg was another bakehouse and another haberdashery.

Next to the chapel lived the proprietor of a taxi and coal merchant's business. There was a fish and chip shop near the top of Gas House Lane. There was another sweet shop on Main Street "with the odd bit of grocery and, of course, paraffin."

Down Seamill Lane a market gardener also did wreaths and there were two houses where people visiting the beach could get a pot of tea.

For shoppers from St Bees, Whitehaven market had attractions. People thought things were cheaper. Other things, which were not available in the village (such as lino and curtains) could be bought there. It was a place to meet friends and stop for a chat. Visiting relatives in Whitehaven might be a regular part of the outing.

The market was not all stalls; there were people with baskets selling produce, perhaps butter and eggs. A market gardener from St Bees took flowers and vegetables to sell. Most people walked from St Bees to Whitehaven, although some went by bus. Mr Butler, coal merchant and haulier, would go every Thursday with his horse and flat cart. He waited in a certain place at a set time and people could have their shopping taken home.

The bus would go down the hill past Greenbank Farm; at the bottom there were bushes and only smoke could be seen rising from a house called Seldom Seen. Sometimes the bus stopped there for a little old lady and a child. (Greenbank Estate had not been built, so there were very few stops on the journey.) Passengers sometimes had to get out and help push the bus up the steep hill by Demesne Farm.'

IT DOESN'T EXIST ANYMORE

'I am writing about a place called Oldside, which doesn't exist any more, just in name. It was mainly an ironworks, plus two rows of workers' cottages. They had two rooms up and two down. The six with bathrooms were for foremen, and the manager had a double-fronted house with a small garden. My grandfather was a blast-furnace man.

I was born at Oldside, in the days when the district nurse attended home confinements. Though I didn't actually live there, I spent as much time as possible at Oldside, because it was very near the sea and we spent a lot of time on the shore. My Granda was a clever man, and made toys from driftwood, and door mats from old rope found on the shore.

The houses were small, fireplace and single cupboard filling one wall, but they had electricity, when no one else had it. My Grandma's house had a bathroom, but no toilet, this being out in the yard. When the works closed, everyone suffered, as they had to revert back to using oil lamps. All cooking had to be done on the fire, or in the oven. They had to wait quite a few years before gas was installed. We didn't go short of food, because Granda grew most of our vegetables in his garden. When the fish-car came around, herring were sold at 16 for one shilling. A grocer's van called twice weekly. It was a big box cart, pulled by a lovely Clydesdale horse. In the front was the hardware – brushes, fire shovels and buckets etc. The food was at the back – sweets, sugar, tea, flour, yeast and most things needed. I can still remember the smell of that van – mint balls, boiled ham and not forgetting the horse! There was even a draper who visited

Oldside works and cottages, Workington. An unpromising site, but when the cottages were about to be demolished, no one wanted to leave.

Oldside, and was always called the "Cockermouth Man" because he lived there.

It was about a mile and a half to town. Not far, but it seemed a long way when carrying shopping. One way into town was across the dock, and the dock bridge, another was across another bridge always known as Halfpenny Billy's Bridge, which was a railway bridge, and a halfpenny toll had to be paid. Going by road, the new bridge had to be crossed.

We always had plenty to amuse us, and our lively imaginations helped a lot. We played shops, using stones or fragments of pots as sweets, and Granda made me some scales from tin lids and picture chain. During summer we had carnivals, using old lace curtains for the queen's train, and bindweed for her crown. We organised concerts, the song of the day being *There's something about a soldier* to which we performed a dance routine. On sunny nights people met at the corner, and someone would produce an accordion, and before long a dance would be in full swing. People danced until after dark, and longer if the moon shone.

It was a wonderful place to live. Not elaborate by today's standard, but we all knew and helped each other, and when the houses were about to be demolished, no one wanted to leave the place. It had its drawbacks, but these were outweighed by the pleasures!'

DOWN THE STREET

Perhaps you would meet the lamplighter, a familiar and loved figure of our childhood, or the 'milk lass' on your journey down the street. You would probably pass the village pub, and the village butcher might be hard at work on slaughtering day. Most of us knew each other in those days – for good or ill! – and even the bank manager took a very personal interest in his 'clients'.

OUR ROAD

'I live at Rosley, by the busy Wigton to Penrith main road. As children, living at Tracen Tree in the 1920s how different it was. We played marbles, hopscotch or ran our hoops on the road – knocking the caulkers off our clogs and making Dad mad. In summer my Dad let his cows graze on the roadside and our job was to watch them. A favourite pastime of Dad and his mates was penny pitching, played on the roadside, while we sat on a wooden seat behind the hedge and watched.

Tuesday, though, the road was always busy – it being market day at Wigton. Horses and traps were driven in, clip clopping smartly along taking country folk to the town, and sheep and cattle were driven to the auction there. Later, John Willie Pearson ran a market bus from Sebergham. It was a funny, high, narrow bus with the door at the back and long seats up each side – so you sat facing one another. Baskets with butter and eggs going, and groceries returning, went on the roof, all put there by John Willie climbing a ladder at the back. In between times he took the top off and used the base as a lorry!

The week before Whit was an exciting time. Gipsies ("potters", we called them) in their horse-drawn caravans were passing along the road one after another, going to the Rosley Hill fair – a big gipsy gathering at the Camp Field where horses were bought and sold. A lot of beer was drunk in the Hope and Anchor pub. On Whit Sunday night we were taken a walk along to see everything. Gipsy grownups ignored us. Grubby children gazed at us and hungry looking dogs roamed everywhere as we wandered about among them. I can still smell the smoke from their wood fires. A tale is told of one gipsy who, when drunk, hid his wad of notes for safety in the wall surrounding the hill and, when sober, had forgotten where it was. I believe it's still there!

During the National coal strike in 1926 the road was a hive of activity. Men, young and old, dug coal out of Coalhole bank across the road from our house. It was hard work lugging the coal up to the road and there was a lot of shouting and swearing. On carts and in all kinds of vehicles – even barrows – it was trundled away, mostly the four miles to Wigton.

We had our regular tramps calling either begging or selling things like pins, needles and shoelaces. A special one was "Tin Whistle Billy" who played his whistle and danced for money. Well known were mother and son, Mary and Jimmy Ruddy, who collected and sold rudd – hence their nicknames. (Rudd was a red stone we used for smartening up doorsteps etc.) They had a pram and she smoked black twist in a clay pipe. In 1962 Jimmy, a very old man, was killed on the road – still pushing the pram containing his belongings and with his dog tied to it. My friend aged 95 remembers a tramp called "Nanny Knockabout". There was also whiskery "Tom Post" on his bike, the scissors grinder and the paraffin oil lady selling the oil off the back of a horse-drawn cart. There was no electricity or gas of course in Rosley. Looking back they were all interesting characters.'

THE VILLAGE PUB

'The Traveller's Rest at Cowrigg was a small farm-cum-jerry – the name for a public house licensed to sell beer, not spirits. The landlord came from farming stock, and had a wife and four daughters. The land was poor and infested with rabbits which, when caught and sold, paid the rent and the wages. The rooms held the bare essentials of furniture – a scrubbed deal table and chairs and a long form, bare stone floors except for the rag rugs made from cast-off clothing.

The farmhouse kitchen doubled as a public bar, and all the cooking was done on a range, which also heated the water brought in by bucket. The parlour was also licensed but only used by the public for special occasions.

The beer was kept in a cellar and drawn from a barrel by tap, and the glasses were served on a tray to customers sitting at table. The patrons were local except at weekends when some came from further afield by the local bus. Cards, darts, dominoes and rings were the popular indoor pastimes, and in the summer there was Cumberland-style wrestling in the garden.

Saturday was market day and the farmers' wives travelled by bus with their butter, poultry and eggs to Carlisle market and brought back the week's shopping. The bus driver loaded everyone's baskets onto the roof, climbing a short ladder fastened to the side of the bus, and anchoring them securely with a rope.

Saturday evenings were the high spot of the week. After a few drinks singing commenced, accompanied on accordion, bagpipes, spoons, bones and mouth organ. The words of songs were often changed to fit local gossip, but best of all were songs composed by locals.

Local christenings featured a lot in pubs. A friend of the family would be sent to the parents' home to steal a dish of rum butter which would be eaten by everyone in the pub and the empty dish used to collect donations and returned to the parents.

Carling Sunday was another memorable day. A two gallon pan was filled with soaked carlings (peas) and cooked in ham stock until "mushy". Everyone in the bar was given a plate of seasoned carlings and a round of ham sandwiches. Men would go from pub to pub partaking of carlings at each, and often laying bets on who could eat the most.

The farmers would insist on taking a portion of their profits from the local auctions in cash. This provided them with spending money and a "snek lifter", which was sixpence or more which they left with the pub landlord to enable them to lift the door snek (latch) and enter the pub later knowing they had enough money to buy a gill, costing threepence and a packet of Woodbines (cigarettes) twopence for five.'

'One old custom held in The Royal Oak was the Court Leet, which according to records in the Carlisle Castle archives can be traced back to 1472. It met to deal with town and country bye-laws and to appoint constables for Braithwaite, Portinscale and Rogerset. The last one was held on 5th June 1931.'

THE LAMPLIGHTER

'As a child, I daily walked two miles to Flimby school with my five brothers and sisters. One summer morning we saw some men digging a series of holes in the roadside. When asked why, we were told they were going to light up the pavement, so that we could see better as we walked to and from school during winter. We thought this a huge joke, and laughed among ourselves, as we had always walked in the dark and never felt afraid. However, as autumn approached, these same men erected a lamp post in every hole, with a four-sided glass box on top of each one, surmounted by an ornamental pinnacle.

We daily followed their every move with childish interest, until one morning our patience was rewarded. We saw a man with a bicycle, who stopped at every lamp post, and using a long thin pole with a hook on the end, he pulled a short chain downward, and behold, a gas mantle lit up inside the glass and cast a glow over the pavement. To say we were fascinated is putting it mildly, as we used oil lamps at home and really had no idea how gaslight worked. To us children it was sheer magic – lights on the roadside! We soon learned to run between each two lamp posts, keeping up with the lamplighter, so that we could watch a repeat performance, and very often made ourselves late for school.

In later years, I was in the senior school when war was declared in 1939, and how life changed! No longer were our magic roadside lamps lit, as everything was under blackout and no light had to be visible from the sky. Our school windows suddenly had thick curtains which were drawn before any light was lit. When victory was declared, it was wonderful to see the wayside lights shining again, and even yet, whenever I hear that phrase from the Bible – "Let there be light" – my mind immediately goes back to those childhood days, when I stood spellbound, watching the lamplighter work his magic.'

THE MILKMAID

'Oh, to be a milkmaid! Immediately one conjures up a picture of a flaxen-haired damsel, with mob cap and snow-white apron, carrying two buckets full of foaming milk, and always the sun streaming in the background. Sounds idyllic, but pictures can be deceiving! In 1947 I worked on a milk round in our village, using a pony and trap to carry milk churns, from which I ladled out pints and gills into various receptacles (not always jugs). As I was an early morning caller, I saw people exactly as they lived. Most had curling pins in their hair, no false teeth in, last night's make-up on, slippers and dressing gown, breakfast dishes on the table, and nappies in the kitchen sink.

The "milk lass" was expected to know many things not even remotely connected with the farming industry, such as, "Is this gingerbread cooked far enough?", "Why isn't my geranium flowering?", "Will six ounces of wool knit our Jack a pullover?", "Have you got a penny for the gas, or the kids will get no breakfast." I often found myself between disputing couples, and very soon learnt to be a "Philadelphia Lawyer". I'm sure I'd have made a good candidate for the Diplomatic Corps any day.

I regularly delivered a basket of dirty washing to a daughter, then returned it, washed and ironed, to "mother" later in the week. One of my other customers was the "hatched, matched, and despatched" lady of the village – midwife at numerous births, served tea at all local weddings, and enjoyed nothing better than laying out anyone who had died. She was a real village character, and could tell many interesting tales. Some were gruesome, if not frightening. Her weekly milk bill was quite low as she bought only one gill daily, yet she would keep the money in her hand, rattling it tantalizingly, but not offer to give me it, until I'd heard every detail of the latest corpse she had laid out, describing the snow white lace-edged pillows, hand crocheted counterpane, laying-out robe and long white silk stockings, saved specially for the occasion. If the deceased was a person she hadn't liked, she would say "He has as much chance of getting into heaven as a celluloid cat walking through hell."

I sold milk at fivepence per pint, but it cost only twopence ha'penny for children under five, and expectant mothers, who had to "register" with me as there were still some wartime restrictions. My old pony was well known in the village, and knew exactly where he would get a crust of bread. He often left me far behind, as he wandered on, seeking the next tit-bit. I was very often soaked to the skin during stormy weather, but the golden rule was to look pleasant at all times. If I complained to my father he would say, "Without rain there'd be no grass. Without grass, there'd be no milk, and without milk you wouldn't have a job, so be thankful it rains."'

POST AND TELEGRAMS

'The postman at Finsthwaite used to carry stamps before the post office was provided. If a parcel needed posting it was taken to the lane end and the postman had a little weighing machine and would say how much it would cost and it was paid, with a little extra for putting on the stamps.'

Telegrams for my parents, living at Low Holme in Cumwhitton parish in the 1920s, came to Armathwaite post office. The method of delivery was for someone to come to the west bank of the river Eden opposite Low Holme and shout or whistle to alert one of us to go down to the river's edge to receive the message. This was done by shouting across the river.

In 1924 a telegram came for my father, and this was being delivered by a woman who came down to the river's edge (west side) but as the river was very swollen and in flood she was unable to make her shouts and whistles heard by anyone at Low Holme farmhouse. Seeing my father's boat moored on the west bank, she got into the boat, hoping to row herself over, but the volume of the water in the river was so strong she lost control of the boat and was being swept down river. Fortunately she got near enough to the east bank and grabbed tree branches, and managed to scramble to dry land. The boat going down water was never seen again. I well remember this lady arriving at the farmhouse drenched through, and my mother getting her in front of the kitchen fire and supplying her with a change of dry clothes.'

THE VILLAGE BUTCHER

'In the 1930s Monday was butchering day at Ivegill. The animals to be slaughtered had been bought the previous week either from Carlisle auction or from local farmers and were kept in a shed next to the slaughterhouse. On Monday mornings they were taken in there, sometimes with great difficulty as if they knew what their fate was.

The afternoon was spent making potted meat and pies. Sausage and black pudding was made at intervals during the week, all to be sold from the van going round the countryside. All this was done without the aid of electricity, the only refrigeration being had from one hundredweight blocks of ice brought from Carlisle once a week and stored in a large insulated cupboard.

At the onset of the war all individual butchers had to stop their work at home as meat was rationed and was distributed by the government from central slaughterhouses.

The only butchering allowed was of the pig, which farmers had a licence to keep for their own use and this took place on the farm.'

A FRIENDLY BANK MANAGER

'In the early 1900s my Aunt Maud was housekeeper for a bachelor bank manager who lived in Brampton. She used to tell me how he would set off, quite often on foot and wearing a plaid, to walk to Shopford, Bewcastle, a distance of eleven miles. He usually went on Friday evening and stayed to Sunday having met some local farmers and dealt with their financial affairs. Apparently he sometimes imbibed too much so when he asked Maud to marry him she decided against it as he fell downstairs one night when he was drunk! Many years ago she gave me a rather attractive knitting stick which he'd made for her with '1906' carved on it.

One day when out on business in the country area with pony and digby he visited an elderly maiden lady who was ill and had to go to hospital. Being poor she was quite distressed because her nightgown was rather shabby. She, like the bank manager, was very large so when he got home he said to Maud, "Do you think any of my nightshirts would fit Margaret Clockey?" That wasn't her real surname but according to country custom people were often called by the place where they lived and her home was Clockey Mill.

My aunt, being a good needlewoman, sat down and made outsize nightdresses for Margaret. The bank manager presented her with them and then took her by pony and digby to the Cumberland Infirmary, which must have been an uncomfortable 14 mile journey for a person who was ill.'

FACING THE WEATHER

Tales of snow, flood, hurricane and tempest can probably be found in every town and village in our county, and we have become used to dealing with the worst that the skies can throw at us. Here are just a few – remember the winter of 1947?

SNOWED IN

'I was brought up at Stephenson Ground, a sheep farm skirting the edge of the Dunnerdale Fells. Early in 1940 there came a big snow storm and the drifts were so high in our farmyard that my father and brother dug a tunnel through for the cattle and sheep to be able to walk to the beck to drink. The roads were more than full of snow, with no walls or trees in sight. Much time was spent getting sheep out of the snow. Many farmers helped the council men dig tracks to outlying houses and farms, to allow people to get out to the shops. The tracks were about two and a half feet wide with 16 foot high sides. It was by far the most snow I have ever seen. Woodend Farm, on the top of Birker Moor was completely covered – the houses, farmhouse and all the buildings, trees and walls were just one blanket of snow.'

'In 1941 we went to live on a farm in the small village of Croglin. The farmers' work was long and hard, and not having mechanical transport they had to walk the fells to shepherd. The Helm wind which is local to this area wasn't easy to battle with on foot. One farmer had sheep five miles up the fell. He would walk up at

Flooding brought damage to roads and houses in Glenridding in 1927.

seven o'clock in the morning and wouldn't get back until very late at night, often carrying a couple of distressed sheep in a sack over his shoulders.

Snow was another element to cope with. I remember the particularly heavy snows of 1947 when we were blocked in for a whole month. I was expecting my fourth baby and was relieved when the midwife managed to get through two days before he was born.'

'Unusual weather can often disrupt people's lives and Cumbrians are no exception to this. In the winter of 1946/7, very heavy falls of snow were experienced all along the west coast of Cumbria, which included Waberthwaite and Corney. In particular, Foldgate Farm at Corney had an unusual experience.

There was a wedding due to take place at Corney church, and snow began to fall just before the bride set out for the church from Foldgate Farm. However, they reached the church safely, and the wedding service went ahead. The time came for the bride and groom and all the guests to leave the church, but dismay came upon them when they saw what confronted them outside. The snow had been falling very heavily, and there was no way that the taxis could get going. Everyone had to make their way on foot as best they could. Even the bride in all her wedding finery.

Foldgate Farm was reached safely, but the taxis were marooned at the church for three weeks.

Meanwhile at Waberthwaite, the snow had blocked the A595 right through Waberthwaite and beyond. Travel was impossible, and none could negotiate Muncaster Hill or Broad Oak. By report, later, it was found that everything was at a standstill from Millom to Whitehaven.

When the snow had ceased men were employed to clear a way along the road, but the snow was so deep that they only cleared enough to allow two people to walk through. Later Italian prisoners of war were brought from Silecroft and provided many more hands to cope with the work, and eventually snow ploughs were able to operate.

Snow remained on Black Combe until June, and over at Foldgate Farm huge drifts as high as the telegraph poles remained for many months.'

'There are so many memories of the terrible early months of 1947 in Dentdale. I remember when my grandfather died in Sedbergh that year. His funeral in Dent had to be delayed for a week because the road from there to Sedbergh was blocked with snow. When we finally had the funeral, we had to walk the mile and a half from Peggleswright through a narrow channel which had been handcut through the snow. The drifts were high above our heads. I was terrified and thought the snow would cave in and we would be buried alive. Local men earned extra money by going out snow-cutting. It took months to get all the roads, especially Dent Head, open again.'

THUNDERBOLT

'Around 1927 a thunderbolt landed in Crosthwaite school yard. In those days The Punch Bowl was also a smallholding, where Mr Howcroft was watering his cows. He was knocked down and a cow was killed. The lightning set fire to the church choir stalls and services had to be held in the Memorial Hall for a while. The thunderbolt made a furrow along the road and ended in a market garden owned by Tom Noble. This storm also hit Tarn-side Farm and threw Mrs Prickett across the room and made cracks in the walls.'

HURRICANE

'I kept a cutting from the *Evening Mail* in 1945 which reported the Bardsea hurricane. It reads: "Some 50 trees, the largest of about four feet in diameter were uprooted during a storm of exceptional violence which struck Bardsea village on Tuesday. During the storm at about 5.45 pm, a strong wind from the direction of Morecambe increased suddenly to what is described as hurricane force. A house on the Coast Road had its slates blown off, but Wellwood was the centre of what looked like a miniature whirlwind. Trees were uprooted in all directions, even though some, when prostrate had roots ten feet long showing above ground. At the same time there was a downpour of rain of tropical intensity and the gutters and spouts were quite unable to cope with the flood. The whole affair lasted only ten minutes and fortunately nobody was hurt and no livestock reported injured. The oldest inhabitants can recall nothing like it having ever happened before.'

FLOOD

'On 26th June 1953 Troutbeck suffered serious flooding, following severe thunderstorms. In the early afternoon a cloudburst occurred at the head of the valley and a torrent of water swept down, carving a ravine ten feet deep and the same width. It carried thousands of tons of earth and rocks into the fields below. Beckside House was undermined and Stonethwaite Farm was ruined. A young man from the south, staying at the Mortal Man Hotel, was washed down Scot Beck while attempting to save poultry. Sadly, he drowned and his body was found at the Ford Bridge a mile down the valley.'

CHURCH AND CHAPEL

Church and chapel were so much part of our lives in the past that a Sunday without attending at least one service and, for the children, Sunday school would have been unthinkable. In fact, Sunday school treats were often the only outings children had and were eagerly awaited each year and fondly remembered. And, of course, it was in church that the old social divisions were often so apparent.

PART OF OUR LIVES

'When I was a little girl I used to walk Miss Ellen Bowman, from Gawthrop, to church in Dent on a Sunday. She always dressed in long black clothes and walked very slowly as she had a limp.

I think one of the biggest changes in my lifetime has been in the part played by the parish church in village life. When I was a girl, 60 years ago, it was the centre of our social life. There were over 40 of us in the choir . . . we overflowed the choir stalls. Today the average congregation is around 40. Choir practice itself was a social occasion and then there were Choir Balls and Churchwardens' Balls and socials throughout the winter. Harvest supper then was at the vicarage and was for all of us who had helped to decorate the church for the Harvest Festival. Then the church was the giver, not the taker as it is now. A church charity paid Tom Mattinson to bake bread specially on Saturday. This was put on to the table at the back before the Sunday morning service and those who needed to, helped themselves. Old ladies would bring a basket lined with a clean cloth, to take their bread home.

It was only a few weeks after Len Pickfold moved to Dent to farm Hugh Croft when his horse died. His fellow churchgoers, knowing that he could not farm his land without a horse, had a collection to buy him another.

Mr Burrow from Gate Manor, who gave Dent the reading room, had a number of tenants. He expected to see all of them and their families in church.'

'The present building at Thwaites is the third church to be built on the present site or near by, there being no trace of the two previous buildings. There were two customs, now extinct. One concerned the parish baptismal robe. This garment was loaned for each baptism, then laundered and returned in readiness for the next time. The other was that of fastening the churchyard gate after a wedding ceremony, until the bridegroom had paid a ransom in pennies thrown to waiting children. The gate was then opened, allowing the wedding party to go on their way.

There is the story of one of the clerks, an old man who kept the Mill Inn. He used to "blow into a little box", put it to his ear, then start the hymn. The little box is still in the church safe, it looks like a wooden mouth organ, but alas – it is quite dumb.

Across the road from the church, there was a building for parishioners to stable their horses, whilst they attended church. This building has now been converted into an additional room for the use of the school.'

'The curfew was rung every night in Kirkby Stephen as a signal for children to go to bed. It is an old custom dating back to the days of William the Conqueror, when the English were compelled to rake out their fires and extinguish their lights at eight o'clock. It is still rung, though the bell is now mechanised. We always referred to the curfew as the "Taggy Bell", and I rang the Taggy Bell many times when I was young in the 1930s.

The "Death Bell" (No 8 Bell, the biggest) was always rung when anyone died.'

SUNDAYS

'Sunday at Troutbeck began with morning church service, with the landed gentry arriving accompanied by uniformed senior members of staff, and always chauffeur driven, there being a lot of bowing and saluting.

Sunday school was in the afternoon, then a visit to grandparents, where aunts, uncles and cousins congregated for tea. It was always a delight to sample the goodies provided by aunties and our mother.

A return to church for evensong at 6.30 pm, being a member of the church choir. We always had a practice on Thursday evenings. Then we took the long route home, harmless fun, but we received many a scolding for arriving home late.'

At the beginning of the century the Rev Simon Inman was vicar of Finsthwaite for 42 years. When encountered in the lane, girls would curtsey and boys raise their caps. He married late in life and he and his new wife gave a party for the schoolchildren, every child receiving a threepenny bit. The children had contributed towards buying a writing cabinet for them, though one little girl, seven years old at the time thought when she saw the gift that it was a salt box.

Thomas Newby Wilson, a local benefactor who was the main contributor towards the building of the Institute, the church and the school, came to church every Sunday in a carriage and pair. He put a golden sovereign in the collection every week! The coachmen stabled the horses across from the church and then came and sat in the back pews. They wore very smart navy blue suits with lots of brass buttons, top boots and top hats with a cockade. They were very much admired and one Sunday during the service a little girl leaned over to look more closely at the hats on the pew in front of her and her prayer book fell into one. She was mortified but her aunt picked it out and never mentioned it again. The coachmen would go out during the last hymn to collect the horses and carriage and were standing outside when the congregation came out, looking magnificent.'

'One of the farmers at Irton used to fancy himself as the Squire.

He used to attend Irton church all dressed up. One Sunday he was at church, which was pretty well full, when a great aunt of my husband's arrived and went into the pew he was occupying. He had his elaborate top hat on the seat by his side where she wanted to sit so she asked him to kindly remove it to enable her to sit down. He refused, so the lady sat on it and squashed it flat! Good for her.'

'Sunday school and school were the framework of my life at five years old. Our vicar at Coniston in the 1920s was the Rev Fred Wilcox, cousin of Charles Lutwidge Dodgson (Lewis Carroll). He too was a mathematician and a story teller of great invention and humour. He visited us with fruit when we were ill and in his prime was vigorous and well liked. He was also an early photographer, showing us his slides as a Christmas treat at school.

Sunday school was enjoyable, especially in the summer when classes could be held in the vicarage garden. Sometimes after Sunday school we went with older children to peep in the windows of Holly Howe, now a Youth Hostel, where during the war a Belgian Count in exile had murdered his family and hanged himself. Alas, I never saw the ghosts I was looking for!'

THE SERVICE IN THE KITCHEN

'Some of my happiest memories are of holidays spent with my grandparents at Challon Hall, a farm by the river Bela, Preston Patrick.

Every Sunday, a Wesleyan Methodist service was held in the stone-flagged kitchen and we sat on wooden forms which were stored in the granary during the week. I sometimes helped by dusting them before the service.

We would carry the harmonium into the kitchen from the hall and also the desk which held the family bible, and rested it on the round table. We sang the hymns heartily and I even accompanied them on two or three occasions.

I can vividly recall sitting beside my grandmother and stroking her black fur tippet while the preacher gave his sermon and the grandfather clock ticked on. Sometimes my eyes would gradually close. There was a large open log fire with a steel fender and a pegged hearth rug. The kettle on the hob would sing while the crickets on the hearth chirruped in harmony.

The service took about an hour and the congregation were local farmers and their families and the other friends and relations. Some of them had walked or cycled quite a distance, but all were dressed in Sunday best.

Once, during the service, on looking through the window into the orchard, I was horrified to see the farm cat run off with one duckling after another and I was powerless to run and rescue them! They had been reared by a broody hen and had escaped from the wire-covered chicken coop.

After the final hymn and prayer, the preacher was always invited to Sunday tea in the sitting room, with silver teapot and best pink china. Cakes and currant pasty were served and jelly and tinned fruit (usually eaten with bread and butter).

We children were allowed to join the adults as soon as we were twelve years old, otherwise we sat with the farm hands at the well-scrubbed kitchen table for our meals. Our Sunday reading was the *Christian Herald* or the *Sunday Companion* but not the *Westmorland Gazette*!

The Harvest Festival service was always a joyful occasion as we brought in stooks of corn and flowers to decorate, as well as the fruit and home grown vegetables. This was followed by a sale of produce on the Monday night, and supper.'

WHY NOT SMILE A LOT?

'The chapel was not only our place of worship, it was also our social life. The Sunday school anniversaries were the highlight of the year. We were all dressed up in new dresses and new suits for the boys, to sing and say our "pieces" (recitations). The first one I remember saying:

"A smile is just a little thing
It does not cost a jot
It's free to beggar and to king
So why not smile a lot?"

The Sunday school trip was also enjoyed. From Hethersgill we went to Whitley Bay generally, from Ravenstonedale it was always Morecambe. Big cases of food were taken on the bus with us, and when we arrived at Morecambe outside a church or chapel hall it was unloaded and members of that church had the tables ready and while we went to enjoy ourselves they prepared our meal (dinner), then we had tea before leaving.

When we moved to Scotby we attended the Railway Mission in East Tower Street, Carlisle (now a carpet showroom). On a Sunday evening after the 6.30 pm service some of the men who attended went on the streets and invited the soldiers and ATS girls into the hall where favourite hymns were sung and sandwiches and tea were served. New Testaments were given if anyone wanted one. On the front row each week were the local tramps (roadsters) but they always treated us with respect. There were army camps at Durranhill (where the Borderway Mart is now) and Hadrians. On a Monday night there was a Christian Endeavour for young people and many of the soldiers attended. Tuesday night was the prayer meeting and Thursday night the Bible Study, on the Saturday nights often Youth Rallies. Other churches were very active too and as we had friends there we always had somewhere to go. People used to love hearing the Salvation Army playing every night outside either the Courts or Town Hall in Carlisle.

Ravenstonedale was full of young people. On a Sunday night about 20 young lads would meet at the bottom of the village when going to chapel. Dad used to invite them in to the service but if they didn't come in they would be playing tricks on someone. One night when going out, the preacher's car was wedged in a farm entrance and it took all the men from the service to lift it up to get it out. One night a turnip rolled in during the service, another night the lights went out, and in winter most people killed pigs so pigs' tails were plentiful, sometimes sent through the post. One night a lady arrived in chapel and the young men had pinned a pig's tail on her back as she had come in.

During the war the "War Agriculture" cut the corn and they generally cut it when they wanted. As father's corn had been cut on the Saturday and hadn't all been stouped that night, while he was in chapel on the Sunday, the lads had put a stoup up the full length of the field and a stack in the corner. He never said anything, just put it right on the Monday. Next Sunday night as he went to chapel the lads were sheltering from the rain and he said, "Rather wet for stouping corn tonight, lads."

In 1945 father was very ill and not expected to get better. No penicillin in those days, but M and B tablets were in use. There were prayers for him in both the chapel and church. We had a lovely Church of England vicar who had a big parish but he made a point of visiting every house in the parish over the year whatever denomination people were. A few weeks later I stayed in with Dad while Mam and two friends who were staying, walked to chapel. After they arrived home a knock came on the door and the lads said, "We've come to see how Mr Calvert is keeping." "Come on in," and 22 young men came in, supper was made, I think every tin in the house would be opened. Father played the piano and great was the singing. Some of these are preachers today. Young people were not condemned, they were loved, but they were mischievous. Often if a young man fancied a young girl and she wasn't very keen on him, he would send a dish of cold rice pudding – it's supposed to be good for love!'

CAMP MEETING

'Every Whit Sunday at Hallbankgate a Camp Meeting was held for the Methodists. Local preachers would take part and there would be music and hymn singing and an address. It was always held outside in a field at Clowsgill Holme and wet or fine, hundreds of people would attend.'

SUNDAY SCHOOL TREATS

'A lovely sunny day in 1938, excitement in the air, waiting for the train to come in at our little railway stop, to take the children of Keekle Sunday school on our outing to St Bees.

I would be up early, washed under the cold tap, and dressed nicely, but not in my best dress. My mother would be organising the case which we would take with our bits and pieces in – towel, lemonade, sandwiches. It was a day I had waited for all year. We would stand on our doorsteps, and when we saw a train coming over the viaduct we'd run down the field, the Sunday school teachers following with clothes baskets full of cakes etc for our treat. It was always a lovely day, something to remember.'

'Memories of meeting at the station at 1 pm prompt on Saturday. A real steam train to Greenroad near Millom and a short walk to the field. An afternoon of games, sack races, egg and spoon and, of course, rounders. Queuing up for tea, a paper bag full of goodies with home-made lemonade and strong sweet tea. Home at 6 pm, exhausted mothers making sure no one had been left behind. Walking home at the end of the day – no cars to ferry us home, but happy thoughts because the sun always shone!'

BAND OF HOPE

'We always had pleasant times at the Band of Hope in Bothel. Temperance hymns were played by the local cobbler. In charge was Mr Johnston, the village butcher, who sold Cumberland sausages from his shop. Mr Tom Nicholson, who worked for Mr Johnston, took the register, answered by saying "present", and we paid a penny. This went towards a trip to Silloth. The meeting was held monthly and after prayers one child read a chapter from the Bible and other children were encouraged to write poetry. Sometimes as a special treat there was a magic lantern show by a Mr Brown.

The trip to Silloth was very special and looked forward to by the children. We were all given a brown paper bag with sandwiches and a cake and also some lemonade. My most vivid memory is of the coloured streamers which we were given to hang out of the windows of Kirkpatrick's buses.'

GETTING ABOUT

From the days of real horse-power, the early obliging buses, the very first motor cars, and the steam trains that were a part of all our childhoods, to the present age of rush and noise is a large step indeed, but not such a long one in terms of years.

CHANGING TIMES

'We start out in a luxurious pram, and I remember my father fitting a bicycle lamp to our pram during the First World War – all prams had to have a light on them. I remember my parents being told "Halt! Who goes there?" whenever we passed the army camp on our way to catch the train after visiting my grandparents.

The train was another experience! Travelling to the junior school, I soon learned to grab a seat with my back to the engine – it saved getting grit in the eyes from the steam engine!

Next came the rattling tram-cars with the backs of the seats that reversed so you could always look forward – wooden seats and an open top if you climbed the stairs. A twopenny return ticket took you to your first job. Then the trolley bus, swift, silent, upholstered and a choice use of the Queen's English when the trolley came off the overhead wires!

Private transport was great – sitting in a tub-trap and bowling along to the accompaniment of a trotting pony. Or when I was a teenager, riding in a side-car, and what a side-car – it was shaped like an Edwardian invalid chair and was made of wickerwork with a big leather apron to keep you dry. The old motorbike that it was attached to was driven by a leather belt composed of solid leather links and it invariably used to snap so we always carried spares. It was replaced by a very smart two-seater carriage-built side-car which always attracted attention – it was a new concept in side-car travelling. Who could forget the musty, leathery smell when you rode in a horse-drawn "mourning coach" at a funeral? Being small and wearing socks I invariably stuck to the leather seats and that bred in me a hatred of leather upholstery that has stayed with me to the present day.'

'In the early 1900s travelling was by spring cart and pony or a digby, this had a door and steps at the back and seats at the side, the occupants facing each other two to a side – more if they were children. Any outing was always by trap and the hotels in Silloth had stables for horses then. My father taught me how to harness a horse to the trap. You had to get the balance just right, if you didn't you got a very jerky motion but getting it right meant you just sailed along as smoothly as can be. I took a pride in that. Of course, we used the Clydesdale horses on the farm for ploughing and what was called a slender horse for the carts. If a journey had to be made by night two candles were lit in lamps at each side of the trap. I remember visiting my grandparents at Aldoth on a black night, pouring with rain. There was a trap rug and also a leather apron which covered your lap. When we got there, there was a great pool of water in this apron.

During the 1920s only one or two people had bicycles since not everyone could afford a bike and I shared one with a friend. If we wanted to go somewhere one of us would start to walk and the other would ride, then they would put the bike in a hedge and start to walk. The walker would then get a turn to ride and went on a bit further and the same thing would be repeated.

There were no coaches or charabancs before 1914 but horse-drawn waggonettes brought trippers from Silloth to the Tarn, where there were boats and canoes for hire and a tea garden. Cars were a rarity until the 1920s. I remember one in 1923, it had a pram hood and the windscreen wiper was pushed by hand. By 1939 one or two farmers owned cars, but in the fields the faithful and intelligent horse still reigned supreme. When I was very small I was lifted on to a cart with a load of hay ready to be returned to the farm. The horse Tommy was told to go home, and he did, negotiating the farm gates to get there, with only me in charge. We were all very attached to the horses and my father wept when Tommy finally had to go. Horse-drawn carts and waggons gradually gave way to motor lorries, the first of these appearing in the Holme area about 1930.'

'At Coniston in the 1920s it was still the age of the horse. An abiding memory is of timber waggons being hauled up Station Hill by a double team of magnificent Shires, with much shouting, grinding of wooden wheels and snorting of the animals. Later, the team returned for the second heavy load, left on its waggon at the foot of the hill.

Horses were used for all transport then; carts took goods from the railway station to shops, hotels and farms. Our groceries were delivered by horse and cart monthly in sacks and large quantities, coal came by the cartload, ash pits and earth closets were cleaned out into a cart.

The hotels had horse-drawn cabs meeting the trains, and every week a cousin of ours drove by horse and trap from Woodland with home-made butter for delivery in the village. I well remember the day the horse took fright coming down the last hill and raced off with the shafts, leaving my cousin in a welter of broken eggs and spilt butter!

Travel locally was by horse. Dr Kendall rode to his distant patients, farmers took horse and trap to market and the local lady, Mrs Barratt, drove out in her Victoria behind coachman Barnes, to wave graciously when we duly curtseyed or doffed caps.

However, in 1920 the day of the motor car was coming. Miss Holt of the Liverpool shipping line used to come to Tent Lodge, where Tennyson spent his honeymoon, in her open Rolls Royce, H12, on which we gazed with awe.

Her Liverpool Boy Scouts on the other hand travelled by train, and marched to camp at Coniston Hall, behind their bugle and drum band, pulling their handcarts, or to church parade on Sundays, to our delight.

The first two cars to be owned by Coniston folk were stabled in our old barn until their proud owners built garages. Charlie Hellen's Model T Ford was taken to pieces and lovingly re-assembled before our eyes. When the time came for its trial run, my father and I were invited to go too. I sat proudly between the two men and we set off down the valley. Over four miles away, as we descended Sunny Bank Hill, I was told that that was Coniston Lake ahead. I declared it could not be, as it was at the bottom of Lake Road near our home. I was early learning geography!'

'In the days when ladies wore skirts down to their feet, elastic was sewn into the bottom and if you rode a bicycle on a windy day you put your feet in the elastic to keep the skirt down.'

'The first cars appeared in the village of Ullock in about 1936. A syndicate in the village had a half share in the Irish sweepstake ticket the day *Mamoud* won the Derby, hence the new cars – and new bicycles for the children.'

FOUR IN HAND

'In the early 1930s my grandfather was a four-in-hand coach driver based at "Fletchers" in Keswick; the stables were in Otley Road. He took tourists on the run through Borrowdale, over Honister Pass to Buttermere where refreshments were taken at the Fish Hotel, then back to Keswick over Newlands Hause.

If there was not a full load of passengers on the coach I was sometimes allowed to go with him. It was quite a frightening experience as the coach was very high and rocked quite alarmingly on the rough road. Most of the lady passengers walked up the Honister Pass and also down the other side, as at the top the "slipper" or brake was applied to the coach and the horses still had difficulty holding the coach back. The slipper was taken off at the bottom, and the coachman had to be very careful as it got to be very hot. The same procedure over Newlands, so the whole trip took quite a long time.

On returning to the stables I helped Granda sponge down the harness and bed down the horses ready for the next day's trip. I sometimes got a sixpence off some of the ladies on the trip!'

'Before 1914 the only transport in Far Sawrey was by horse or in an open Victoria. The roads were of dirt and many had potholes. In summer the highlight for many people was watching the coaches, some two-horse and some four, coming from the hotels in Bowness and Windermere and crossing the ferry on their way to Coniston. All able-bodied passengers had to get out and walk up the hills. No wonder they called in at the hotels on the way.'

'My father remembered the old coaching days well. A toll had to be paid at Waterhead when travelling into and out of Ambleside, and they were not always paid willingly. The wood waggoners who paid their toll into Ambleside strongly objected to paying again on the way out! They gained nothing by argument so decided on other measures. One dark morning, on arriving at Waterhead, they took their horses out of the traces, parking their waggons down by the pier, and then hitched their horses to the stoup of the toll booth. One determined effort and they had detached the booth from the toll house and towed it away. This happened around 1870 and in 1874 the toll houses in the district were sold off. I do not know what retribution, if any, overtook the miscreants.

When my father was a young man he worked for a time as a postillion on the coaches going over the Kirkstone Pass. Six horses were needed to get the coach up to the pass and only four were needed for the rest of the journey. So, he would travel as far as the pass and then bring the two extra horses back to Ambleside to be ready for the next outward trip.'

CROSSING THE FORD

The last known horse carriage crossing of the river Esk at the Roman Ford in Hall Waberthwaite, was undertaken by Mr and Mrs J. Jackson.

In those days, flower shows were held in the grounds of Muncaster Castle, and the people in the trap were en route for their afternoon's entertainment. The ford was just downriver from the church. There was a sloping, well marked entry and exit.

The trap entered the ford as usual, but before they had made much headway, water was seeping through the carriage floor. Some alarm was felt by the occupants of the carriage. A short distance further on, the horse was unable to find bottom and started swimming, leaving the carriage virtually afloat. However, luck was on their side and they reached the other side safely. And they went on to enjoy their afternoon in the castle grounds.

As far as can be ascertained there were no further crossings at this ford, but there is a rumour of some motorbikes which crossed shortly afterwards.

A notice board was put up, warning of the danger of the crossing. Shifting quick-sands further complicated the situation, and a violent storm later destroyed the chance of further crossings at that point. The ford is not in operation today.'

ON THE TRAIN

'My father-in-law grew up in the Station House at Penrith, his father being the stationmaster at the turn of the century. The Earl of Lowther (known as "The Yellow Earl") frequently entertained royalty and the nobility. King Edward VII and the German Kaiser would be greeted on arrival at the station by Robert Phizackerley dressed in his uniform of top hat and tails. The family would receive gifts of game from the Lowther estates and the stationmaster was a highly respected figure.'

'The railway station called Ravenstonedale was situated at Newbiggin on Lune. The stationmaster would go along the platform shouting "Ravenstonedale, Ravenstonedale", while the porter followed on behind shouting "Russendale, Russendale", which was the local name.'

'For many years Windermere railway station was very busy around 8 am on weekday mornings, with businessmen living in the district arriving to catch the special train to Manchester.

Until as late as 1948–9, one solicitor would arrive by carriage pulled by two and sometimes four horses, and always driven by Bert Postlethwaite. Others would arrive by chauffeur-driven car.

The luxury train was made up of club cars only, taking businessmen to their work in Manchester.'

'Can you imagine making a train journey today, where children could approach the guard on a train and ask him if he could stop the train to allow them to pick wild flowers from the embankment to decorate their country cottage? This was known to have happened in the 1930s when children were travelling from Carlisle to Port Carlisle on board *The Dandy*.'

'Flocks of sheep were walked to the Lazonby auction market by drovers. The animals came from the Pennine fellside and as far away as Alston, the drovers having a peculiar shout and flapping their coats to keep the sheep moving as they filled the surrounding roads. Sheep and cattle were also transported by rail to and from Lazonby station. There were extensive cattle pens and a loading dock which was so busy that they needed a special "cattle dock porter". There were five other staff and a good train service. The 8.25 pm express service from Carlisle stopped each night at Lazonby to pick up hampers of rabbits for Leeds market. Catching this allowed time to go to the first house at the pictures in Carlisle, and there was a special late train on Saturdays, so you could stay for the second house or even the Palace of Varieties.'

'Every one in Dentdale had turbary rights. When they had cut and dried the peats, they brought them down from the moor with a horse and cart. When the railway (Settle-Carlisle) reached the Dale in 1876, they could buy coal for the first time but at sixpence a hundredweight, it was too dear, "like burning silver".

Candle Willie came on the train. He walked down the Dale with two baskets of candles to sell from house to house.

The ladies of upper Dentdale have happy memories of travelling to Settle market every Tuesday. They left home, by bicycle, around 9.15, parked their cycles by the old reading room at Lea Yeat and walked the long hill to Dent station to catch the 9.50 train. They returned on the 12.10 train from Settle and were home again with their shopping in time for lunch at 1 pm. "The carriage was humming with chatter as we exchanged our weekly news until Dr Beeching put an end to our jaunts".

Jonty's father was killed in an accident on the road near Nellie Bridge. His mother had to try and make a living and she borrowed a horse once a week and went round the Dale collecting eggs, butter, hens and rabbits to sell via the railway. She boxed and labelled about 30 dozen eggs a week, getting half a crown a dozen for them. She put them on the train at Dent station and they went as far afield as Preston and Liverpool. Eventually she was able to buy a house for £24.'

'Shortly after being married in 1948, my husband was transferred from Barnard Castle to work in Ulverston.

We caught an early morning train at Barnard Castle station and, after crossing the Tees and Deepdale viaducts, ground up the long gradient through Bowes to the Stainmore Summit. We left the wild moorland scenery through the railway cuttings near Barras, which only the previous year had been blocked with snow for several weeks.

As we ran downhill to Kirkby Stephen the view over the Eden Valley was magnificent, with the Lake District mountains in the distance. It was then only a short haul to Tebay station, where we changed onto a southbound express train for Carnforth.

It is sad that this journey is no longer possible as the railway was later closed and only small sections of it converted into roads.

In those days a number of main line trains stopped at Tebay and Carnforth, and we were able to change from the express train to the Furness line connection at Carnforth for Ulverston.

The next part of the journey, which included the crossing of viaducts over the Kent and Leven estuaries, only served to emphasise how far Ulverston was in time and distance from the North East.

Nowadays a car trip takes only one and a half hours and my sense of isolation has vanished, as the M6 motorway can be reached in 30 minutes.

Since 1948 we have travelled afar, but nothing exceeds the excitement of returning to our Furness home with its beautiful surroundings and overlooking Morecambe Bay.'

OUR BUSES

'The bus service in Lorton was begun by my father in the early 1920s, when there was a regular service to Cockermouth from Lorton, Loweswater and Buttermere, with more buses on market day. The farmers previously cycled, walked or went to the auction by pony and

The first regular bus from Lorton to Cockermouth in the early 1920s, owned by George Scott. Buses were used for everything, from livestock to choir trips!

trap or horse and cart. My father's bus was used for everything – choir trips, school outings, visits to flower and agricultural shows included. It was even used to bring coal to the village from Bullgill Colliery during the General Strike of 1926. He regularly took parties to the Isle of Man in June, to the TT races, for the princely sum of 21 shillings per day.'

'From 1924 onwards we could get to Carlisle from Alston by Percival's Bus. As well as passengers, this carried quite a lot of goods and shopping on the roof. At Christmastime live geese and turkeys in hessian sacks with a hole cut out for their heads were transported this way.'

'I remember the first double decker bus that came through Rowrah. We used to rush out and wave every time it came, it seemed such a huge thing and we thought it would topple over!'

THE BUTTER BUS

'In the early 1920s in the village farms, dairying was one of the main occupations. After the cows were milked, it was put into a separator and the cream was drawn from the milk and ran into a separate container. The skimmed milk ran into another bucket and was later fed to the young calves. The cream was stored in a basement dairy, ten steps down and quite dark, as there was no electricity, in a big earthenware pot.

Wednesday, each week, was churning day. Two children were assigned to churn, one handle at each side and it could be tiring and laborious. The consistency of the curds had to be just right. That night in the dairy there would be rows of pounds and a few half pounds of butter, which had been shaped and patted, as well as decorated to entice customers. These were all laid out on a plate base and sometimes cradled in big, washed dock leaves, ready for the "Butter Bus", otherwise known by its correct name of the Maryport market bus, on Friday.

It is not known how it originated but Johnny Johnston, the celebrated sausage maker of Bothel, would take some farmers' wives in his waggonette to Maryport along with very delectable fare and it probably followed on from that.

The Butter Bus was motorized, a type of charabanc, open roofed in summer but roofed in canvas in winter to withstand the elements. He started in Ireby with one lady passenger from Uldale at approximately 9 am. My mother was the second passenger at Torpenhow where the children helped to load the butter baskets and possibly eggs too. Other ladies joined the bus at Threapland, Plumbland, Gilcrux etc en route to Maryport. The bus stopped at the covered Market Square, which has now disappeared, and baskets were laid out on the allotted stalls and selling began. As mining was a profitable industry there was no dearth of customers. The nicest part of the day was counting up the takings, having a light lunch and boarding the bus for home. Then the chatter would begin as to who bought what and why. If prices were down, goods were sometimes bought to be sold again another day at a higher price.

Mother returned home after a welcome break in the daily routine and the Butter Bus was put back in its garage ready for another Friday.'

JOHN WILLIE'S BUS

'As a child in Welton, around 60 years ago, I remember the Saturday morning market bus. Rain, hail or snow, Mr Pearson from Sebergham picked up his passengers and their produce, and drove off to the market in Carlisle.

The little bus, driven by its owner, was affectionately known as "John Willie's Bus". It was a small square Chevrolet vehicle with a rack around the top and a very steep ladder up the back. Inside it carried about twelve people. The seats faced each other and this gave the passengers, mostly farmers' wives, the opportunity to discuss local news, and any other gossip of the day. Children sat very quietly. They were rather afraid of those stern ladies, especially the older ones who were of the school of thought that children ought to be seen and not heard. This in no way took away the thrill of riding in the bus and spending the day in Carlisle.

That hard working little bus and its driver were kept busy all the week. Tuesday was market day in Wigton, and there were always goods to be delivered – even those heavy library boxes for schools were carried by Mr Pearson onto the top of the bus. The body was removable, leaving a flat waggon which took anything from hay, straw and turnips to sand and gravel.

Mr Pearson was a pleasant, slim little man, but he must have been very strong – he climbed that steep ladder with the heavy baskets on to the bus roof. There were baskets of butter and eggs, apples and other fruits from the farm orchards, but what is most clear in my memory are the chickens and hens in swills (shallow baskets) with hessian sewn over the tops. Small holes were cut in this for their heads to poke through. A sheet of oilcloth covered the butter baskets to keep the contents dry, but the poor hens must often have been soaked before they reached the market.

Sale was fairly brisk – most people had their regular customers, and by lunch time most of the produce had changed hands. Then came the shopping for provisions, and anything else needed on the farms for the next week.

For the homeward journey the baskets had to be loaded on top again, almost as heavy as they were in the morning. The conversation then was mostly about prices – how butter and eggs were much too cheap, and anything they had to buy was far too expensive.

If there was a dance in the district the bus was out again. Young people this time – girls in long dresses and young men in their best suits. The Welton Brass Band also hired the bus for outside events, and Mr Pearson played the drums.

Sadly, the little bus grew old and had to be retired. Everyone was sorry to see it go, but it will always have a place in local history, and it is certain we shall never see anything like it again.'

HOUSE & HOME

Weekly wash day on the farm

THE WAY WE LIVED THEN

No 'mod cons' that we take so much for granted today; dark, cold and draughty – those picturesque cottages and farmhouses were very different in the not-so-distant past. It was the way our families had lived for generations and we took it all for granted.

HOME LIFE ON THE FARM

'I was born on a small farm, three miles south of Keswick, in 1928. The farmhouse was over 300 years old. The staircase was carved out of the rock first and the house built around it.

My father had just recovered from double pneumonia. Times were hard but we had plenty of food, having our own milk, butter and eggs. Some of the poultry were table birds and we killed a pig and cured it each year. We had full-board visitors during the summer months which was our main income.

Our water was drawn from a well in the yard with buckets and when on the odd occasion that dried up we carried water from a stream on the fellside (a ghyll). In 1940 we had a hand pump installed in the back kitchen. We bathed in a tin bath in front of the fire, the floors were blue "flags" and a rug (home-made) only went down at night. We had linoleum in the parlour and mats in the bedrooms.

The earth closet was down the garden. It was kept dry with ashes and emptied by a barrow each week. We used squares of newspaper for toilet paper. Some of the cottages shared one toilet between three households. Some toilets had up to three holes in the wooden seats to sit on – all different sizes.

Our groceries were delivered once a fortnight. Flour came in four-stone bags which were later boiled, halved and used as tea towels. The women all wore cotton print overalls and "rough brats" for dirty work, which was a hessian sack made into a half apron.

We bought our first wireless in 1935. It was a Decca made by a local man who also made and delivered our hen-houses. While we were of school age we had always to be in bed by 9 pm when Big Ben struck so my parents could listen to the news in peace. We had no electricity until the 1950s so used paraffin oil lamps downstairs and candles to go to bed.

Jim Benson with his wife and daughter in the farmyard at Knott Houses, Grasmere in 1902.

The *Daily Mail* was sent by post each day – couldn't be done now. Any important news was delivered by telegram as there was only one telephone in the valley.

On the odd occasion we had a holiday, we went to Morecambe where you were able to have "apartments". We provided our own food and the landlady cooked it.

At local weddings, children tied ropes across the road until the wedding party threw coppers for them on the way out. There was no vandalism. It was quite safe to leave your cycles anywhere, or your doors unlocked. The only people we were a bit wary of were tramps and they were usually well known and harmless.'

'I remember on our farm at Rosley in the 1920s we had no tap water, no sink. All the water had to be carried from the pump at the top of the yard. We had an outdoor closet across the yard and through the orchard, round the back of a building. Ours had two holes. If it was dark we lit the paraffin stable lamp and we went in twos.

The grocer came once a month for the order. It was delivered by horse and cart from Little and Johnstone's, Carlisle.

The cows had to be let out for a drink at the pond in winter. My two sisters and I had to keep them there until Dad mucked the byre out. In the summer Mother had to milk the cows by herself. We had to hold the cows' tails so that they wouldn't switch her face and one of us flapped a piece of tin to fan her.

When it was haytime we had our tea in the field. Mother made a can of water with oatmeal in for the men to drink. It was supposed to be good for hot days.

We had to plant potatoes and gather them. We couldn't wash our hands so we ate some gay smelly teas.

If we wanted a doctor Dad had to bike to Dalston for one and he came on horseback. Mother had a medicine chest which consisted of camphorated oil, syrup of figs, Veno's and iodine. If we had a sore throat she used to blow sulphur through a rolled up piece of paper into our throats. It nearly choked us. Not forgetting "bi-carb" that cured burns, scalds, headaches and stomach pains!

A man came from Wigton with his horse and cart selling fresh herring, shouting, "Twenty for a shilling."

My Dad went to Carlisle every Saturday with the horse and cart taking vegetables like potatoes, carrots and turnips to sell. He stood on the Crescent at Carlisle for years. He put his horse in the Red Lion stables. He fetched and carried for folks on the way.

We had to walk two miles to school. There was 14 of us by the time we got there. If we stopped to talk one of us had to walk on then we ran to catch her up.

If we went to Wigton Dad used to put a box on the cart. Mother and Dad sat on that and we sat on the cart with our backs to them. That's how we travelled about.

There was a blacksmith's on our way to school. He let us blow the bellows to make the fire red. We watched him making horseshoes. He chewed 'bacca and kept spitting.'

'All the cooking in the 1940s was done on the open fire in the black kitchen range with its large oven. Many loaves of bread were put to rise on the fender in front of the fire, many plate cakes were made using the fruit in season. We had a large orchard and kitchen garden and fruit was bottled and made into jam. We picked burnets in the hayfield, which Mam made into wine. She also made lemonade and ginger beer, which were taken into the fields to drink in hot weather.

Monday was always washday. A fire was lit in the washhouse to boil the white clothes, which were given a final blue rinse. When dry, sheets and towels were folded and put through the large mangle and garments were ironed with a heavy iron heated by charcoal. Mam made most of our clothes on her treadle sewing machine, and I used to knit thick wool socks on a sock knitting machine, for Dad and my two brothers to wear with their working boots. Old clothes were cut up into lengths to make prodded hearthrugs.

Lamps were the only lights; the Aladdin lamps had to be filled with paraffin, the lamp glasses cleaned, the wicks trimmed and the mantles fitted. It was a great boon when we had calor gas lights installed in the three main rooms downstairs. The house and buildings were wired for electricity in the early 1950s and we were able to have lights only from a generator attached to the milking machine engine.

Although mains electricity was installed in nearby Gaitsgill in 1948 it took much campaigning to bring it to Stockdalewath and the nearby hamlets. Mr Glyn of Thistlewood wrote to Colonel Dower, MP, to ask for his support; his letter ends, "I look forward when a wave of your magic wand will both lighten our path and warm our bodies." He asked Dad to help him to visit local houses to see how much electricity they would guarantee to use in a year. This varied from £5 for a cottage to £40 for a farm or large house. We eventually received mains electricity in 1958.'

'Our farmhouse in Caldbeck in 1954 had little in the way of "mod cons". We did have a water closet next to the door into the farm yard; the earth closet in the garden was in the most inaccessible place (fortunately no longer in use). We bathed in a tin bath in front of the fire or went to our grandparents once a week for a "civilised" bath. The back kitchen had a tiny window over a flat sink which allowed the water to splash out. There *was* hot and cold running water – the supply came from a tank up the field which filled from a spring which ran down a gutter shared by sheep and cows. My "towny" cousin once came to stay and when she ran the tap to fill a glass she got a tiny frog in the water. Until we got mains water many years later she always bought a bottle of lemonade at the village shop on the way here.

The door into the living room was flush with the wall and the draught was terrible – a calendar on the wall flapped in the breeze. The Triplex grate smoked continuously and smuts covered everything. The sandstone flags in the back kitchen were always damp, smelly and uneven and had to be scrubbed regularly. We did have bottled lighting gas installed in the kitchen and living room and had a gas cooker, boiler and iron; only candles upstairs, and when we woke in the night we used a torch – many a time my mother nearly knocked herself out when she forgot to bend down to avoid the low doorway into the bedroom.

In wintertime the curtains blew in the draught from the windows. We had plenty of entertainment on winter nights when mice and rats ran across the boarded ceilings. One night my brother shouted that there was a mouse scratching in his waste paper bin. We managed to turn the bin over and capture it. By next morning it had eaten a hole in the carpet and escaped.

Although we had a car we depended on vans bringing our supplies: the gas man came every other week; the butcher on Saturday afternoon; Ivinson's traveller came and eventually a travelling shop; Robertson's bread van came on Friday evening (sometimes after we had gone to bed) – our special treat was to stay up to get crisps and sweets; Bardgett's (draper's) traveller came with a large suitcase of clothes and household linen.

In winter my mother wore a heavy tweed skirt and at least two woollen jumpers and a pair of my Dad's socks (very few ladies wore trousers then) – and this was in the back kitchen.

One incident stands out in my memory of my brother's first Christmas. He was given a chocolate Santa which was fixed on the top of the small tree. It would be there for a week or more and when he went to open it all that remained was the silver paper – a mouse had eaten poor old Santa.'

TWO UP, TWO DOWN

'We started married life in the 1930s in a rented two up, two down house in the village of Newtown in Irthington parish. It cost us five shillings and sixpence a week. There was no water or electricity and the toilet was up the garden. Water had to be carried from the tap on the village green and rainwater was collected for washing.

The living room fire grate had an oven at one side and a boiler at the other which was very useful as long as the fire was on. Water was put into the boiler in a bucket and pitchered out as it was needed – not all grates had boilers at that time.

We bought a new bedroom suite for one room and for the other, a bed, chest of drawers and two chairs. Linoleum covered the floor with a carpet rug at the side of the bed. Willie bought me a new Jones sewing machine and I made curtains and matching bedspreads – rather grand in those days.

Next the living room: linoleum on the floor, a sideboard, a scrubbed table top with a velvet cover for Sundays and special occasions, and a stobbed hearthrug made by Willie and his mother before we married. There were four secondhand chairs and a three piece suite which was sold off cheap having been rescued from a factory fire.

Two pictures decorated the living room walls – "When did you last see your father?" and "The boyhood of Raleigh". Both had been received in return for so many cigarette cards collected by the family. Cutlery, towels and bed linen were all wedding presents. The stairs were varnished and had a carpet runner in the middle with wooden stair rods to hold it in place. The back kitchen was quite a good size and meant we could keep all the washing tubs in there.'

OUR MODERN BUNGALOW

'Our bungalow at Natland, modern in the 1920s, cost £210 to build. My father, who built it with the assistance of a friend, obtained a subsidy of £100 from the Government towards the cost. It took nine months to complete. It was heated by coal fires with a back boiler supplying the hot water, and the lighting was by oil lamps (Aladdin, I believe). We still went to bed by candlelight. We cooked on a Valor Perfection oil stove and woe betide us if we ran out of paraffin!

The advent of electricity in the early 1930s was a great event, the great switch-on being eagerly awaited. This meant we could have a wireless to listen to Children's Hour, dance music and Monday Night at Seven (later Monday Night at Eight), as well as the news.'

THE HOUSEHOLD ROUTINE

Without modern appliances, the household routine filled each week and it really did seem as if a woman's work was never done. Springcleaning was a chore which seemed to come around all too soon, and even day to day housework involved a great deal of physical effort and drudgery.

EVERY DAY OF THE WEEK

'On Monday it was always washday. We always had a maid and farm lad who also lived in the house. The "set-pot" was filled with water and the fire lit early. After milking and breakfast, in the washhouse the work began. Washing was an all day job and as I arrived home from school the washhouse was being swilled out and brushed. Tuesday was ironing – generally box irons heated by the fire or flat irons, for which a shield was placed on the bottom. Then when we were at Ravenstonedale we had calor gas installed for cooking and a calor iron. When we went to Scotby in 1950 we wired the house for electricity.

On Wednesday the garden was tidied. We had great pride in the garden and with a big vegetable garden plenty of fresh vegetables and fruit were available. At the very end of this was the building containing the two-seater, a lovely building with a dovecote above. The paper was newspaper and it was a bit draughty on a wild day. I can't understand why it was so far to go. I once went to visit friends and their loo was a round building in the middle of a field, I was terrified.

Thursday was bedroom day – most of the rooms had lino but the best had a carpet square with lino around. Mattresses were flock or hair and feather beds were very cosy and warm in winter. The best room had a washstand and bowl and jug with lovely toilet dishes, and of course all our beds had "potties" underneath. Towel rails were used and all the beds had ends on; some bedsteads were brass, iron or oak, but the best room had mahogany furniture. Carpets were brushed by hand.

Friday was baking day. The oven was at the side of the fire. The big Glendinning range was well stoked with long branches and planks of wood, posts or anything that would burn well. Bread was prepared and while it was "raising" scones were cooked, and pastry made, or always rock buns. After the bread was baked, came sponges or gingerbread. Bread was cut by hand and was generally very thick slices. When I was small I used to call them doorsteps and liked to go and see my aunt at Carlisle because her bread was thin. We didn't have fancy cakes but the apple cakes were so lovely and juicy, the currant cakes also. We had lots of home-made jam, lemon curd and honey – we had beehives.

On Saturday the floors were washed on hands and knees – the back kitchen and the kitchen. The black grate was given a special clean and blackleaded and the steelwork cleaned. The lovely fender was also cleaned, but of course first the bucket was lifted out under the grate where the ashes had fallen from the grate. It was called the ash pit. The lovely stobbed or hookie rugs were shaken. In the kitchen was an oak press (cost £4 in 1929 when my father started farming), an oak settle, long table and kitchen chairs. In the kitchen, around the door entrance, was a screen with a seat beside the fire, built into the wall – I loved this seat. Furniture was polished and everything looked so clean.

Sunday the milking was done and cattle fed, but no extra work. My father was a local preacher in the Methodist church and he was busy preparing his sermon and choosing hymns for a service at night. We generally had cold meat for dinner or something easy as my mother said she had made a dinner all week. We had the roast on the Saturday and she wanted a rest.'

EVERYDAY LIFE

'Many generations of my fore-elders were Cumberland dales farmers. In 1906 my parents transferred their belongings to Cross Canonby, then a small hamlet with three other farms near and a few houses. Horses and carts were used for transportation of furniture, implements etc, a journey of approximately 40 miles each way, as to and fro my father and helpers travelled many times.

Cumberland dialect and country life never seemed strange to me and oil lamps and lanterns and coal fires were everyday life, as was an earth closet. Washstands with a wash basin, jug, soapdish etc and chamberpots to match provided bedroom requirements and when guests were staying a hot water can was filled and taken up to the bedroom in the morning. Iron or wooden bedsteads were used with either chain mattresses or wooden slats and a horsehair, straw or flock mattress, a feather bed, blankets, foot pad and quilt or counterpane (knitted or crocheted). Linen or cotton sheets were used in summer. Large rooms can be quite cold in winter. Electric blankets, gas or central heating, telephones and fridges were never thought of. Rooms were swept with a brush, or mop if linoleum was the floor covering. Carpets were not fixed down as every room was thoroughly cleaned twice a year and swept and polished weekly.

Each day was mapped out as washing day, churning day, baking day, market day, room day etc. Knives and forks were cleaned with bathbrick, on a board. Spoons and brasses and doorknobs were polished, grates blackleaded. There were lamps to fill with paraffin, wicks to clean and glass to polish at least twice a week, pantry shelves and dairy sconces and floor to scrub. Our household usually numbered 14 and all the food used was home-made, large quantities being required. My father often said, "If you can't eat you can't work," and in those days work meant physical labour, not sitting on a machine.

Our home was often visited by relatives as my great-grandfather and his daughter lived with us, and as years passed other relatives when needing help found an ever open door. Elders were looked after by their families. Many an old saying still comes to my mind as I remember my happy childhood, and how true it is to say, "What you haven't had you never miss".'

A WONDERFUL PLACE TO SIT

'Our outdoor toilet, or closet as they were called, was at the top of the farmyard, through a gate. It was a wonderful place to sit and have a chat with one's best friend, as the wooden top had two holes and two wooden lids. Ashes from the fire grate were put down every day and at the appropriate time the horse and cart were commandeered, and the contents shovelled into the cart to be spread on the fields.'

SPRING CLEANING WAS AWFUL

'Spring cleaning was awful: two weeks of beating carpets, scrubbing floors and washing paint. Feather beds and pillows would be warmed in the set-pot (boiler) to fluff them up; curtains, the overmantel and anything else washable would be washed. Washing anyhow was a big chore, with water to be heated and ironing with flat irons. Electricity came to Eskdale just after the Second World War, but not to the more distant parts of the valley.

There was more work in running a home in those days and everyone had their chores; water had to be brought from the well or pump, oil for the lamps came from the grocer, and lamp glasses had to be cleaned and wicks trimmed. They made pit props near us at Bigrigg, and on Saturdays we'd go there and collect the bark for boiling the set-pot for washday.'

SCRUBBING AND POLISHING

'A day might be spent scrubbing steps and reddening them with kidney-ore found locally at Lamplugh on the slag heaps of the iron ore mines, or whitening them with a donkey-stone. Flagstones were washed with water to which a drop of milk had been added to help keep their colour. Furniture was polished with a mixture of beeswax and turpentine, the range was blackleaded and the steel fender cleaned with a mixture of ash and spit!'

'My great aunt could remember boys going up to collect sand from the tarn on Whernside, which they sold for a penny a measure. Housewives bought it to scrub floors instead of the more expensive soap.'

TELLING THE TIME

'As a child at play, I heard the gun placed in Serpentine Woods fired promptly at one o'clock certain days of the week. This was to allow people in Kendal to set clocks, before many people had wireless sets. The first gun, used for many years, was then placed in Abbot Hall Park; the replacement was eventually stolen, a mystery which has never been solved.'

TEA LEAVES

'There were no fitted carpets, but mostly rugs with linoleum surrounds. I can remember my aunt throwing damp tea leaves down on a carpet before brushing it. This was to keep the dust down.'

MOWING THE LAWN

'When I was young a donkey pulled a lawn mower to cut the grass in my grandfather's garden. He wore felt shoes to prevent his hooves damaging the lawn.'

CLEANING THE CHIMNEY

'My mother would often complain about the smoke blowing back into the kitchen on baking day. To clean the chimney we would get the mason and he would go up on the roof and rattle a stick down. He wore clogs as well and it used to frighten me to see him up there. Another method of cleaning was to push straw up the chimney and set a light to it, but you had to be very careful when you did that because of the wind.'

'There was no chimney sweep at Dent. We swept them ourselves with a bunch of holly on a rope.'

WATER & WASHDAY

Most of us had to fetch our water from wells, pumps or streams not so long ago, a heavy task for women and children. Every drop of water, for personal use, for drinking, for cooking, for bathing and for washing was precious. Washday was, of course, one of the abiding memories of childhood – always a Monday, and a day

when the woman of the house toiled at washing, rinsing, starching, blueing, mangling, drying and ironing!

FETCHING THE WATER

'I was born in an old toll-bar house on the A684 between Kendal and Sedbergh. An old gentleman who called there one day, said that when his aunts lived there, there was a wheel in the living room, something like a ship's wheel, which could be turned from inside the house to open the toll gates in bad weather. The house had two windows nearly side by side but facing in opposite directions, to see the travellers approaching from either side, and through which their toll money could be handed.

I can remember having to carry water from the well on the roadside, which was beautiful in summer but in winter used to get flooded and my mother made us boil it all before we could use it. The well water was always put into a white enamel bucket for drinking and stood on the kitchen table. The rainwater from a big tank at the back of the house was put into zinc buckets and stood on the floor. It was used for washing floors and general use.'

'When I was a child in the 1920s we had no piped drinking water supply in our village. There were two pumps for this purpose, one at each end of the village. The one we used would sometimes run dry and when it was my turn to bring the water I secretly hoped this would happen. Then I would have to go to the beck for a bucket of water and bring it back to the pump, empty it into the top of the pump to prime it, then pump like mad until the water started to flow again. One elderly lady had quite a long walk to this pump and used a wooden yoke across her shoulders with a bucket hooked on either side. For other household purposes rainwater was used.'

'Prior to 1937, drinking water at Holme St Cuthbert was either from a pump or a well. However, when I was staying with my grandmother at Edderside an elderly man used to come to collect water from her yard. He always stopped for a chat after he had filled his two buckets. The ducks in the yard used to come over and drink from them and splash their heads about. He didn't take any notice, would just lift the buckets and go home. That was his drinking water.

The main toilet facilities in the area were bucket or earth closets, the contents of which had to be taken away and buried. Although piped water was installed in 1937, these toilet arrangements still prevailed well into the 1950s. They were usually situated at the bottom of the garden or in an outbuilding across a farm yard. At the Tarns "there was an earth closet outside the farm house and if you wanted to go at night a stable lamp had to be lit and you were taken across the yard – there were five of us being trailed over." Hot baths were taken in a large tin bath placed in front of the kitchen fire but even so the cold rising from the kitchen flags could be quite daunting.'

BRINGING WATER TO CARLISLE

'The decision once made to ensure a supply of clean water for Carlisle citizens, the undertaking began in earnest in 1905; it was to take four years. The work included the tapping of seven springs in the valleys of the New Water and Old Water, the rivers which combine to form the Gelt; the taking of some water from both the New and Old Waters; and piping the combined whole through underground pipes over two miles to a reservoir, to be built at Castle Carrock, as the bedrock in the Gelt valley was thought to be unsuitable. Constraints were laid down so that there would always be sufficient water in the Gelt to supply watering for stock along its route and for the operation of the corn mill, "Gelt Mill", near Greenwell, below Castle Carrock. The Castle Carrock beck was piped under the "works", and left untouched so that farms still had the beck available for their uses.

The enterprise was extremely labour intensive in those days of picks and shovels and sundry other hand tools. The work involved building the dam at Castle Carrock to hold the water, 27 feet deep at this point, plus foundations; the adjacent sand and gravel filter beds; a house at Castle Carrock for the Superintendent of the works; the 20 inch cast iron pipe from Geltsdale intake works to Castle Carrock; and, at Geltsdale, the catchment chambers for tapping the springs; the sluices and weirs on the two rivers; the pipes to bring the tamed spring and river water to the intake works, where it was to be measured and monitored before beginning its journey to the reservoir at Castle Carrock; a house for the occupation of the person in charge of this regulation, built where the New and Old Waters join, three miles from Castle Carrock; and a house for metering the flow in the Gelt at Hynam, two miles downriver from Geltsdale.

The average number of men employed was 400, a vast increase in the population of Castle Carrock. A few came from the surrounding area but most were from Ireland, housed in wooden "bunk-houses" built on site in Castle Carrock and at Geltsdale when work began there in 1906. To serve the men in their leisure time, after working six days per week from 6 am to 6 pm, the two public houses were supplemented by three alehouses, an extra sweet shop and a home-made cake and pie shop. On Sundays, six volunteers moved a piano up to a hut on the site which became a Catholic mission, for the benefit of the Irish workers, where the church organist, Mr Shipman, (also headmaster at the school and postmaster) played for their service. Mr Shipman, helped by a Mrs Watson, also acted as a letter writer and reader for those who, away from home, could neither read nor write.

The transport for the machinery, pipes etc needed was by rail to How Mill and thence by teams of as many as eight horses to Castle Carrock, along the rough, metalled road. The blacksmith at Castle Carrock employed six men to keep horses well shod and tools mended, the horses being hired out to the contractors by farmers in the district. An overhead pulley hauled stone from the quarry above the works to the site, and around the perimeter of the proposed reservoir ran a narrow gauge railway, hauling stone, pipes etc. A similar narrow gauge railway was built at Geltsdale to help in laying the pipes and building the weirs etc and laying the main cast iron pipe. A new bridge was built over the Gelt, just below the intake works, together with a new road to provide vehicle (horse-drawn) access. The position of the bridge and new road was intended to accommodate the farm at Geltsdale, on whose land the springs rise, and to provide easier access to existing barns beside the river. A ford and footbridge were made for access to the house at the intake works.

The pipeline from Geltsdale to Castle Carrock follows the river Gelt for about two miles until it escapes from the valley, below Hynam, and sweeps round to the reservoir. The pipeline is only apparent by reason of iron-covered air valves along its route and the gates in hedges which it crosses.

The whole undertaking was completed in 1909, when Castle Carrock settled back into its uninterrupted, peaceful, rural existence. The only reminders are the odd piece of rail, some pipes left at Geltsdale, the gunpowder house on the bank above the reservoir (disintegrated in the 1970s) and, of course, a clean water supply for Carlisle.'

MEMORIES OF WASHDAY

'I was twelve years old in the year of 1935, and lived on the west side of the seaside town of Silloth. Our house was situated in a terrace and was quite big, as our family was big too. Besides Mother and Father, I also had seven brothers and two sisters, so you can imagine the amount of washing my mother had to get through every week.

In those days we had not even heard of washing machines or tumble driers. The washhouse was a small building in a communal yard, and was shared with six other families, each one allocated a day of the week to do the wash. My mother's day was always Tuesday, the one I hated most, as I knew I would have to stay off school to help her. The morning began very early, as the copper or boiler, as we called it, had to be filled with water from the tap in the corner. Then the fire which was already laid the night before, was set alight. While the water was getting hot, the two dolly tubs were set ready – these were made of zinc and were quite heavy. One was placed underneath the big mangle, which had wooden rollers. This had to be turned by a wheel with a handle, and took a lot of strength and muscle power!

The dirty clothes were sorted into piles and whites such as sheets, pillowslips and tablecloths were always done first in the hot water from the boiler, which had been put in the tub, together with the soap powder, usually Rinso – fivepence per packet. These were given a good thumping with the wooden poss stick, then put through the mangle and into the copper, which had been filled again and powder added, where they were left to boil for the required time. Meanwhile the fire was stoked up again, and the second tub filled with clean water and a Reckitts blue bag added, ready for the whites to have a final rinse when they came out of the boiler. The blue bag was to give extra whiteness.

After the rinse they were put through the mangle and into a wicker basket. Part of my chores was to help carry the basket and peg the clothes on the line if it was a fine day.

Mother then started on the next pile, shirts, underclothes etc. This was when the rubbing board came into use for any articles badly soiled. It was made of lightweight corrugated zinc, set between wooden sides. The clothes were soaped and rubbed up and down on the board to remove any stains, then received the same treatment as the whites. Towels were always left until last as they needed extra boiling.

Then I had what I considered a horrible task – washing the socks in a small tin bath set upon a stool. Each sock was rubbed by hand with carbolic soap! To this day, I can remember the smell of sweaty socks and that soap. To do this, I was enveloped in a coarse apron (made out of a hessian bag) and had old fashioned clogs on my feet, as I was inclined to splash the water about.

As I grew older, I was entrusted to use Robin's starch on special items, such as the collars on my father's best white shirts. In those days the collars were loose and fastened to the shirt by studs, one at the back of the neck and one at the front. The collars were washed separately by hand. It took me quite some time before I got the starch to the right consistency.

Another very busy day was blanket washing, usually on a warm March day with a good wind blowing. Helping to lift heavy, damp woollen blankets onto the lines in a stiff breeze certainly took some doing, but it was worth it for the clean softness and fresh air smell on your bed.

After the washing was finished, the fire under the copper had to be left to go out, then the ashes raked out. It was then re-set for the next person and the washhouse floor was scrubbed with any left-over suds and a good stiff yard brush.

I often think of those days and wonder how my mother withstood all that hard work bringing up a big family with no modern conveniences. If I moaned about my lot, which I did often, her reply was always the same – "It's good training for when you get married." Nowadays when I switch on my washing machine and spin drier, my heartfelt thanks go to the man who had the brains to invent them. As far as I'm concerned he deserves a medal as big as a frying pan!'

'Before the advent of piped water in the village of Lorton, most people had access to their own water supply, albeit a well, trough, stream, spring or river. Those who had not, carried buckets of water from their nearest source. This was done on the Sunday evening to fill the set-pot ready for washday on the Monday morning, when a fire was lit underneath.

When the water boiled this was ladled out into dolly tubs and sheets and blankets were "possed" in the tubs. Turning the mangle, which had wooden rollers, was quite an achievement, as the clothes had to be fed through the rollers evenly and a suitable receptacle was placed behind to catch the newly-washed bedding, towels and clothing. There was no plastic line for drying then, it was a cord which had to be wiped scrupulously clean before pegging anything out to dry. Many is the time the wet washing was hanging up in the kitchen for days – there seemed to be an awful lot of rainy Mondays.

When the time came for ironing, the box-iron was put into use. Wedge-shaped pieces of metal were put into the fire until hot and transferred to the iron with tongs. Two "heaters" for the iron were used, one to be heating in the fire and one to use in the iron. The cottons had to be done first and then afterwards the clothes which needed a cooler temperature, when the heater had cooled down. When electricity came to the village in the 1930s it was certainly a red-letter day!'

'Gran and I spent many happy hours together at Appleby in the 1930s. On ironing day we would go over the road to the smithy. Gran would carry the box iron and Grandad's coffee. I carried his bite to eat in a little blue Co-op sugar bag. When we got into the smithy, the iron-tables were taken from inside the box-iron and put into the forge fire, and the hot ones put back into the iron with the aid of long tongs. Gran went back to continue her ironing, but I sat up beside Grandad on the fire hearth. He pulled the bellows to make a "lobby low", then we looked for pictures in the fire – castles and caves, faces and fairies, I eating the contents of the sugar bag and he drinking his coffee with the stray grounds swirling over the top.'

BATH AND BED

'Life in a tiny farm cottage as one of six brothers and sisters was hectic, enjoyable and well worth recalling. We had no gas, electricity, hot water, or bathroom, and oil lamps provided our only light. Everything we ate was either cooked on the fire or in the brick oven beside it.

Each evening during cold weather, after the dinner had been taken out, six bricks were placed on the oven shelf to warm. When bedtime came each brick was wrapped in a sheet of old newspaper and popped into our beds, which soon made a warm cosy place for each child to lie in. Three sisters and myself slept in one bedroom, which contained two black iron bedsteads decorated with ivy leaves and brass rosettes. Each mattress consisted of a large bag made from "ticking" material, and filled with chaff, which is husks of corn. This chaff was changed annually, when the travelling threshing machine visited Granda's nearby farm every autumn. Our pillows too were refilled. It was a red letter day when we did this, as we all had such fun burying each other under mounds of chaff, plus numerous pillow fights during the proceedings. After the job was finished and the beds remade, we all needed a bath.

This took place in the scullery where a large boiler, known as the set-pot, had a fire under it to keep the water hot. It was ladled into a large wooden dolly tub, and cooled with water from a zinc bucket which stood under the cold tap. When the tub was three parts full we all six followed each other into the water, where we sat cross-legged, with the soap suds coming up to our chin. Before we had time to blow bubbles Mam had washed us all over, using a large bar of red carbolic soap and a piece of flannel as a face cloth. Our hair was then rinsed with cold water from the bucket. As the next in the queue clambered in we jumped out of the tub onto the cold stone floor and ran through into the kitchen, where Dad dried us with a coarse towel in front of a roaring fire. Our nighties were made from calico bags which had originally held calf-meal. When boiled they became lovely soft material and made pure white nighties, but on close examination one could see "Pattinson's Oats" printed in the most unexpected places!

However, before we put our nighties on we were rubbed back and front with goose grease, saved from Christmas. This was to prevent "croup" developing, which was a common childhood chest complaint. I also had a piece of pink thermal wadding called Thermogene stitched inside my vest to protect my chest. It was restitched on to each clean vest until it naturally disintegrated – just in time for spring. Because of these precautions we seldom ailed, and every night we had a basin full of warm bread and milk, and were soon fast asleep, tucked up beside our nice warm bricks.'

MAKING THE MATS

Warm mats were essential in the days before carpets came into such general use, to keep our feet warm on cold winter days and to add just a little comfort to life. Making the mats was a family occupation, and no scrap of material was allowed to go to waste.

HOOKIE MATS

'When I was young and lived on the farm, our back kitchen was huge with a very uneven flagged floor. To make it more comfortable hookie mats were laid in front of the cupboards, the old wooden settle and at the doorways. They were home-made mats worked on hessian with rags.

Matting frames were used – these were long pieces of wood to which the hessian was fixed. Two wooden stretchers with holes and pegs made the hessian firm, and starting to work at one end of the mat it was rolled on as each section was worked. The rags were cut into long strips about an inch wide, and pulled through with a metal hook, leaving a loop on the top and tight on the underside.

Coats, suits, skirts, dresses and jackets were all used to make mats. Ours were kept in a tea chest until that cold winter afternoon when the matting frames were brought out and the hessian was sewn to the frame. It was always fun sorting through the old clothes and remembering how we liked or disliked that particular coat or dress.

Then came the dusty job of clipping or tearing the rags into strips. The different colours were mostly kept separate to help create a simple design. It took a few afternoons to cut up enough rags for a mat, and the mess in the kitchen was unbelievable. All buttons were cut off and kept for the button box, and linings and stiffening had to be removed, along with the other pieces which could not be used. We always had a rush to get the place tidied up for the men coming in for tea.

When at last we got started to hook, the place was still untidy with ends to be cut off, and always a few strips of rag got away. The designs were simple with the bright colours to the middle, and always a black border. Light colours were used sparingly – it was said they showed the dirt.

It took quite a long time to hook a mat, but it was a grand way to spend a cold afternoon and evening, with the frames in front of a big red fire in the old black grate and the cosy light of the Aladdin lamp. When the mat was the size we wanted it was removed from the frame, the edges of the hessian were neatly sewn to the back and another hookie mat was complete.

The new mat was always laid in front of the kitchen fire – often "for Christmas" – and the old one relegated to the back kitchen, perhaps in front of the sink. All these mats told their own story of coats and suits of days gone by. They were very cosy and very hard wearing.'

MOTHER'S MATTING CAREER

'Most winters before the war, my mother would make a prodded hearth rug. She would have been cutting up clippings for some time beforehand. In those days clothes were handed down and passed on in the family; sometimes they were patched or darned, but their final resting place was as clippings for a mat. The sound parts were cut up into pieces, using the side of a matchbox as a guide for size. We were once given some outdated tailors' pattern books. These were as absorbing as story books, with smooth suitings and hairy tweeds. There were stripes and checks and many different weaves, and all manner of colour combinations, but all were sacrificed to the scissors.

People liked patterns on their mats, and hessian could be bought with a design ready stamped on, or you could buy plain and draw your own. The patterns were usually flowers and leaves amid a general mixture of clippings and all set off in a black border. There was no shortage of black material in the days when people went into mourning after a death in the family.

When sufficient clippings had been cut, the hessian was stitched into the frames, using a very strong thread. The unravelled fine string that fastened flour sacks was just right, as was my mother's packing needle for the sewing.

My father groaned when he saw the matting frames come out. He hated the upheaval caused in a small house by an operation that took up so much space. So once started the object was to get on and get finished as soon as possible. Anyone was welcome to sit down and do a few rows. We girls could be encouraged by being allowed to do the flowers or the leaves, even a little boy could fill in the pencilled shape of a car or a boat with mixed clippings which wouldn't show on the right side when the mat was finished.

Matting is unavoidably dusty and dirty work. The clippings shed bits on to your lap and the floor from the underside as you work. The mat was put aside each evening when everyone was in, and at weekends, but even so it could usually be finished in two to three weeks. It was a great feeling putting in the final few clippings and then unpicking the stitches that had kept it in the frames. It was rolled out on the floor and we competed to be the first to jump on it. The mat was finished off by hemming the edges and sometimes a backing piece of hessian was stitched on though this made the mat very heavy to shake. Any odd, over-long bits were trimmed off with scissors, like a barber giving a hair cut, until there was a nice even surface. Then it was outside for its first vigorous shake. It took quite a few shakings before the bits stopped coming off.

Then the mat began, like most things on earth, to go through a life-cycle. At first it was the Best Mat and was only put down at weekends after the big Friday clean-up and was put away again on Monday morning. As the next new mat came on the scene, this one became the ordinary everyday mat, in front of the fire. Next it was relegated to the back kitchen and its final duty was done inside the back door where it got the hardest wear of its life.

Later, during the war, when Dad was far away serving king and country in Africa, I remember Mother trying something different. We were all roped in to help when she made two mats for the bedrooms, using our old knitted jumpers, cardigans etc. These were all unpicked and the pieces were unravelled and wound into balls. The balls were then made into hanks which were washed to get out the wrinkles. The first mat was a hooked rug with a pattern in two opposite corners resembling searchlights. The hanks of different colours were hung on the silver knobs of the black range and as she worked we gave Mother a long length of six or eight strands for her to hook into the hessian. Hooked rugs are worked with the right side uppermost and all the loops on this mat were cut, giving a short dense pile. The second mat was different, the loops were left uncut and Mother worked it without frames on her knee. However this was on hessian, not modern rug canvas so the finished mat was not a rectangle but a parallelogram. Still, it stood many years of hard wear.

Mother ended her matting career with a work of heroic proportions. After we had all left home, except for our younger brother who had been born after an eleven year gap, they moved to a larger house and she tackled the job of covering a hall, a staircase with half-landing and a square upstairs landing. She now had a spare downstairs room to work in, so the length of time it took was not important. The mats were all hooked and all blended beautifully. The pattern was simplicity itself, consisting of double rows of eight inches in one colour with the following double rows covering two halves of the previous colours, like slim bricks in a wall. The borders on all the pieces were two rows of brown, one row of green and an inner row of brown again. As work progressed the appeal for material went further and further afield among family and friends. I remember someone sending a yellow scarf through the post to be cut up and used. I was married by this time and decided I would like to make a hooked rug for myself. I had four or five nice balls of material in a box as a start, when my mother got her eye on them, and I have still never made a hooked rug. However, making prodded rugs has always been a real pleasure and enjoyment for me.'

FOOD & DRINK

The kitchen was the heart of the house, warm and cosy with the heat of the fire or range and filled with the smells of baking day. The food of our childhood is remembered with nostalgia – tatie pot and sad cakes, fresh butter and the bread to go with it!

THE HEART OF THE HOUSE

'The kitchen had a paved floor which had to be scrubbed and then chalked round the edges of the slabs, making a pattern. The hearth had to be whitened as well. There were home-made proddy rugs on the floor and also a rocking chair, most farms had them. We had a large settle which had a lifting seat and you could store papers underneath. The cushions were stuffed with chaff. This was produced while threshing was under way – nothing was ever wasted. There was something called bass matting, but the dust went right through and it had to be lifted to be cleaned. A large wooden table and wooden chairs completed the furnishings, together with a dresser in some cases.

We lived in the kitchen during the week and a fire was lit in the parlour on a Sunday only – this was the "best" room. Lighting was by oil lamp, candles and Tilley paraffin pressure lamps although one enterprising farmer at Holme had built a windmill onto a Dutch barn, which drove a generator to charge batteries. When the wind was blowing hard the light was quite bright but it dimmed when the wind dropped to a gentle breeze. Before supply authority electric lighting (and power) reached the area in the 1950s stock men had to use paraffin lamps to inspect the stock. Sets of lamps would be lit and lined up ready for them to take on their rounds. There were two hanging up in the milking byre and all these lamps had to be cleaned every week. However, accumulator-powered radios were making an appearance by the 1930s in most homes.

Another prominent feature to all farm kitchens during this period was the great black range used for cooking and water heating. The kitchen range was very crude, having a heavy oven with a steel handle and hinges, and there was also a hob and a girdle which swung over the fire for cooking scones on. In 1951 in one home the kettle was on a hook that could be swung from the fire and there was a cloth for the kettle handle as it got so hot. The ranges had to be blackleaded and polished up and the handles and hinges cleaned; this was not a popular task but very necessary. Coal was used mainly, although wood was also used, and the farmers near to the sea shore, for example at Mawbray, were able to collect sea coal washed up on the shore from the mines lower down the firth.

Baking day was a special occasion and the fire had to be just right to bring the oven up to temperature. We as children used to have to go and collect sticks for the oven so that my mother could get the extra boost to get it right. There was also a damper at the side of the oven in order to control the heat but on windy days it was very troublesome as the oven would get too hot and the cooking would be wasted.

Tatie pot featured in most diets in the area and we had rabbit pie, which was delicious; this was well before myxomatosis was introduced. We kept pigs and the butcher would be called to kill one, which would be salted and hung to be used over the winter – of course this was very useful during the war. We also kept hens and collected the eggs. We always had porridge, bacon and eggs, and tatie hash – another popular dish. Bread and teacakes, cakes and tarts were all home-made. Sometimes there would be roast beef which would be made into tatie hash for the next day. I remember the rice puddings and also the steamed ones such as spotted dick cooked in a cloth. We had the type of food that could be left to cook in the oven or on the stove while you were busy with something else.

When catering was for large numbers, such as when farm workers were employed, the baking was done twice a week and would include "great big ginger cakes". There was also milk, and home-made butter. For a real treat we used to have trifle. I can remember my first sight of tinned fruit. I'd been taken out to tea and looked in this bowl to see what I thought was a number of egg yolks with the whites. It was actually peach halves with juice – it amazed me.

The food was basically very simple and wholesome and as there were orchards, fruit in the form of apples, pears and soft fruit was plentiful. Other provisions such as flour, sugar, dried fruit etc would be brought out to the area from nearby Silloth. Half a hundredweight of flour would last all winter.'

SAD CAKES AND HAVERBREAD

'In the early years of the century every dales kitchen was dominated by the blackleaded "firespot". Many still had the old fashioned "reckon", which was a hinged bar swinging out over the fire, on which kettles and pans were hung. The baking was done in strict sequence, so that items needing the hottest oven were made first. My mother's sequence was first, scones and pastry; second, sponges and sandwich cakes; third, bread; fourth, fruit cakes and gingerbread; and last, a casserole for dinner while the oven was "falling".

Haverbread was one of the most important items in the local diet in Dentdale. There are many versions of this oatcake. The one most generally made was very thin and crisp. A little flour was added and it was mixed with boiling water, giving it a greater elasticity and enabling the cook to roll it out very thinly. It was eaten with every meal; for breakfast with bacon, soaked in the fat, at dinnertime broken into the gravy, at supper and breakfast broken into buttermilk. It apparently took the place of both bread and potatoes.

Sad cakes seem to have been peculiar to a small area of the dales. They appear to have been one of the main items in the diet of Dentdale from farther back than anyone living can now remember. They were eaten at every meal as well as at "drinking time". Six ounces of bacon fat or lard was rubbed into a pound of flour, with a pinch of salt and of bicarbonate of soda, then it was mixed to a stiff dough with buttermilk. A handful of dried fruit was optional. The half inch thick cakes were then cooked in a hot oven for about 15 minutes, though many swore they tasted better if fried in a pan or on a griddle.

Anyone who stayed with my husband's granny in the summer earned their bed and board picking burnets for her famous wine. Her grandchildren were given a sip as a treat, for their first taste of alcohol! It was light and flowery and a beautiful ruby red.

My grandparents always had a whole Wensleydale cheese. It often used to be crawling with maggots before it was used up but that didn't deter them. My grandfather would just push them to one side, but my friend's father, the blacksmith, would eat the maggots as well!

On Saturday night they used to have pies and peas at Tom Mattinson's shop. Dad would go down into the village shopping, and take a can for the peas. The shops were open until nine o'clock. When I got bigger we all went down. You used to meet people and all of us children would play around.

Batty Bros ran their business largely on the barter system. They gave groceries in return for butter and eggs. They kept enough to sell in the shop and sold the surplus elsewhere. The barter trade ceased in the early 1930s.'

SUNDAY TATIE POT

'There was a long narrow pantry at our farmhouse in Bassenthwaite in the 1920s, with sandstone sconces. Eggs were preserved in isinglass in a large crock behind the door, and meat was kept in a safe on the wall outside the back door protected by a lead grille.

On Sundays we always had a tatie pot (made with beef as my mother was brought up on the coast and maintained it was the custom there because the Irish cattle came into Workington docks; lamb or mutton was traditional to the central Lake District). The tatie pot was put into the oven at breakfast time. When we came back from church we all had a mug of Bovril while the tatie pot was moved up to the top shelf to brown the potatoes.

Saturday was a great baking day; dough was put to rise in front of the kitchen range. Enough cakes, scones and platecakes were made to last the week.'

THE CHRISTMAS GOOSE

'Nothing was wasted. The goose was brought into the kitchen along with a basin of red liquid, to which Gran added a few handfuls of oatmeal. This was fried as black pudding. The bird was plucked and the feathers put into a bag in the warm fire oven with the door left open, to dry them so they could be used to replenish fillings for pillows and feather beds. The giblets were made into a pie. The wings were put on the fender to sweep in the ash from the fire. The grease in the roasting tin when the bird was cooked went into stone jars for rubbing on bad chests in the winter.'

BUTTERMAKING

'Cream was churned twice a week by hand, then made up into one pound and half pound pats. The pounds were oblong and shaped with scotch hands which were made of wood. The half pounds were

Isaac and Mary Fleming at Broadrayne Farm, Grasmere in 1920. Helping with the stock, as well as buttermaking and cheesemaking, was part of everyday life for most women on the farms.

round in the shape of a cow. This, along with eggs, potatoes and vegetables, was loaded onto a cart and taken into town.

The Butter Bell at Kirkby Stephen was always rung at ten o'clock on Mondays to begin the selling of butter in the cloisters at the entrance to the church. Potatoes were sold from two carts in the streets and women sat along a low wall selling their fruit, eggs etc from baskets.'

'Every Thursday at Highberries Scaleby was a churning day. The housemaid carried the large cans of cream from the cellar dairy to the churn house and rinsed the large end-over-end churn with cold water ready to start making the butter after breakfast. The churn would hold 30 gallons of cream. My mother would wash her hands thoroughly in water and oatmeal before starting. My father attached the churn to a long rod connected to a large wheel with cogs, then fastened it to a long pole whereby a horse was yoked and was driven round and round for about an hour until the butter was ready.

During the school holidays my sister or myself did this tedious job but the horse seemed to be content and happy. Then the butter had to be washed, salted, then rolled to get the water away. My mother weighed it into pounds and worked it with the wooden pats until it was in good shape, making about 90 to 100 pounds of butter, which was sold in the market and to local people.

In the winter it was a very cold job and in summer it was difficult getting it to set, with the heat, as there was a tin roof. So my mother had to wait until the cool of the evening to make up the butter. When my sister and I came from school we had to take a large five gallon tin down to the well to get ice cold water. That was a mile away.

The butter was placed on large slates and put on shelves down in the dairy. The housemaid washed and scrubbed all the utensils ready for the following Thursday.

Friday night I used to help my mother pack the butter into baskets ready for the market and customers on the Saturday morning, each piece wrapped in greaseproof paper. The cellar dairy was very cold and we only had lamps so it wasn't a pleasant job. I was glad when it was over. Then to market we went on the Saturday morning after my Dad got it all loaded into his car. The market was a wonderful place, full of stalls, of country produce and farmers' wives selling their produce.'

EGG WINE

'This is a good pick-me-up after an illness, a wineglass to be taken before breakfast. Put five newlaid eggs unbroken into a basin and squeeze over them the juice of six lemons and allow to stand for 48 hours, turning the eggs after 24 hours. The egg shells should then be dissolved by the lemon juice. Take away any skin that is left and stir in half a pound of honey, a gill of cream and a gill of rum. Beat all up thoroughly and bottle carefully.'

THE PUDDING BASIN

'Grandmother, Grandfather and the three girls, my mother being the eldest, lived in a small two up, two down terraced house in the 1920s in Wigton, with toilets out the back and across the communal yard.

This is my mother's story of their next door neighbour's pudding basin. They were a large family; scruffy, snotty-nosed kids of all ages running around, and not two ha'pennies to rub together. Bread doorsteps and treacle were handed out liberally to keep the kids full, but on Sundays a proper "dinner" was always served, with rice pudding for afters. The only basin big enough to hold the rice pudding to feed all of the family was an old, large, enamel washing up bowl.

For as long as my mother can remember that enamel bowl sat "steeping" on top of the yard wall from one Sunday to the next when it was brought in, wiped, and used to make the pudding in. One day the old enamel bowl went missing, but that's another story, and perhaps best not told, although Grandfather is no longer around to take the consequences.

To this day our family still does "a Bessie Burton" when a dirty pan or basin is left to steep.'

EASIER TO DO WITHOUT

'My husband hasn't taken milk in his tea since he was eight years old. The reason is that as a child he had to walk about three miles to the farm for the milk or do without, and in the winter it was easier to do without.'

BREAD AND TRIPE

'I remember at Barrow taking my Nanna's bread to be baked in the big ovens of the bakery at the top of the street for a charge of a halfpenny a loaf. Then calling at the tripe shop for a cowheel for my Grandad, and also taking a jug for a pint of beer at the "selling out spot" (outdoor licence). Jugs were put out on the doorsteps each day for the morning delivery of milk which the milkman ladled out of a big churn carried in the back of a pony and trap.

Most household deliveries were made by horse and cart and it was a common sight to see someone following with bucket and shovel collecting the horse dung.'

RECYCLING THE FLOUR SACKS

'In the 1930s flour was delivered to my family home in large cloth sacks. They came by horse and cart over the fell from Newbiggin-on-Lune to Crosby Garrett. These sacks were greatly prized by my mother. As soon as they were empty they were washed, scrubbed, boiled and bleached until they were snow white. This material varied in texture and was used accordingly. Rough cloth was made into dishcloths, tea towels and mattress covers. Medium grade made tablecloths, traycloths etc, and the finest cloth made pillowcases, petticoats and knickers.'

KILLING THE PIG

The pig was once the mainstay of cottage life, and during the Second World War it came into its own once again. Everything could be used but the squeal, so they said.

A MONTH OF PLENTY

'During my childhood on the farm it was commonplace to slaughter at least two pigs each winter for consumption by the family and farm workers. I believe that this was allowed during the war years as long as you surrendered your bacon coupons. The bacon produced was much superior to anything in the shops today, but the present generation don't enjoy this richness so the custom died out. I expect it wouldn't be allowed today with all the stringent regulations.

At home we had a local butcher come out to slaughter the pig. At this stage I would go missing! The boiler fire would be lit as endless supplies of hot water were needed to scrape the skin.

The first job was to stir the blood when warm to prevent coagulation. This would be used that, or next, day to make black puddings

– with hot fat, barley and seasoning added. In those days skins from the intestines were thoroughly cleaned and washed and made a strong casing for black puddings. A quicker method was to pour blood into a roasting tin, roast in an oven and eat fresh. Those in skins would be boiled in a deep pan for hours and would keep for some time.

The carcase of the pig would hang for a day or two to allow the fat and meat to set. The butcher would then return to cut it up and separate meat from bacon. This was the big day! All the neighbours and friends enjoyed samples – spare rib, sausage and black pudding. The fat was taken out, cut up and rendered down for lard to be used for pastry in winter.

It was said that the only thing not used from the pig was the squeal. The head would be dissected, cheeks taken off and the rest salted in a brine for two to three weeks. The feet would either be made into a pie or used in the brawn. Some people might roast them.

After all the pork was taken out the bacon would be in six pieces to salt – flitches, shoulders and hams. This was allowed to drain and then rubbed with a mixture of salt, saltpetre and brown sugar either on slate slabs or in a wooden tub. The cheeks would have the same treatment but were taken out and dried within a week or ten days. This would be used first, very good roasted with a chicken.

Flitches came out next and might be rolled and tied with string. Shoulder hams would be in for three weeks. After hanging in the warm kitchen they were wrapped in white flour bags to keep out flies. It was never advisable to have bacon about in summer.

There was always a lot of trimming from the pork joint – this was minced and made into sausages, again using the skins. Families had their own recipes; we used sage, plenty of salt and pepper and breadcrumbs – a much meatier sausage than that bought. Later in life, we used a large cast-iron sausage filler which compressed the meat into a funnel – it came out at an unbelievable rate. Brawn would be made in about a month – it took a lot of cooking. The result was very tasty.

There were no deep freezes in those days so it was usual to prolong the keeping by salting some of the pork. After a week or two it was delicious roasted or in a hot pot with black pudding added.

This time in the farming calendar brought a lot of work for the ladies but the result was so rewarding. Where would we have been without a ham hanging to use for unexpected visitors or late night suppers for all the extra help at harvest time? It was certainly a month of plenty!'

ALWAYS IN NOVEMBER

'We always killed the pigs in November. The bacon lasted us a year. Bacon, taties and oatcakes were a grand meal.

The pig was the mainstay of the family economy in Dentdale. They were always kept until they were as fat as possible, and were dry salted. It was thought that if a woman was menstruating she must not touch the meat while it was being prepared and cured or the bacon would not keep. This superstition was very widespread.

On the more prosperous farms they would have a woman in to make the pies, black puddings, sausages and brawn. The hams and sides of bacon were salted and dried and would keep for over a year, and were not considered good eating until well matured. There were many anxious conferences about whether the bacon was going to keep and everyone sniffed at the shank and gave their opinion.'

OUR FAMILY PET

'Our family pig was always called Suzie, and each night when our water supply was carried from the village spout, Suzie had her exercise and ran along behind us like a dog. Pig killing time brought tears. We all broke our hearts, as the pig was our family pet.'

SHOPPING & CALLERS TO THE DOOR

Many everyday goods were brought direct to our doors in the past, orders taken and deliveries made by traders who became almost part of the family.

BRINGING GOODS TO THE VILLAGES

'It is a balmy summer evening sometime in the 1930s. Children play happily together, parents occupy themselves in their various abodes. Suddenly, in the distance, there is the clip-clop of a horse's hooves, accompanied by the rumble of cart wheels. The children stop and listen, knowing full well what these noises signify. As the sounds draw nearer the children dash madly, each to his own home, for they know that soon they will hear a voice calling, "Ice cream". The ice cream seller has travelled from the town to the villages in his colourful yellow cart, pulled by a pony. The ice cream is in a metal container. Children have been given a penny which will purchase a cornet, whilst adults indulge in a twopenny wafer sandwich. The visit of the ice cream seller is a luxury in the days when no house in the village boasts any form of refrigeration.

Not quite so exciting is the visit of the grocer's traveller on his bicycle, though it does arouse a certain amount of anticipation. When the delivery van arrives a day or so later, bringing goods which have been ordered from the traveller, the box will contain a complimentary packet of sweets, appreciated by children with very few pennies to spend.

The arrival of the baker's van is welcomed by Mother, enabling her to purchase extra bread or cakes to supplement her own home baking.

There are also the weekly visits of the butcher and fishmonger. Milk, however, is not delivered. Each customer takes his own can or jug to the farm where it is filled. Butter and eggs can also be purchased from the farmer's wife.

Once in a while there is the visit of the draper's van, and a travelling van with shoes for sale. The shoe man will take shoes in need of repair into town and bring them back on his next visit.

This is not the age of the universal ownership of the car, and so it is to the advantage of both trader and customer to bring the goods to the villages.'

'At Far Sawrey village before 1914, we had several callers selling bobbins, tapes, pins and needles. They each usually had a tin box which was put on the doorstep and opened. They were always welcomed and offered cups of tea. They had regular times for their visits and were always most polite.'

'At Troutbeck butchers, bakers, greengrocers and fishmen all called. One of the latter we called "Fishy Dick" and he rode a bicycle with a huge hamper on the front and shouted "Fresh herring" in a most peculiar voice.

A curly haired little man pushed his bicycle round the area, sharpening scissors and repairing doormats. Mr Langhorn from Kendal came round with shoes to try on, then delivered the orders the following month. The drapers came with material and patterns, while the ironmonger had everything on his cart from a clothes peg to a bucket.'

THE TRAVELLING DRAPER

'When I was a little girl in the early 1920s I greatly enjoyed the three times yearly visits of Tom Tweddle the draper. He was always dressed in a long black coat and tile hat as he walked from farm to farm in the quiet countryside. My brothers and I sometimes met him when we were walking home from school and he would usually bring out a bag of strong mints saying, "PTO, PTO Please take one," in his quick voice and we never thought of refusing!

He carried a long pack wrapped in black waterproof oilcloth and my mother allowed me to sit on the end of the large kitchen table while he showed off the fascinating contents. There were samples of suitings – the Fifty Shilling Tailors hadn't yet arrived – and the most popular material seemed to be navy blue serge or a bright ginger-coloured Harris tweed. The latter must have been everlasting as two of the local farmers wore nothing else in all the years I knew them. The striped flannelette shirts never had attached collars, they were bought separately, stiff white starched ones with large fronts like bats' wings which must have been very uncomfortable and difficult to launder. There was striped ticking for making feather-proof beds and pillows and also huckaback towelling. The white variety was kept for "best" and my mother added hand-crocheted edging.

Another delight was a selection of elaborately pleated cotton "clootie bonnets" with a wide frill at the back to protect one's neck from the sun. They were very sensible headgear on a hot day in the hayfield. Most of all I liked to see and feel samples of dress materials and specially remember cream or grey alpaca used to make the very long skirts still worn in those days. The haberdashery contained strong linen threads, crochet cottons and white linen buttons used on hand-made linen pillowcases, some of which I still own.

Tom was a colourful character and purveyor of all the rural news and views from miles around, always offered a cup of tea and also free overnight hospitality at some of his favourite farm houses on his rounds.'

FROM THE CRADLE TO THE GRAVE

In the old days, we were far more likely to be born, to suffer our illnesses and finally to die, in our own homes. Home remedies were often resorted to in place of expensive visits from the local doctor, though both he and the District Nurse were respected figures in village life. Before today's drugs and medical care, scarlet fever or diphtheria could be childhood killers, and a simple operation such as having our tonsils out might be performed on the kitchen table. Weddings, christenings and funerals all had their own time-honoured customs.

ROMANCE STARTS IN THE ODDEST WAYS

'My mother led a very busy life. Being a farmer's wife and having four children under five years old left her very little spare time – but she did promise to help me make a new dress for my dolly on a special Friday afternoon school holiday.

Coming home that day, my little playmate from the neighbouring farm asked if he could come and play, and I told him "No" most decidedly. Imagine my horror when he still came, and just as I'd planned to have my mother to myself for half an hour. I was so annoyed, I threw a chain at him and swore! I was promptly sent to bed for being so rude.

He told his Mom that I had sworn and said "Damn", to which she replied that I wasn't a very nice little girl to play with, and to stay away. He never took the hint, because I've been married to him for over 40 years.'

TYING THE GATES

'At weddings at Dean (and the custom still goes on in some places) the lychgates were tied with string and not undone until the bride and groom had thrown pennies for the village children. All the children turned out for weddings. Neighbours would view the presents at the bride's home, and were given a piece of cake and a glass of sherry or home-made wine.'

Tying the gates at weddings, as here at Kirkby Stephen parish church, has been the delight of generations of Cumbrian children.

CHILDBIRTH AT HOME

'Preparations for home deliveries included collecting brown paper and newspapers with which to protect the mattress and the provision of a large jug and basin for washing mother and baby. A drawer might be used if a cradle was not available. An experienced local woman would be taken on to look after the mother, the other children and the home for three to four weeks as it was common practice for the mother to remain in bed for at least two weeks following childbirth.

The midwife either walked or cycled and it was not unusual for her to have two or three deliveries in a day, perhaps in Arlecdon, Lamplugh or Dean. She must have been fit! Labour may have been induced by the administration of an enema and a dose of castor oil. The doctor would be called upon only if complications occurred, bearing in mind that his services would have to be paid for before the days of the National Health Service.

A piece of lint was placed over the umbilical cord and a flannel binder kept it in place. Baby would be dressed in a "Barra" coat; this went over the long nightie and buttoned up at the bottom like a sleeping bag. A shawl was then firmly wrapped round the baby before placing him on his side to sleep. It was thought that placing him on alternate sides would prevent his ears from sticking out!

If he had wind, a hot cinder from the fire would be dropped into a cup of water and a teaspoon of the cooled liquid administered. Sticky eyes were cleaned with milk, spit or rubbed with a wedding ring.

Although complications and sometimes death were a common feature of childbirth, Lamplugh mothers proved capable of producing hearty offspring, the heaviest recalled at 14 pounds!'

'On the birth of a baby at Lorton in the 1930s, usually at home, the District Nurse was required to visit twice a day for the first week and once in the second week, travelling by bicycle as much as ten miles each way. If the doctor was needed at the confinement, then she was lucky, she got a ride in his car on the first day.'

'Villagers at Dean paid into a health club, a small weekly amount to pay for visits from the District Nurse and for care when babies were born. Usually a neighbour in the village acted as a midwife to all expectant mothers; the District Nurse had to cycle from Kirkland. If the payments to the health club were in arrears then a very hurried payment was made as the expected date of birth drew near.'

'My youngest sister was born in May 1941, during a particularly bad air raid on Barrow. I, aged five, was fascinated by the midwife's bags and packages and for many years I thought all babies were "born" in a dark suitcase at very short notice!'

RUM BUTTER

'When a baby was christened a dish of rum butter was passed round the tea table with crackers or bread and the empty dish was passed around everyone on the way back and a collection made in it for the new baby.'

'Rum butter is still made for a baby's christening party in the Lake District. When my father was young the youth of the valley made a practice of raiding the house where there was to be a christening and making off with a bowl of rum butter and a loaf of bread. When this had been eaten, the lads returned the bowl, in which they left money for the baby. There are many old rum butter bowls still in existence.

Another curious custom told to me by my grandmother, was that when a single girl in the village had a baby she was obliged to go to the village church and walk the length of the aisle carrying the baby, thereby making public what was regarded as her disgrace. I think this happened in Grasmere years and years since.'

WHEN PRAMS WERE PRAMS

'Babies were pushed around in *real* prams with big deep bodies and springs which made them bounce as they were pushed along. Most baby items were plain and ordinary, built to last and serve their purpose well, because the large items such as prams, cots etc had to serve each baby as it came along until the family was complete. Then, the prams could be used for collecting wood on country walks, transporting vegetables from the allotment, or the wheels could be used to build a "Jordie", which was a flat, low cart with a rope to steer it.'

HOME REMEDIES

'Use carbolic soap and sugar made into a paste for boils, or to draw a boil to a head, fill a bottle with very hot water, empty it quickly and put the neck of the bottle over the boil and leave to cool (sure to make your eyes water if nothing else).

Jean and Bobby Clark in the 1920s, when prams were built to last!

Use a dolly blue bag for stings. To pull out a loose tooth, tie a piece of thread around the tooth and tie the other end to the open oven door (old range, of course) and push the door shut quickly.

First thing in the morning, dip your chilblains in the full chamber pot.

Have a shampoo Friday night with paraffin to prevent nits.'

'How I hated that goose grease spread on a piece of red flannel and pinned inside my vest! It was so difficult to fasten my liberty bodice over it. Buttons were shed left, right and centre.

Another of my Gran's cures was from a gipsy woman who came hawking to the door during New Fair Week. The substance was put into a saucer with torn up brown paper, then vinegar was poured over it. It was put near the bed of a sufferer of a "bad chest", the fumes helping to ease breathing.

My Gran did not put soap on her face. She would wash it with a handful of oatmeal tied up in a piece of muslin; in summer she used a handful of elder flowers in a muslin bag.'

'On Friday nights, syrup of figs, Epsom salts and lemon, or sulphur and treacle were administered for "inner cleanliness"! Children's hair was carefully checked with a fine tooth comb (much pulling and tugging), then washed with Derbac soap in an effort to combat the dreaded head-louse or "biddies" so prevalent before the introduction of modern insecticides.'

'Springtime seemed to coincide with the outbreak of a number of illnesses which affect children – measles, colds, spots, scarlet fever, chicken pox etc. As there was no National Health Service, parents used traditional remedies handed down by grandparents. If they were worried about anything, they would also seek advice from relatives or neighbours. It had to be very serious before a doctor was called.

In the spring we were usually given home-made drinks of salts and lemon, a mixture of brimstone and treacle, plenty of soups, vegetables, boiled leeks and onions, with butter and pepper. These were given to "purify the blood".'

'For coughs and colds we had our chests and backs rubbed with eucalyptus and camphorated oil, which smelled very strong. This, however, was an improvement on the goose grease (saved from the Michaelmas and Christmas goose) with which Mother and her family were anointed. We also had to have a woollen sock, which had been worn, fastened around our necks at bedtime. Some children wore them at school. These children were sewn into their clothes for the winter, with reputedly a layer of brown paper under them.

Local chemists at Broughton Beck made up cough medicines, of which the best remembered was "Tonsilline", dispensed by Fleming and Farrar in Market Street, Ulverston. It was brown and not unpleasant but could have been lethal, as it contained morphine and strychnine.

There was a fashion in the 1930s to wear iodine lockets, small bakelite containers holding something soaked in iodine. I think these were worn to prevent goitre.'

'My grandfather was a keen herbalist. He treated my knee infection by bandaging it with a plantain leaf, and it soon cleared up. To stop bleeding, he would use powdered rice on a piece of lint.'

DOCTORS AND DENTISTS

'Early this century, the bone-setter, forerunner of the modern osteopath, operated in the Broughton Beck area. He was a member of the Dennison family from Kendal, more than one of whom were gifted in this way. He used to visit The Queen's Head each Thursday, setting broken bones and putting right dislocations. Several of our family have reason to be grateful to this man who drove from Kendal in a pony and trap.'

'At the Hiring Fair in Kendal, anyone wanting to see the visiting dentist for the extraction of a bad tooth would also have the benefit of a small band playing whilst the dentist did his work!'

'When I had pneumonia in the late 1950s, the doctor walked the three miles from Ravenstonedale every day to visit me. It was winter and thick with snow. My father and brothers had to dig out every day to meet him and it kept filling in again behind them.'

THE DISTRICT NURSE

'I have happy memories of commencing my District Nursing career at Patterdale on bicycle – and more unhappy ones in the rain and snow.

In those days there were no pre-packed dressings or disposable instruments. Dressings were cut and then sterilised in a biscuit tin, popped in the oven at home, and all instruments were boiled in the patient's kitchen as required. It took me a long time to get used to using a pair of forceps once and then throwing them away.

I remember I frequently inherited bedpans and commodes and having acquired a heavy solid wood commode realised it was just what was needed for Mrs A. I'd soon sort out her problem! I had passed my driving test by then and after a great deal of manoeuvring, the cumbersome item was placed on the passenger seat. Still a lot of hard work ahead to deliver it up a narrow alleyway. After several visits I noticed the absence of this elegant piece of furniture. After a gentle enquiry I was informed it had been chopped up for firewood by another member of the family!

In those far-away days the village nurse was involved in so many incidents from first aid through road and mountain accidents to drink problems and marital upsets, the last offices, school nurse and child care. You name it and we tried to serve to the best of our ability. There was frequently an item in my personal diary which might have read – "Check TPR and BP Fish." The latter word meant I had promised to pick up a nice piece of fish to tempt my patient's appetite.

There weren't the number of tourists in our valley way back and everybody knew everybody. The elderly could teach us a thing or two and we had to tread carefully with our advice and instructions. I like to think I became a friend to all my patients and was privileged to share their troubles as well as their joys.'

FEVERS

'1935 is a year I will always remember. I was seven years old and there was an epidemic of diphtheria to which I succumbed. Perhaps I was greedy but I also caught scarlet fever simultaneously.'

I recall my father carrying me down to the ambulance which took me to the fever hospital for the next seven weeks. At home all the rooms were sealed and fumigated. The family were put into quarantine and amazingly none of them were infected.

How different that ward was from the cheerful, sunny children's ward of today. Because of double infection I was isolated, off the main adult ward, with a view of the cemetery and no visitors. The family were allowed to view me through glass!

Odd memories stay in my mind. The revolting bread and milk – they only tried that once; the bed full of skin each morning (it peeled off in quantity); the orange I wasn't allowed to take home because it couldn't be fumigated.

About Eastertime I went home, very feeble, very skinny and unable to walk. I remember with pleasure the afternoons when Horlicks and Virol featured while my twin sister was of course at school. Not so pleasant was having my legs rubbed with Neat's foot oil – a horrible smell.

I was so disappointed that I was unable to stand with the rest of the Brownies who formed a guard of honour for the Duke and Duchess of York who came to open the Jubilee Bridge. I did however have the perfect compensation. I was given a new bike (my legs now worked) while my sister had to make do with a secondhand one!'

'Scarlet fever was common and involved a seven week stay at the Fever Hospital at High Carley, where there were also wards for diphtheria and other infectious diseases. On the other side of the wall was a sanitorium for the treatment of tuberculosis patients from all over Lancashire. Local children with TB were treated at Oubas House Hospital where their beds, with red blankets and white sheets, lined up on the verandah, could be seen from Hoad.'

'I well remember the "Fever Ambulance" – it used to be very busy picking up patients from round the south of the county and taking them to the sanitorium in Parkside Road, Kendal. The attending nurse made a splash of colour with the bright red blankets she carried for wrapping round the unfortunate patients.'

'In 1943, aged 17 years, I started training at the Carlisle City Hospital for Infectious Diseases, which had about 400 beds and treated patients with diphtheria, scarlet fever, meningitis, typhoid, dysentry, measles, chicken-pox, whooping cough and TB. The nurses wore long striped dresses, "butterfly" caps and thick black stockings. In the first year we received £2 0s 8d a month, food and a bedroom and worked 98 hours a fortnight. We could get bread and dripping and cocoa for tenpence.

There were only sulphonamides available in 1943 and daily baths and cold sponge-downs were used to reduce temperatures. In 1944 the American Army gave penicillin to treat a meningitis epidemic and in the following year new drugs became available for TB and meningitis. Scarlet fever patients were kept in hospital a month and could only shout to visitors through the windows. The home bedroom was stoved (fumigated) and possessions used in hospital were treated the same way before they could be taken home.

After my fever training I went on to general nursing, but back on the TB/meningitis ward in 1950 streptomycin was giving wonderful results with children who would previously have died. I ended my career as a District Nurse.'

HAVING OUR TONSILS OUT

'When Mother had her tonsils out (c1906) her father took her from Broughton Beck by horse and cart to Dr Robinson in Ulverston. She was laid on the kitchen table with her father holding her head while the doctor ripped out her tonsils. The following week she went to the doctor for a check-up and when he said there was a little bit more to come out, she ran off up the street, leaving her hat behind. She never did have that bit removed and always had throat trouble.

Joyce had her tonsils removed in Ulverston Cottage Hospital about 20 years later, walking there in the morning and back at tea time. Her only abiding memory is that Mother gave the little boy in the next bed sixpence, but didn't give her anything!'

'One man at Soulby remembers as a child having his tonsils out lying on the kitchen table, the doctor coming to the house. When his friends called to see him the next day they were shown his tonsils on a tin plate.'

'Remember the world before antibiotics? Keswick school, nearly 60 years ago, relied on fresh air, open windows, Lysol disinfectant in the bath, and frequent medical inspections.

Around 1935 there was a measles epidemic. The school was closed for work but boarders could not go home so each day we went for walks – and each day the numbers shrank as more spots appeared.

I remember going up Cat Bells – then came spots! A darkened room and bed. My friend, Christopher, aged five years, died in the school so the staff did their very best to help the others to recover. We had to keep very quiet.

At Keswick cottage hospital – the room is still much the same – I had my tonsils removed. My mother told me that we were going to visit someone in hospital but I was suspicious as she carried a small case. In no time my clothes were off and I was lying on a trolley being wheeled along, my mother and, by then, my father too holding my hands. A nurse's white starched cap was put over my face and a liquid with a funny smell poured on – chloroform. I yelled, then went out. Later, on recovery, being asked what I'd like to eat, I replied, "Mutton and mint sauce!" As an acquaintance had died having his tonsils out, no wonder my parents were anxious.

Thank heavens for antibiotics!'

'Tonsils were removed at the local hospital, with as many as 30 to 40 children in the same ward. I well remember in the 1930s sleeping "top to toe" with a boy, and going home to ice cream and jelly next day.'

BEATRIX POTTER'S WEDDING GIFT

'Mrs Amanda Thistlethwaite, married in June 1932 at Hawkshead, was visited by Beatrix Potter to view the wedding presents. On her arrival she said that she had been sent by her husband, Mr Heelis, to see what was needed. She looked around and finally said, "You have got everything, you don't need a present, but Mr Heelis says you have to have one, so I will give you a cheque." This she did and Amanda received a cheque for £2.'

FUNERAL CUSTOMS

'Since the early years of this century, funeral practices have changed dramatically as better transport and communications have become the norm. Also, before the Second World War, most people died in their homes, not in hospital.

In those days not many people in the countryside owned cars and even fewer households had a telephone so that when a death occurred the funeral arrangements were usually passed on by word of mouth.

A local lady who was an expert at such things was usually asked to do the "laying out" – preparing the body before the arrival of the undertaker. The one I remember had a bicycle and in later years a motorbike. In many homes there was a special drawer which held a white shroud and stockings, a drawsheet with strong tapes for lifting, and white linen sheets for the death bed.

I remember my father, or a friend of the deceased person's family, walking round the parish to farms and cottages "bidding" people to a funeral, informing them of "lifting time" – the time the coffin left the residence – and also the time of the burial service. Friends gathered at the house and were asked if they would like to view the corpse, supervised by the undertaker. At one funeral he was heard to say, "Aye, poor old body, isn't she leyke hersel'!" All the men wore bowlers, usually called hard hats, some of them slightly green with age, and the womenfolk, especially near relatives, wore unrelieved black for about a year and were not expected to go out much at all during that time. My father thought that was an unnecessary and cruel custom and spoke of families who incurred heavy debts buying mourning clothes which they simply couldn't afford.

The parish hearse was a horse-drawn vehicle housed in a nearby building and it was usually driven by a local farmer with a Clydesdale horse in shining harness between the shafts.

My mother died in 1925 when I was a little girl and I was sent to stay with a neighbour on the funeral day but I remember watching the hearse making its slow progress down to Lanercost Abbey. Some mourners walked but there was stabling for a few ponies and traps nearby.

In the churchyard there were still relics of Victorian days with glass globes full of wax flowers beside the gravestones.'

'A most interesting custom in Dentdale was the giving of funeral cakes. These were rather like raspberry buns without the jam. They were coated in white icing (the shroud?) and were handed out in individual glass dishes. These little dishes still turn up at local sales. Mrs Mattinson was the last to make funeral cakes for sale and her recipe called for one pound of flour and one pound of sugar, with half a pound of butter rubbed in and eight eggs. The mixture was baked in small pieces until done but not brown, and covered with icing.

My father, who was born in 1880, told me that in the church at a funeral service there was a reserved pew which was called "Neighbours Row". On leaving the church, as well as being given a card or bookmark with the deceased's name and age, mourners would be given a funeral cake.'

'When anyone died at Hallbankgate, a friend or neighbour would lay out the body and it would be kept at home until the day of interment in the churchyard. The night before the burial a local man, Tom Jefferson, would go round the village knocking on the doors and saying, "Your company is desired at the funeral of . . . Lifting at 1.30 pm. Church at 2 pm."'

'When someone died at Braithwaite, a village woman usually went to lay them out and this was done in the best parlour and the relatives and friends were invited to go and say goodbye. The hearse used to be kept at Force Beck and was drawn by a horse.

Nearly all women wore a veil at funerals and the departed's wife wore widow's weeds – a bonnet with white frilling in front and a yard of black crepe hanging down the back.'

'When a death occurred all the mirrors in the house were covered over, so that the dead could not see their own soul. Death cards were sent out to inform the neighbours and the body was laid out in the front room for people to view. All blinds were drawn. Graves were dug by hand by Mr Beattie, the local gravedigger and sexton at Dean, and in 1917 it cost six shillings if you lived in the village and twelve shillings if you lived outside, while in 1948 the cost was 22 shillings and 30 shillings respectively.'

'Funerals weren't talked about, but we always knew when there was one because Dad's hatbox would come down.'

'Following a death, a trusted friend was invited to do 'the bidding'. He would visit all the homesteads for miles around, bidding the men to assemble at the house of the deceased at the appropriate time.

The mourners would be welcomed with a glass of whisky and a chance to bid a last farewell to their friend before setting off along the 'Corpse Road' to the church.

Returning, everyone enjoyed a meal of Cumberland ham and Nikkie cake (a traditional plate cake filled with currants and mixed peel, well soaked in spirit) before going on their respective ways.'

CHILDHOOD & SCHOOLDAYS

VISITS WITH THE PAST

To many children, visits with grandparents or other relatives were journeys into the past, where "mod cons" were few and far between and life still went on much as it had done since the early years of the century. Some loved it, and some hated it, but those visits had a magic all their own.

IT WAS MAGIC

'These memories are of 1925, when I was seven years old. My sister Bo and I visited our grandparents at Waterside Cottage, situated near Hawkshead, each year for two or three weeks. This was my father's old home and he drove us up in his Humber from Lincolnshire, where we lived. The journey took between five and six hours via Ilkley, Settle, Windermere and the ferry. There was not much traffic but in bottom gear up the hill from the ferry the car was quite noisy. How wonderful it was though, to come over from Kendal and see Windermere lake and to then arrive at the ferry. I cannot remember the ferryman's name but he knew us and was always glad to see us. The ferryboat would take up to six cars, traps or carts but we were usually the only car.

And so we arrived at Waterside, or home as my father always called it, so happy he was to see his old house and his parents. In 1925 my grandmother was a beautiful person in her early sixties and my grandfather, over 80 years old, was a rather slow, old man and completely deaf. He had a long white beard and firm features and we were in awe of him. They greeted us with lots of happiness when we arrived and into the house we went. Here, it was magic!

My grandfather was full of imagination – he had made little shelves out of growths on trees and they were varnished black. On them were stuffed birds and animals of which the most startling was halfway up the stairs – an otter. Also halfway up the stairs was a door with little diamond panes which opened into the "pink room". This was a little room on stilts built by my grandfather for his wife one year while she was away on holiday. A glass roof was covered in see-through material, pink panes in some of the long windows looked onto the garden behind the house, and little pink upholstered chairs, a table and desk and a pink carpet filled the room. We were allowed to play Racing Demon (a card game) on the carpet on wet days. Sadly the room rotted away and was pulled down after the war.

My sister Bo and I always slept in the bedroom which looked both over Esthwaite Water and the back garden. We could see the pier by the lake where we sat and fished for perch with worms. There were lots of shoals in those days and we would make potted perch. We could also see the tiny glass house where our grandfather sat all day, looking at the lake and the boathouses. Granny sent us shopping to Hawkshead by boat, which was about three quarters of a mile, with one oar each, and we were there in no time. We ran from where we had pulled up the boat, near a farm, to the village with the list and back again with full baskets. We rowed over the lake again and manoeuvred the boat into the boathouse. We were quite proud of ourselves.

From the east window we looked at the lawn with the summer-house built by my grandfather round the trunk of a weeping elm. There was a wooden table inside and a seat along the back. We played here endlessly but now the trunk of the tree has grown and broken the table and the whole house has tilted and the elm is dead. Further up the garden were two wire cages with decorative Chinese pheasants inside and then a wired part for hens. We fed them and collected eggs every day. Also from this east window we could see the fernery, which was just fairyland! Also invented by my grandfather, it was a glass house with a stream running through it into a pool with a little fountain: a little path from the pool led to steps which took you to a seat very near the roof. Near the pool was a door, and wonder of wonders, this opened into the dining room of the house. We were only allowed in the fernery with a grown-up!

I must mention the dynamo that could be found in the stone-built house by the lake. My grandfather had built tarns on the tops near Flagstaff Hill and these gave a head of water to the hatchery just north of Waterside, where trout were bred, and then a pipe took the water down a field to the road and along to the dynamo. Every day at dusk my grandfather went to the dynamo house and pulled a lever to set the engine in motion and then the lights came on in the house. We usually went with him and in later years one of us pulled the lever. It had to be pushed down before my grandfather went to bed so there were oil lamps in the house as well.

Part of the magic of our visit was our grandfather himself. Each day we woke him by knocking on the bedroom door, which had a metal knocker that was very loud. We then left Granny to dress and give him breakfast after which we took him by the hand for a walk towards Sawrey – as far as the water trough (still the same) where we would sit for a few minutes before starting back home. High Crag and its lovely garden wasn't there; there was only a field. All the trees along the way are now much taller. We only saw a farm cart or two, hardly ever did we see a car; we also saw several people walking including Beatrix Potter (who knew my grandfather well) in her long coat and pulled down hat. She would pleasantly pass the time of day to us and then continue walking to look round her sheep. There were also a few bicycles and an occasional pony and trap.

When we arrived back at Waterside, Grandpa would go over to his little glass box and sit there all day. We would have to call him in when meals were ready. Another outing was to walk to Colthouse with Granny to have tea with elderly ladies. On Sunday mornings we went to meetings at the old Quaker meeting house. The road has hardly altered nor the meeting house, farmyard and other homes we visited, except they now have more orderly gardens and new breeds of shrub! It was good to get back to Waterside after these "well behaved" visits, into the cosy bathroom and so to bed.

The boat was the only means of transport for my grandparents in 1925 as my grandfather was too old to drive his electric car in which he used to go to work at Troutbeck Bridge until he retired in 1904. This was a small open car run by batteries which were charged up every day by the engine that produced the electricity for the house, and then again at the electricity works at Troutbeck Bridge for the home journey. Even with all this charging up the car was not powerful enough to get up the ferry hill and the brakes would not hold it going down either; so my grandfather had to go round by Ambleside to get to work.

Unfortunately the electric car was neglected after my grandfather died so it is lost. I don't remember ever seeing it although it existed unused until 1940.

This ends my magic memories. There are many more to think about: the stream running under the lawn and the road into the lake, the window boxes on the west side of the house, the special smell of Waterside and of the dynamo house and fishing on the tarns.'

AWAY FROM CIVILISATION

'Aged four in 1950, I spent my summers with my Nanna and Granda at Blennerhasset, away from all the trappings of civilisation, while my Mum looked after my baby twin sisters in Carlisle.

There was no electricity, a cold water tap and no sanitation. One half of the house was virtually derelict and we lived in a large kitchen lit by oil lamps. Chips were a special treat cooked on a large primus stove and all the other meals were cooked on a black range, which turned out the most delicious cakes and scones. If Granda caught a rabbit we had rabbit pie, and he grew a lovely selection of vegetables in the garden and flowers which he sold from his greenhouse.

We went to bed in a huge brass bedstead with a candle to light the way and a potty under the bed. A large proddy mat was beside the bed, warm to put your feet on first thing in the morning. We often listened to the radio, powered by acid batteries, which had to be taken to the village to be re-charged.

My Mum used to regularly send me parcels of comics and other treats, especially sweets which had just come off ration, and the postman was eagerly awaited.

Our toilet was an earth closet at the bottom of the garden and I hated the dark, warm, smelly place with its spiders and cobwebs. Each evening I walked down to the farm to help the farmer bring the cows in. "How up" came easily to my small lips and the stick I carried was taller than me. I loved the smell of the cowshed and helping the farmer to milk his cows by hand, but I hated the taste of milk and still do.

My Nanna and I walked everywhere and she took me round the fields and patiently taught me the names of flowers, trees and animals we watched. The dry stone walls seemed ten feet tall and I frequently scabbed my knees climbing on – and falling off. One day she took me on a trip "on the chara". We went to Allonby and it was the first time I had seen the sea. I still remember the sheer awe at this expanse of sparkling water which stretched all the way up to the sky and when I got the chance to paddle with my dress tucked in my knickers I revelled in the fun of it all.

Each year when it was nearly time to go back to school we picked brambles and rose hips. We had National Milk tins with a piece of string through and every day gathered the fruit which was then sold to a man in a van who used to visit the village to buy them. Each time I look at rose hip syrup I fondly remember those days in the fields with my Nanna, who was well over 70 years old at the time and always wore a flowery wrap-round pinny and a dark coloured beret on her snow white hair – treasured memories indeed.'

'I was a town child and every year with my family I went to spend holidays in the country with my grandparents. This was a place where every one spoke a rather obscure language. My father assumed this language as soon as he set foot in his native village. My mother understood it but thankfully did not speak it. I neither understood nor spoke it which gave rise to the belief in the family that "t'child was deef"!

My grandparents lived in the centre of the village, and an aunt, uncle and cousin lived on the outskirts, or up t'village. Sometimes in the evenings I would go up t'village to play with my cousin. If it was an Easter holiday, when it came time to return to Grannie's night had fallen. I would step out of the house into a darkness that was solid and almost touchable. On each side of the road there were tall trees, and on looking up I could just discern a pale streak that was the sky. I would shuffle, run, stumble down the road with my eyes fixed on that narrow strip of sky, convinced that one day the trees would meet overhead and I would never see the sky again. Seen in daylight the road had a hedge on one side and a wall on the other. The level of the field behind this wall was much higher than the road level so that cows – big cows – looked down on one.

The alternative to coming down the village was to sleep with my cousin. She was younger than me and had a lighted candle beside the bed all night. In the summer months I would cower under the bedclothes watching the foot-long shadows on the ceiling of the moths and daddy-long-legs that circled the flame.

These were my holidays and I longed passionately for each one to finish so that I could return home to the place where light came on at the touch of a button, hot water came out of taps both upstairs and downstairs and, oh blessings, there were lights in the streets at night.'

MY CORNISH GRANDMA

'The family came to Millom when the Cornish mines closed, to work in Hodbarrow mines. We often visited Grandma, who lived in a terraced house in Devonshire Road. The parlour contained a black horsehair sofa which always prickled my legs. The toilet was in the back yard beside the washhouse, the Wesleyan calendar hanging up alongside neatly cut squares of newspaper.

Grandma always wore long black dresses, and a gold locket. Being a Cornish lady she had a lovely accent, and called everyone "my dear". Her Cornish pasties were out of this world, but I disliked the caraway seed cake which was a Cornish speciality. Of course there was always Cornish cream and apple pie. She was a "real" Grandma with her rocking chair by the fire, knitting outfits for my dolls. I recall her showing her nails broken and roughened with sewing and scrubbing, telling me never to bite mine or they would grow like hers, so I never did! When we walked to Devonshire Road from the station, I used to run ahead – the door was always open. Grandma would be sitting rocking and took no notice of me creeping in to hide under the chenille covered table and when Mum and Dad arrived, Grandma pretended I wasn't there, until I couldn't keep quiet any longer.

When Grandma died in 1929 aged 70, I was six years old and was taken to the bedroom where her little figure was lying, covered in a white sheet. A plate of salt was on her tummy and a penny on each eye. The mirrors were covered with sheets. I think the salt was to keep the "evil spirits" away.'

SUNNY SUMMERS

'Holidays during the war years were spent in a little village not far from Carlisle called Cumwhitton, where one of my aunts lived. It was a lovely place to spend summer, always sunny and warm. As Auntie lived near a farm I was sent each morning to collect the milk for breakfast, taking a little milk can with me. I would watch the cows being milked by hand. The farmer's wife had a name for each cow.

Afterwards my cousin and I would go to the village shop; the lady was called Mrs Bacon which really amused us. The smell in that shop was one which I have never encountered since. Then further on to the village post office, another small place with everything from a stamp to an elephant (toy, of course). We paddled in the small stream which ran along the side of the road leading us to another farm where the lady let us feed the hens and collect eggs still warm in the nests. Sometimes she allowed us to feed the calves; their rough tongues licked our hands and they looked at us with big brown eyes under long eyelashes.

Most afternoons we played in the meadow near the church – loads of buttercups, daisies and cowslips grew there and butterflies hovered everywhere. We nearly always had meals outdoors in the garden, which had apple and plum trees, and we enjoyed picking the fruit. The worst part of staying in the country was a visit to the toilet, which was at the far end of the garden in a little wooden hut with a bucket beneath a wooden seat. This one had two holes which I thought was for twins to use.

Sometimes we went with Auntie to the common where she cut lumps of peat for the fire. Most houses in the village had peat cutting rights. We loaded up the old pram and trundled it back and helped to unload peat into a shed. Some was always put in the hearth to dry. The smell as it burned is another I shall not forget, but the most noticeable smell of all was from the blacksmith's shop which was just across the road. Many an hour was spent watching Frank the blacksmith putting shoes on the farm horses that came. He had a big roaring fire and great bellows to fan the flames to get it red hot for the metal to make the shoes.

All too soon the holiday was over and the bus which ran twice a day would draw up outside the gate. Anthony the driver would help with luggage. He knew everyone who travelled on his bus, and their relations, and he would tell stories on the journey back to Carlisle and give a big smile and wave as you got off. Looking back I suppose I had good holidays in the peace of the countryside away from all the noise of wartime.'

DAYS OF FREEDOM

Wandering off for the day into the countryside and the farmyard, greeting friend and stranger alike, and returning home just in time for tea – how many of our children, sadly, have the freedom we had and took for granted? It really did seem that the sun shone every day through those long summer holidays.

WE HAD FREEDOM

'We had freedom, something today's children will never know. We'd sit on the fence waiting to collect car numbers in our little notebooks. We had patience then, and just as well, as perhaps only two cars went past each day!

We played hopscotch on the road; even if we couldn't afford toys and games we could manage to buy a piece of chalk. That same piece of chalk enabled us to play rambling hide and seek games, with an arrow on a tree, or a gate, or a stone. We'd walk and run, and hide for miles. Our parents didn't have to worry about our whereabouts – Cumberland was a safe place then!

The orchard was full of trees, apples, pears, plums. We had a swing on the big old apple tree, a piece of string and a block of wood, flying through the air, not a care in the world. We played hide and seek in the orchard as well, where the buttercups grew tall and we could wriggle amongst them and not be found for ages.

Everything stopped on a Sunday afternoon, when the old folk slept. All the local youth, maybe 50 of them, arrived in the meadow and played football or cricket. The teams were big but it was fun, six foot tall youths letting a nine year old girl bowl them out or save their penalties.

We'd pack our jam sandwiches in our saddle-bag and go for a bike ride – it didn't matter where we went or how long we were away.

We had freedom!'

WANDERING THE COUNTRYSIDE

'Children in Eskdale would walk long distances to school, and dawdle home in the afternoon, eating "bread and cheese" (hawthorn leaves), nuts, berries, sorrel leaves, young nettles or pignuts. They would talk to the roadmen, who would be breaking stones or clearing the edges of their section. If it was a windy day when the steam roller came, with the man walking ahead with a red flag, there would be clouds of dust and grit.

The children would see the farmworkers and other familiar people about the valley; indeed, a stranger would occasion comment. Freedom and friendliness are in all the memories of those who were children during the inter-war years, although they had to show respect. The policeman in Eskdale had a walking stick, with which he could deal a swift blow to a lad who was cheeky.

Harvest time at Ravenstonedale in 1947. The farms drew children like a magnet and many helped out at harvest by taking food and drink out to the men in the fields.

Farms were like magnets to all the boys, and they would go there after school and at weekends, whether or not they belonged to a farming family. There was the rabbiting, rat hunts and fishing, besides the many chores to be done, and at harvest times they would all be helping in the oatfield or picking up potatoes, along with the quarry folk who would come after work.

Longrigg Farm had four work horses, besides the yearlings to be broken, the working mares and the foals, and in the evenings boys would walk the horses home, water them and help to feed them, whilst girls remember taking tea in a billycan to the fields at haytime, and being allowed to ride the horse back to the farm. The first tractor wasn't seen in the valley before 1948, and that would have been the big, heavy Fordson, with iron wheels.

We country boys really did get a better education than townies. At the farms we were learning all the time; we were involved with older people, listening to their talk and seeing their ways. And those farming people were marvellously adaptable, able to turn their hands to any new skills. Farms affected communities, and we lived and breathed farming.'

BUSY DAYS

'You certainly didn't cast a clout until May was out and even if it was a lovely summery day and you wanted your summer dress on, you couldn't take off your winter things, so we just put our dresses over them! Last year's clothes were brought out and lengthened, false hems put on, etc. When no more could be done to make them fit you, they were passed on to someone who perhaps didn't have a dress to wear. (I can remember having such a frock!) My mum made my dresses with pants to match (a pocket for your hankie). A number of us had dresses the same, with a small rosebud pattern. Our mothers went to the same sewing afternoon at Enyeat and they must have got rolls of cheap cotton from somewhere. The dresses had a little saddle and full skirt and we were always looking for some sort of belt to pull our waists in! We had to clean our shoes each evening, ready for school or church and on our return we always had to change our clothes and shoes to play in.

When you were particular friends of people, you were invited into the living room and they talked and talked, more people would come in and then we were sent out into the back garden to play so that we didn't hear their conversations! I often wondered what they spoke about.

We used to enjoy throwing a stick in the river and watch for it coming out at the other side of Challon Hall Bridge (ideal for that game). However, it was not so good for running down Rostard with your iron "booly" in case the horses were crossing the tramlines at the bottom of the hill. I was forbidden to ride my bike down Rostard but I eventually got brave and got on it near the bottom, where a gang of us went over the bridge, missed the sharp turn and ended up in a heap amongst the stinking ramps (onions) in Challon Hall Wood. We then had to go home and try to hide our scars and bruises and buckled bikes after all the strong warnings we had had of steep hills, trams, horses, tramlines, sharp turns and hazardous bits of road!

We had hens and a hen-house in the little Rostard field and we fed them twice a day and collected the eggs. We had a Rhode Island Red cockerel whom we called Nebuchadnezzar and he used to stroll in the road as if it belonged to him. He ran after white socks and black patent leather ankle-strap shoes! He was always around and lived to a great age. With his scaly legs he was a friend to everyone, even though they did poke him with walking sticks to annoy him. He then started performing – he loved to attract a group of children around him so that he could show off. Poor Nebby! He never got in the way of horses or the gunpowder trams – he was wiser than that.

It was a lovely walk down the tramlines to Crooklands, by the beck and the weir, which you had to cross twice across the "slush" which was very deep and if you had fallen in you would have drowned. The best primroses and violets and cowslips grew on the feeder side, but how we were lectured not to go near the slush. We often got our feet wet, and sometimes a lot more than our feet – as far as our liberty bodices and "combs"!

A job I did enjoy was "going sticking" – looking for fuel for our various needs. We had to wear a lot of clothes to keep warm for this job. We tried to get thickish logs to saw if we could find them. We had to fill the paraffin lamps each evening and clean the lamp glasses daily, after school. We took a cake or a loaf of new baked bread to someone who wasn't so well, brought back a pile of washing or a scribbled note asking if Mum could sit up with someone at night, and went back with the answer. We were kept busy, what with all this and homework too. Sometimes we had a composition to write, or a bit of sewing or knitting, or a poem to learn which we would have to recite the next day in front of the class.

I loved the summers playing in the beck and helping with hay-making – having a picnic in the field after you had been raking or turning the hay, getting a ride in the horse and cart back to the field for another load, and having a drink of cold tea in a blue enamel can with a lid which was supposed to be white inside but had seen better days and was stained brown! We had lovely ham sandwiches, all home-cured. Lots of hams and flitches hung at Kaker Mill I remember. I never waste my crusts, even today, as I think of the home-made bread baking in the big black ovens – you could recognise the smell miles away! It was lovely to eat the little cobs with butter which had just been churned – we helped with that too, taking our turn at turning the big barrel. Did we ever get time to relax?

I had my first driving lesson when I was twelve when my dad got a fresh vehicle – Dennis, the old Model T Ford. It was like a new toy. The local lads all learned to drive it round Park End Field (which was a bit boggy) and spent all their pocket money going down the trams to Dick Wall's Garage for a can of petrol, cheap in those days, and I was the only girl but I was allowed because it was our vehicle. The lads were mostly grammar school boys (later to become vets and dental surgeons) and they would tell me when to let the brake off! We've ended up in the beck before now and I often wonder if these old men, as they will be now, can remember our antics.

I did enjoy learning the alphabet in Mrs Earnshaw's infants class at Endmoor school. The blackboard was on the wall and each letter had a chalked picture – A for apple, B for ball, etc. I can remember them all. When it came to X we said Oxo, I don't know why. We all stood round Mrs Earnshaw and she pointed to each letter with a long cane. We chanted them and remembered them by heart, but we always seemed to stick at F for feather – we seemed to have to say it a dozen times and Mrs Earnshaw had to say "Please, boys, do not spit." They had all lost their front teeth! We used to say the fairies had kissed them out. (You got a silver threepenny bit under your pillow for each lost tooth. You used to take it to school in a clean white hankie to show the teacher how brave you had been.)

The children at Kaker Mill had a donkey called Gipsy. One summer I was ill in bed and waiting for the doctor. The door was wide open and in came Gipsy. I wondered what was happening. I heard the clomp, clomp of her hooves on the stairs. Suddenly she fell down and almost knocked the doctor off her feet. We all laughed and I felt much better!

Weddings were lovely – we always tried to get to see them. The boys tied the gate at Preston Patrick church and would not allow the bride and groom out until the groom and his best man had thrown pennies. Then the fun started – all of us scrambling about for who could get the most to spend at Nannie Black's sweet shop at School Houses.

When Merlyn Green foundations were being put in we had great fun walking on the ledges. When it was completed, Nurse Stockton moved in with Granny Wilton. She used to tell me all kinds of stories and I used to pick dandelions and burnip for her home-made wine. I thought it was great when she offered me a glass with a piece of home-made cake, but it made me sick and I never did get the liking for it. Poor Tom Stockings used to sleep in the loft – "Why does Tom go up there," I would ask, "when he could sleep with you?"

Nurse Stockton used to come to school and we lined up for inspection for "biddies" in the cloakroom. If you were found to have them you took a note home or "Auntie Alice" would call on Mum. As I had two long plaits my mother was always brushing my hair and combing it with a small-tooth comb. Then she put Harrison's Pomade on it, which was supposed to stop biddies jumping onto your hair. It wasn't a particularly nice smell at all. One of my mum's friends had a daughter and she had something similar put on her hair for the same reasons. When asked by her teacher what it was she had on her hair, she replied, "What my dad puts on dead folks"!'

GAMES AND CHORES

Without television or any of the other modern "toys", we played the games our parents had played – and probably their parents too. Toys often had to be improvised in the days when money was scarce, but imagination made them just as much fun. Sometimes the pranks that were played must have sorely tried the adults, though! We had chores to do too, around the house and on the farm, before and after school and at weekends. Pocket money was in short supply, but oh! the delight of spending the Saturday Penny.

TOYS WERE OF THE SIMPLEST

'I once asked my father what sort of mischief the children in the village got up to in his boyhood. After thinking for a while he remembered a group of boys fixed up a button dangling from black cotton, and tied it to a tree alongside the headmaster's house. They stood, well hidden, outside the garden gate and pulled the cotton so that the button tap, tap, tapped on the window pane. The headmaster came out repeatedly before he traced the cause of the irritating noise, by which time the gang had fled.

When I was young in the 1920s, toys were of the simplest, and cost very little. I can remember my younger sister sitting in her high chair playing with a "Nigroid" tin with a couple of buttons in it, which she shook and shook and banged and banged on the tray until we could stand it no longer! Later our parents made us kites out of strong paper and string, which we tried so hard to fly as we dashed up and down the garden. We spent hours playing with rubber balls which we bounced against the garage door – over our shoulders, behind our backs, under our legs, left handed or right handed. We played with cheap little spinning tops, and bowled hoops around the school playground and kept ourselves busy for hours.'

'As a little girl I lived in a place called Wet Sleddale, four miles from Shap. We never had any toys to play with so we used to collect fir cones. We made fields with little stones and the different kinds of fir cones were different kinds of sheep. We would pretend to have a shearing and dipping day, then they were all moved into another field. We were farm children, as you may have guessed.

After we got bored playing sheep we would make puddle pies. We had a hole in the wall as a pretend oven to bake them. These were for our tea after a hard day's work among the pretend sheep.'

'I enjoyed watching my grandchildren when they were small, blowing bubbles using the wire or plastic ring and thick, sticky liquid sold nowadays. Was it the fun we had, with an old clay pipe and "Rinso" or coal tar soap worked to a froth? Can you remember the awful taste we got if we sucked instead of blowing, and the excitement of chasing the rainbow coloured spheres as they sailed into the air? The clay pipe cost about twopence, and was given with the sharp admonition, "Don't break it!".'

THE GAMES WE PLAYED

'The local lads enjoyed the game of "Knock and Nash" around the village of Dalston. Very annoying I'm sure, but relatively harmless. They would fill a water barrel and lean it against a door, then knock on the door. The door would open and in went the water.'

'Football was often played with an empty syrup tin at the Co-op corner in Moresby – no traffic problems then. The lad lucky enough to get a football for his birthday or Christmas was always picked for the teams. The time our football burst and we patched it with a halfpenny stamp, it lasted all day.

We played a lot of games, including Duck, Cannon, Relievo, hide and seek, skipping and Hoppy Beds (the local name for hopscotch and played with a piece of slate). Whip and top or wooden tops was a playground game; a wooden spinning top was decorated with chalk so that when it was spun you could see the pretty pattern. Stick, or Roger or Bummer, was a five a side game. One person stands beside a wall and the other four bend over to make a caterpillar. The other team have to run up one at a time and leapfrog onto the caterpillar. The aim is for all five to hang on.

We used to go fishing with a bobbin, cotton and a bent pin, for "blophins" (small rock cod). We took them home and fed them to the cats.

Pitch and toss was a betting game played by some of the miners. Coins were tossed in the air and bets taken on which side they would land. Lookouts were posted in case the policemen came along as this was illegal betting.

Children didn't have a lot of toys – a few home-made wooden ones if they were lucky. The radio took pride of place in the parlour. Programmes such as *Children's Hour* with Auntie Vi and Uncle Mac were daily favourites. *Dick Barton – Special Agent*, and later on *Journey into Space* were very popular.'

'Games in the playground included skipping to chants such as:

"I'm a girl guide
Dressed in blue
These are the actions I can do
Stand at ease
Bend your knee
Right about
Left about
Out goes she".'

'Guinea Pig was a game with a piece of thick stick about four or five inches long, tapered at one end and laid over a stone. It was hit with another stick and the player who sent it furthest was the winner. Kick Can Knirky was a game of hide and seek when a can was kicked and whilst the catcher retrieved the can, the rest ran and hid.'

'In the 1940s we used to play a game called Buttony at Distington. We drew a square or circle on the ground, and someone put in a button. The aim was for other people to throw their buttons close to the first one. The winner then picked up as many as possible by spitting on her thumb, pressing it on a button and dropping it into her other

Crowning the May Queen on Beetham sports field in 1935.

hand. It must have been very unhygienic but we didn't care about that then.

I was particularly lucky as I knew someone who worked in the local button factory and I got lots of blanks and seconds for my collection. What's more, we played on the main street and only had to listen for the odd bus – not like the hundreds of vehicles that tear through the village today.'

'Playing in the street after tea, when the Crosby shops had closed, was great fun. Very few cars passed down our road. A cushioned seat tied to the lamppost was as great a thrill as a ride on Fletcher's roundabouts.

With a ball, we played Cannon. The others were a bit older than me and sometimes I was only allowed to play if the numbers were uneven. We took three sticks and set them in the corner of the electricity wall. Having arranged ourselves into two teams, we took turns standing in the gutter to knock down the sticks. Then we scooted. The opposing team had to catch us and in the meantime we had to set up Cannon again and scream "Cannon!"

The fair always came to the Market Square on Whit Saturday and the last Saturday in October's potato week. On Whit Saturday morning we had a Scram-mally. My uncle stood at the top of the stairs, up in the attic, and threw down a handful of coppers. We were finding money until the afternoon, counting it out and sharing it. Then up to the fair with heavy pockets, always returning much lighter but with a straw ball in a red, white and blue net or a clacketty-clack thing or something on a stick. The ball was what we coveted most – our Shirley Temple ball on a bit of elastic. We sang songs about Shirley and practised our skills against the wall. Up and down the ball would go on its long elastic, then it would be shortened and we sang the rhymes as we sprang the ball over our hands, over our legs, over our heads if we dared, against the wall. Once the elastic gave way we used an old stocking. The bigger girls were better than me and they seemed to be "in" for hours, but it was fun to watch them and await my turn with the rest.'

WE ALL HAD SLEDGES

'Hoar frost and icicles hanging on the wall and in the beck. Small ice floes in the estuary and frozen dubs (pools) on the shore hard enough to slide on.

Inside, homes were cosy and warm with coal and log fires. Outside, everywhere was quiet and still, the sky heavily laden with snow waiting to fall.

Every morning I would look out of the bedroom window hoping there had been a fall during the night, longing to make igloos, snowmen, huge snowballs and have snowball fights with the boys, and go sledging.

Then it started, slowly at first, twirling down, softly reaching the ground and quickly covering everything.

Sledges trundled up the road, up the lane, into the field. I would beg to join them. Getting ready to go out meant coat, pixie hood, scarf and mitts, long brown woolly stockings with garters, and clogs (or wellies if you were lucky enough to live a certain distance from school to qualify for them during the war). My clogs were red with metal caulkers. They were good for sliding on the pavement, but best on ice. I loved my red clogs.

From the top of the hill, girls and boys on sledges raced down, some sitting, some two together, some on tummies one on top of the other. Some landed in the hedge at the bottom. All of us got wet with wellies full of snow and damp bottoms. Gradually they would leave, feeling cold or ready for tea, and I would be left all alone sitting on my sledge, reluctant to go in. Snowing again. No sound except for the quiet touch of snow swirling around in a white wonderland. Then mother would call and come to look for me wondering what had happened. So I went inside, to get warm and dry and watch through the window the snow still coming down. Winter was fun.'

'As children in Windermere, during the war, we all had sledges. Our

Winter brought its own delights. Here on Mill Moss, Patterdale in the 1920s, a few hardy souls test the ice for skating.

dad had made ours, heavy, solid, wooden ones with metal runners and old rope for the handle. We were good at sledging for there seemed to be plenty of snowy days. The council didn't waste its money on grit – people put their own ashes on the pavement from their coal fires, but the roads were wonderfully "slape" (slippery). The sledges were good runners down but like pulling a baby tank back up.

We used to sledge in the field where Droomer estate is now, sliding down towards the beck. I only remember falling into the beck once and getting wet. It was perishing cold – how welcoming the hot cup of Bovril and the hot bath at home. I can remember well a boy flying down Hazel Street and on to Oak Street right under the milkman's horse. Luckily there was no mishap.

The "Cresta Run" of Windermere went from the Kendal Road A591, down to the lake at Bowness. There were always a few people waiting to set off at the top of Cuckoo Lane. You set off down the steep bit towards the LMS goods yard, now Lakeland Plastics, then under the railway bridge, hurtling down Thwaites Lane – then a lovely country lane, now part of the Droomer estate. The road has been changed since those sledging days. It used to go straight down on to Woodland Road past Oak Street, past our house (hope Mother isn't watching), the St Mary's boys school, Broad Street, then down Dick Fell's hill, past the quarry where the fire station now is, past the Brookside Hotel, and up the Carver Hill. Bellyflopping gave you a chance to kick and push up. Then down past the Baddeley Clock, the Circus field, now Goodly Dale, and the police station. It was a long flat to the top of the rise and usually you had to get off and push. Then the last bit hurtling down past the shops and flashing down Crag Brow, round Queen's Corner, down past St Martin's church, around the corner to the Promenade.

The thrill and excitement of having made it was suddenly replaced by the horrible thought of the long haul back up. Then we had a new police inspector and he banned sledging in the road.'

YOU'RE GOING TO DANCING CLASSES!

'"You're going to dancing classes," my mother announced. I was about seven years of age at the time. I was so excited, imagining myself as another Ginger Rogers. I duly set forth clutching a shilling for the class and sixpence to cover bus fares. The classes were to be held in a village called Houghton approximately three miles north of Carlisle.

In those days Houghton consisted of a village hall, a shop, a school, a church, the Co-operative and a few cottages. I remember vividly standing outside a clay cottage waiting for the bus to take us home (no cars for us in those days), and the teacher telling us ghost stories. It was very dark, everything being blacked out as it was wartime. We suddenly heard a noise behind us and we were clinging to each other in absolute terror. When the bus arrived the driver said it was probably a cow in a field; it took a while to convince us that it wasn't a ghost. For many months poor Miss Davies tried to teach us the art of tap dancing and graceful movement, but as we all had either two left feet or were suffering from puppy fat she did not succeed.'

I HAD CHORES TO DO

'I was born at 26 Old Smithfield, Egremont. We were a small family consisting of mother, father, one brother and myself. My father died very young so times were not so rosy. There were only 34 houses; three rows, top, middle and bottom. It was very healthy, clean and a safe place for all the children to play as it was surrounded by fields. One thing I always had was a good clean home, my mother doing all the baking of bread, biskies (not teacakes in those days), cakes, pies and home-made brawn. On baking day my brother and I always had spoons to scrape out the gingerbread dish – lovely.

When school finished on Friday I had chores to do, such as washing the front steps, eight altogether. But first I had to have a good piece of red ore. I usually found it on the nearby pit top. After spitting on a stone a few times and trying for the best red colour I eventually found what I was looking for. When I finished I felt proud to see how nice they looked. Sometimes I did the neighbour's steps too. I didn't get much pocket money so a friend and I collected about eight milk cans and went to Howbank Farm for the neighbours' milk – for which we were paid sixpence from our customers (a princely sum).

On Saturday afternoons I went to Wallace's Picture House in South Street. It cost one penny and a bag of sweets were also one penny. The picture "Pearl White and Elmo", eyes glued to the screen, would she get away from the oncoming train, and would the crocodiles eat Elmo? Continued next week!

In the light nights and sunny days out came the skipping ropes and the top and whip with different colours of chalk on the top so it looked nice when spinning, also bat and ball and hoop and stick.

Winter nights were spent making prodded and hookey rugs. The days rolled on and teenage time came when Cleator Moor lads met Egremont lassies on the famous Cleator Road. No money in our pockets but plenty to chat and laugh about.'

WE ALL HELPED

'All the childen at Holme St Cuthbert, both boys and girls, had work to do before and after school, and when they left school many went straight into farm work. They were all capable of hand milking cows, having been taught by their parents from an early age.

At Low Tarns Farm, we all had special jobs to do before we went to school – I had to feed the hens and collect the eggs and my sister washed the dishes. In those days the boys were privileged and there were some things they didn't have to do. I could hand milk and make butter in a big wooden churn, and was helping with the baking from the age of ten.

At Mawbray in the 1950s Geoff was responsible for the hens. "I had to shut them in at night – it was expected of me and I just did it. Even if I was with friends I would leave them and go back home to do it. It never occurred to me to ask someone else, it was my job. I would clean them out at weekends and feed them occasionally.

There were about seven or eight farms in the area and I used to help out on them as well."'

'I was the only girl in a family of six children and we all had jobs to do to earn our pocket money. I used to polish the floor on Fridays, one brother would scrub the kitchen floor, another chose to swill the backyard – which with hindsight was a clever choice as it seemed to rain on a number of Fridays, especially in winter! (We always did our jobs on Fridays then, I suppose because my mother liked everything tidy for the weekend.)

Having a lot of boys in the family and me the only girl, there were always a lot of socks to darn, so Saturday night sitting by the fire I helped my mother to darn the socks, listening to *Saturday Night Theatre* on the radio.'

'We had many jobs to do about the farm as children. We fetched water from the river with a bucket on a rope to water the cattle; we also caught minnows in jam jars to see how long we could keep them, but despite feeding them with breadcrumbs they usually ended up in the water trough and were swallowed by the cows. It never seemed to do them any harm. One of our favourite games was half filling metal calf buckets with water and swinging them over our heads round and round so fast the water stayed in the bucket.

We would walk a mile down the fields to feed the hens and collect the eggs. Until it was made illegal, we used to wash the eggs with Vim, then we used dry sand and a paper block. Another job was having to stand and keep the cow and the bull in a confined space while the bull did his job.

When we were hoeing turnips we tried to push back into the ground the ones we knocked out by mistake but we were always caught out. We had hessian bags wrapped round our shoulders when it rained.

Every Sunday morning we helped to wash the milk units. They had an extra special wash then and we had to stand and hold the ends of the long rubber tubes, over eight feet long, while our mother pushed a long-handled brush halfway along the tube, then changed ends. It was always a very cold job. Cooking Sunday lunch or on baking day, extra long oven sticks were used to heat the old black range. Each time we walked past we had to push the sticks in a bit further. They would be about ten to twelve feet long.

We regularly got ringworm; our youngest sister got it in her hair and had to wear a mob cap and pay frequent visits to the doctor. We were the last family in the village to wear clogs with caulkers and the other children banned us from the slide in the playground.

We had to get up early to help Dad deliver milk. We always got some lovely apples and oranges at Christmas from the customers, much appreciated in a large family when all Christmas presents were shared.'

TATIE PICKING

'When I was in my early teens (1950–52) I looked forward to "tatie picking week" in October – now called half-term. My friends and I would gather outside the War-Ag office in Penrith waiting for our transport which was usually a covered wagon, then off we would go to the farm. We were usually quiet in the morning but coming home at night we used to sing and one song was "Bless 'em all" but we didn't sing the usual words, something quite different!

I remember one day while picking taties the farmer walked up and down the stitches to make sure we picked them all and he used to shout, "Scrat, yer buggers, scrat." We were always hungry with working outside and enjoyed our packed dinner sitting on bales of straw. One day my friend got a mouse up her trouser leg which had come out of the straw. That caused a lot of excitement and laughter.

We were paid one shilling and one penny an hour and we usually worked seven hours so at the end of the day we were very rich. I used to save all my wages and buy some new clothes. One year I bought a pale blue twin set and a brown and yellow checked skirt from the Co-op.

The highlight of the week was being allowed to go to the second house at the pictures. I felt really grown up then.'

THE SATURDAY PENNY

'What pleasure we derived from spending our Saturday pennies. Being twins, we shared the spending of two pennies between us. We went to the little sweet shop nearby, where we stood and gazed at the array of sweets in open glass dishes. We usually chose some small ones to fit in the little bottles with which we played "shop". These were chocolate dragees and chewing nuts, dolly mixtures, liquorice torpedoes and laces and occasionally kali, though never chewing gum – that was forbidden.

Each Saturday we usually chose a halfpenny's worth of two different kinds, and it took a long time!

My father could always be relied upon to produce a small bar of chocolate – Cadbury's Milk, or a Barker & Dobson's barley sugar, like a round cushion with a dent in the middle. But none of these gave us the pleasure of the sweets we bought ourselves with our Saturday Penny.'

A MISHAP IN SMITHY SQUARE

'In our small village of Frizington in the year 1930, I was just seven years old. In the centre of the village, opposite what we call Griffin Corner, there was a Smithy Square with a blacksmith's shop at the back. Next to this was the slaughterhouse. As children we loved to go and see the horses shod. On the middle of the Smithy Square was a big concrete block with a black iron ring in the centre, which was used to tether the horses whilst they were being shod. We used to sit on this big stone to watch the blacksmith as he took the horseshoes out of the furnace and into cold water before he put them on the horse's hooves. Of course we didn't know, as children, that the horse could not feel this, so we all winced every time he hammered the horseshoe on the hoof.

In the summer holidays we spent many hours here. Of course he was a very busy man, the blacksmith. There were three milk floats, all horse-drawn, as were the three coal waggons and the carrier waggon which brought the parcels every day from Parkside station, not British Rail in those days. Monday was the day the butcher slaughtered the animals, you could hear the poor things bawling as they were led to slaughter.

It was on one of these summer days, when Mother and I were on our own until 4.30 pm and dinner was always made at that time for the men coming in from the quarry, that she decided we would have a handy snack. She said, "Just go and get two pies at the baker's shop"; this is still on the go today only under new management. So off I went for the pies.

Before this Mother had said to me that when she was a little girl they had to curtsy to the vicar and the boys had to doff their caps. So on the way back home with the pies, who did I meet on Smithy Square but the vicar. Not to be outdone I thought I would curtsy to him. To my horror down went the pies, rolling out of the bag on to the black dust. Well you can imagine how I felt. In those days we all had a piece of rag (no handkerchief) so I picked them up and rubbed the black dust off with the rag; they looked as good as new.

Off I went home. Mother and I ate the pies with relish. I then plucked up courage to tell her how they had rolled on the Smithy Square. She howled with laughter and said in the true Cumbrian fashion, "Ah well, we have all got to eat a peck of muck before we die, so I reckon we've just eaten ours."'

SNAILS AND TOMMY

'Often during the summer holidays, my brother and I would go to Grandma's house for the weekend. We travelled on the bus from Ellonby to Caldbeck, then walked the last two miles to Greenrigg (the house John Peel lived in when he lived at Caldbeck). One particular night while walking there, we picked up, out of the hedgerow, lots of brown and yellow snail shells; we soon filled a brown paper bag. On arrival, these were left in the bag on a small round side table, and promptly forgotten about until the next morning. You can imagine Grandma's dismay when going into the living room she found snails climbing everywhere, up the dresser, over the wallpaper, down the table leg, snails going in all directions. I can't remember the consequences!

My mother would often recall the days she spent looking after Tommy. He was the son of the family she was in service with, around the early 1930s. On one occasion Tommy was lost and everybody was called out to search for him. After looking everywhere Mother heard a whimper coming from the outside lavatory. On looking inside she found him hanging by his fingertips, down the hole, sobbing, "Nommy fall down."

Another day Father was working with two big shire horses in the ploughing field, when the horses suddenly stopped and no amount of coaxing could get them to move forward. On further investigation he found little Tommy asleep in the next row.'

PRANKS AT BELMOUNT HALL

'In the 1930s my sister and I and two friends often used to go exploring Belmount Hall, a large Georgian residence. At the time it had just been bought by Beatrix Potter (Mrs William Heelis). The house stood in the middle of a large, overgrown, neglected garden and was darkened by the density of shrubs and trees around it. It was said to be haunted. I was always very nervous and anxious as we wandered through the grounds, staying very close to the others, in part because of the ghost and also in case Beatrix Potter turned up.

One day we came across a trapdoor under the window of a large room, through which the four of us squeezed. We then had a lot of fun sliding down the bannisters. At least the other three did, I was too fearful of the ghost but dare not tell the others how I felt since they might have laughed and made me last out through the trapdoor, possibly holding it down while I was panicking inside. It was so eerie in the house and our voices echoed. We thought there was a chapel somewhereabouts but didn't come across it.

Many years later, a friend came upon a book of the letters of Beatrix Potter written to various people over the years. In one letter dated 18th March, 1939 Beatrix Potter described to her cousin the state of Belmount Hall when she bought it from a Miss Owen and of the ghost she had seen in the garden by a laurel bush. It was of a monk. Miss Owen had also seen the ghost on one occasion and had hung a rosary on the laurel bush to entice the monk to reappear. Beatrix Potter recalls how when she first explored the house she came across a shroud in a box and worse still some "unpleasant early Christian remains" which Father Taylor from Coniston took away and had buried in consecrated ground. I think I had every reason to feel fearful!

Beatrix Potter and her husband were quite active at the time of my early teens and on another occasion we four friends skirted the back of Belmount Hall, climbed up the kitchen garden wall and peeped over the top to see both Mr and Mrs Heelis gardening. It looked like a scene from the *Tale of Peter Rabbit*, the kitchen garden with its potting shed and Mr Heelis looking for all the world like Mr McGregor as he dug the garden.

We four laid along the top of the wall and broke the stillness of the afternoon by making owl noises by cupping our hands together and blowing between our thumbs. I don't think the gardeners were fooled.

There were many occasions when, by telephoning Beatrix Potter, she allowed us to go into the garden to pick flowers to decorate the church during the various festivals.'

WHAT'S AN ELIVINO?

'One year we had exam papers at school and one of the questions was, "What animal is found in Africa?" Well, I didn't know, so I asked Dorothy who was in the desk next to mine and whose mother was a schoolteacher. She answered, "Elivino." So I put that down on the paper. At playtime I asked her what kind of animal it was. I thought it was some kind of elephant. She said, "I meant, 'hell if I know!'" Of course, the teacher wanted to know what kind of animal it was. I got no marks for that.'

WHAT WE WORE

'One of my earliest memories of clothes is, as a toddler, having to wear leggings in the winter (these alternated with woollen "pullups" which had elastic which went under the foot). The leggings were rather stiff, and buttoned from top to bottom. They had to be fastened by means of a buttonhook (used for buttoned boots), which often seemed to pull my skin – I hated them.'

'Times were hard in Ulverston during the 1920s and 1930s. Amongst others, Mr Preston North, who had a coal business in Brewery Street, did a great deal for the kids in need. Through a fund initiated by him, they were able to obtain essential items of clothing, such as jumpers, stockings, clogs etc, from certain shops in the town. I remember Purdy's was one of them. A pair of new clogs was a real treat for any lad. There was never any shame felt about this as so many of us were in the same boat.

Another bonus for the kids was what they termed the "Free Breakfast". This was an annual event, held in the Coronation Hall each Boxing Day. After a free film show at the Palladium, where talking pictures were beginning to be shown and were a great excitement for all, we would go back to "The Coro". This would be packed with healthy appetites and the big hotpots and the mince pies were soon devoured. We were then given an apple, an orange and three brand new pennies. Wealth indeed, and the best part of Christmas for many.'

'Boys at Eskdale and elsewhere wore corduroy breeches and jackets, whilst girls wore dresses with white pinafores, and all wore hand-knitted stockings with clogs or boots. Every few months, travelling salesmen visited the village bringing great packs of household linen, haberdashery and clothes. Liberty bodices with rubber buttons to hold up one's stockings are common and hated memories for little girls right up to the 1950s, worn with thick knickers with a pocket in them. Though by then pinafores were out, and boys wore short trousers.'

THE BEST YEARS OF OUR LIVES?

Long walks to school, wet clothes drying round the classroom stove, small classrooms and large classes, slates to write on – memories shared by decades of Cumbrian children. Schools changed very little until the 1960s, and small village schools were still the norm for most children. Discipline was strict, but many teachers are remembered with affection and respect.

EARLY SCHOOLDAYS

'In 1910, aged five, I started school at Crosthwaite infants school. On my first day I found some chalk and scribbled on a toilet door. For that offence I was taken into both classrooms and given a stroke of the cane in front of the children.

Everyone walked to school and in bad weather we got soaked, our clothes being hung to dry around the classroom stove. If a pupil lived too far from home, they took sandwiches and ate them in the empty classroom at dinnertime with a drink of water, or, if the teacher was very kindhearted, a drink of milk.'

'The road to Chapel Stile was often flooded during very bad weather, and we children from the head of the valley often had to wade through deep floods and thick snowfalls to get home. The new road was not made until 1925, long after I left school.

One of my earliest memories, in about 1908, is the "scrawls" at school at Christmas. We all had to kneel on the floor and the headteacher and helpers threw nuts on the floor, which we scrambled for, then we were given an apple and an orange.

Once, the older boys were given an essay to write on "air". The whole school was assembled to hear one boy's essay. It consisted of five words – "My father has 'airy legs."'

'I started school in 1911 when I was five years old and was at the same school, Lees Hill, until I left at 14. We all looked forward to the big treat of the year – the summer outing. The older children with some of the parents would be taken by motor waggons to the coast at Silloth. They were driven by Mr Bill Nixon of Brampton. Mr Joe Elliot and Mr Bill Hetherington. The waggons had forms placed across them

The pupils of Hayton school in 1906. Girls commonly wore starched pinafores, while the boys wore breeches and jackets. The shiny caulkers on their clogs can just be seen.

for seats and there were covers that could be raised over the top if it rained. They were not considered safe for the smaller children who were collected up by some of the local farmers in their horse-drawn carts and taken the shorter journey to Talkin Tarn. If it happened to rain then the outing was cancelled and it was lessons as usual!

It was very exciting when I was big enough to go to Silloth. It seemed such a long journey and it was the furthest most of us had been from home. I remember my mother coming on one of the outings. We took our own food and all played games on the sands and had donkey rides.

The outings to Silloth stopped while the Great War (1914–18) was on but we all went to Talkin Tarn instead, usually by farm carts. I know one year the whole school walked there and back. Some of the children would have walked several miles already to get to school. You had to have good legs in those days.'

GETTING THERE

'I lived at Mockerkin from the age of six years to twelve, walking every day to Dean school approximately three miles away. Children started school at five years and no parents ever accompanied a child to or from school. The largest of the three rooms in the school had a round, iron solid-fuel combustion stove and many a time, when wet, children stood in front of it with steam rising as their clothes dried on them. Most children took sandwiches, no school dinners in those days and some took tea in tin bottles as used by miners and in winter time were allowed to stand them on the stove to warm, minus corks of course. Occasionally someone managed to get one on with a cork which eventually shot out with a loud bang.

On our walks to and from school we learned the names of all the wild flowers and which we could and could not eat; sour dockings, sometimes with a nettle leaf between, made very nice sandwiches, and wood sorrel was very sweet. If we were stung by a nettle we knew there would be a dock leaf nearby to rub on it. We knew which nests belonged to which birds and woe betide anyone who robbed one.

The school had an allotment where the older boys learned to grow vegetables and crop rotation etc, while the older girls went to cookery. It is almost unbelievable, we walked to school to get our mark, then to Branthwaite to catch the train to Bridgefoot and up the hill to a wooden building in the school yard where we learned to cook on a huge coal-fired iron range. Before the summer holidays all the old books and papers were torn up and put in bags and two boys set off across the field to lead a trail for a paperchase, great fun. Another memory was the sewing lesson and rubbing our needles with a cinder to remove the rust.

During the hot summer days we would stop at Ullock to "cup our hands" and have a drink from the well beside the river, from which quite a number of nearby houses collected their water in buckets.'

'When we went to school at Preston Patrick, if they were repairing the road we used to beg for a ride in the steam roller. All the road men were our friends and we had chats with them when we went to and from school. The grass verges were kept like new pins, the ditches were all dug out and the sides cleaned. We knew where all the violets grew and the strawberries.'

'As a young child of six, going to Church Walk infants school from Hollowmire, Osmotherly, I was collected by Jolly's Taxi Service.

Going along with my elder sister and brothers and neighbours' children, this was indeed a great treat. There were twelve to 14 of us packed in the taxi like sardines in a tin. The vivid memory of me falling out remains 60 years later! I wasn't seriously hurt, just badly grazed and with cut legs and arm, so I went on to school. The teacher cleaned me up and told me what a brave girl I was. This didn't cheer me greatly – it was the fact that nobody missed me until half a mile later that caused the real hurt!'

'I was an only child on a farm situated three miles from school and three miles from the village church. When schooldays began the way was long and lonely. Most mornings, in all weathers, my father attached a cushion to the carrier of his bicycle for me to ride on, a small pillion passenger holding on tightly. In this way I was conveyed to within about a quarter of a mile of school, at which point I usually met with other children for the remaining distance. After school my mother met me at a similar point and we walked home again.

My maternal grandparents lived in a village about two miles from this same school and when I was six I used to stay with them from Sunday night to Friday night, as other children from the village walked to school and we were company for each other. So little did we worry about distance that if we were ever lucky enough to have a halfpenny or penny to spend we went to the shop in the next village during lunch hour, and that was a mile each way. Along the way in season we picked flowers, caught grasshoppers, watched the swallows come and go from some deserted buildings along the way and even (shame!) picked sweet yellow gooseberries from a garden and apples from an orchard.'

'A railway ran through the village of Hallbankgate when we were children, steam trains from Kirkhouse to Midgeholme. On our way to school we used to put a penny on the line and wait for a train to run over it and flatten it.'

SCHOOLS BETWEEN THE WARS

'We usually walked home to Oxenholme from Natland school for lunch but on wet days took sandwiches and an Oxo tin containing a mixture of cocoa and sugar for drinks, which must have been very weak because quite a lot of the cocoa and sugar was eaten on the way to school.

In the infants class we counted with coloured beads and wrote the alphabet in sand trays with our fingers. We also learned to knit, but never produced a finished article as our work was pulled back so that the wool could be reused by beginners. It was a great treat to be promoted and given a ball of new wool!'

'My mother in law remembered how all the schoolchildren from Dent were taken down the Dale to see the first flush toilet.'

'Starting school at the age of four, I attended the Kirkby Stephen council school, where most pupils stayed until they were 14, unless they were fortunate to win a scholarship or had parents who could pay the necessary fees (£6 per term), the girls going to Kirkby Stephen grammar school and the boys travelling to Appleby grammar school.

Looking back at minor scholarship papers of 1921, we were expected to answer questions on Scripture, History, Geography, Elementary Science and Current Affairs. The following are some of the questions:

> Why did the people of Israel rebel against Rehoboam?
> Write out the Beatitudes.
> Explain clearly why the annual rainfall is greater in Westmorland than in Norfolk.
> Explain Reparations, Sinn Fein, The Big Four, Indirect Tax.

A needlework test was also included – drawing a pattern for a pair of knickers, estimating the amount of material, darning a hole in a sock, and making two buttonholes.

Transfer to Kirkby Stephen grammar school meant everyone had to wear uniform – navy gym slips and white blouses: hair had to be worn in two plaits until you reached the fifth form when it became one. Short or bobbed hair only came in the late 1920s. Indoor shoes had to be worn and buttoned or laced boots in winter which could also be worn for hockey.

Subjects were the usual ones with French and Latin included, and Arithmetic was expanded to Mathematics including algebra, geometry and trigonometry.

There were only 70 pupils, taught by six mistresses who were subject teachers. Homework was set each day and had to be handed in the following morning for the headmistress to inspect.

The school produced two or three pupils each year who went to training college or university, some to faraway London – a great contrast, yet the training we had stood us in good stead.'

BEFORE THE ELEVEN PLUS

'One Saturday morning in the spring of 1928 my father took me by pony and trap to Brampton to take an exam for a free place at the local secondary school. I spent a very nervous, unhappy day, not knowing any of the other pupils who were there. After a few weeks some of us were called for interview and then there was silence, and as summer holidays approached it was all but forgotten. In those days the grammar schools had six weeks' holiday and elementary schools only had a month so I duly went back to my small country school after the holiday.

A fortnight later the postman handed a letter to the headmaster who came to me and said, "Can you walk home [more than a mile] and tell your father that you've got a place at the secondary school and you must start tomorrow!" I walked home and then back to school for the rest of the day and ended my primary education.

I had no uniform and no bicycle so an old boneshaker was borrowed from a neighbour and thus began the four and a half mile journey in all weathers until I was 16.

My mother had died three years previously so a family friend took me to Samuel Jesper's store in Carlisle where I was fitted out with uniform which included expensive cashmere stockings – very unfashionable at that time, shiny navy sateen knickers, always worn for PE lessons, a navy hat like nurses used to wear and also a panama hat. It was against school rules to be seen on the street without a hat. A memory from my first day was that for homework I had to read a chapter from *Legends of Greece and Rome*. Thirty years later when my daughter came home from her first day at the same school she opened her satchel, brought out an old green, hard backed book and said, "There you are Mum, *Legends of Greece and Rome*!" Time had stood still.'

COOKERY AND NEEDLEWORK

'During the 1930s the senior girls went, by bus, from Castle Carrock school to Warwick Bridge school on one day a week for cookery lessons. Giggling and chattering, we occupied the back seat of the bus to Warwick Bridge, armed with our baskets full of ingredients, carefully weighed out at home (1 oz rice, 3 oz steak, ½ teaspoon salt etc) plus newly washed and ironed cookery aprons and caps.

Under the instruction of the Warwick Bridge cookery mistress, we laid out utensils to an exact pattern on the scrubbed tables and, using the cookery room with its stoves and sinks, prepared, cooked and ate our own dinners (stew and rice pudding).

After a dinner-hour excursion to the delights of the Warwick Bridge Co-op, our afternoon was filled with an introduction to the art of making rock buns or similar delights. Cooking over, before leaving we carefully wrote down the next week's recipe, list of ingredients and method to be used, scrubbed down the tables and left everything clean and in its rightful place, as befits visitors.

The day's adventure over, we returned, by bus, to Castle Carrock, carrying with care our baskets containing the cakes made during the afternoon, crumpled aprons, and next week's instructions. At home, the cakes were revealed with pride and eaten, hopefully with approval, by the rest of the family; while next week's list was noted by a long-suffering but helpful parent.

Great importance was given to the art of needlework at Castle Carrock, the infants teacher being herself an expert. Every girl, from her first entry, was taught to do excellent "plain sewing" and embroidery. First article to be made was a "sewing bag", in strong coloured cotton, neatly hemmed, oversewn and decorated with "snail-trail", and with tapes attached to tie round the waist. This was the bag in which all subsequent sewing "in progress" was placed – tidily. Very rare was the day which did not include "sewing" and woe betide the girl who left her bag on the village seat or at home. Nightdresses with shell edging, camisoles with faggoting, petticoats with tucks were produced, all hand-sewn, winning prizes at Brampton show. Christmas presents of table runners, nightdress cases and embroidered pictures were in abundance. When a smoking stove made lessons in the big room impossible, while the boys were sent out to play football, the girls were "allowed" to sew in the small room. Many a seam was taken out and redone until declared fit for its purpose – long before British Standards were introduced.

No girl left the school without an excellent grounding in the art of needlework, standing all in good stead in later years, the art painstakingly learnt under an exacting but fair taskmistress.'

FROM DACRE TO PENRITH

'I started at Dacre school in 1919. There were eleven pupils and the teacher was Mrs Tibbs. She wore long black skirts and a little woollen shoulder shawl. We girls wore holland pinafores with shoulder frills, home-knitted woollen stockings (black and itchy) and clasped clogs with iron caulkers; the boys wore corduroy knickerbockers and high-topped "duck nebbed" clogs. There was one schoolroom with an open fire and a porch used as a cloakroom. We sat on long benches with a desk top in front but no backrest.

Every day began with Scripture followed by Arithmetic, then English, Grammar, Composition and Dictation. We learned to read from large charts slung over an easel, crude maybe but quite effective. We also did History, Geography, Nature Study and Drawing (using both sides of foolscap paper). We learned our tables by heart and reams of poetry – eg *Lochinvar* and *The Forsaken Merman*, which I still recite on sleepless nights. The bigger girls did sewing whilst the boys drew or modelled with clay. At playtimes we played marbles and spun tops, skipped and chased "boolies", ie bowling hoops, as well as playing singing games and made up games like chevy chase and carriage horses.

In 1925 I gained a county minor scholarship to Penrith Queen Elizabeth grammar school. There was a preliminary test at Dacre school then two more tests in Penrith schools. My mother and I walked the six miles to and from the two in Penrith. When news came that I had passed, my elder brother was ploughing at a nearby farm so I ran to tell him my news. He dropped the reins and flung his cap in the air (fortunately the horses stayed to watch!). My brother bought me a bicycle for 30 shillings, taught me to ride it and I travelled the six miles to grammar school on it for seven years.

How I enjoyed all the new lessons, it was the opening up of a whole new world. My younger brother won a scholarship in 1928 and we weathered many storms together – wind and rain, snow and ice, none of which did us any harm. On Monday mornings we had to set off earlier as we had to thread our way through large flocks of sheep being driven to Penrith auction mart, a nuisance maybe but not so dangerous as motor traffic. We were free to cycle without fear of danger from traffic or molestation from strangers in those far-off days.'

NATLAND ELEMENTARY SCHOOL

'Natland school in the 1930s had four classes, four teachers including the head, and about 90 to 100 pupils. Of these pupils, over 30 were "Home Boys" from the Waifs and Strays home in the village. These boys wore navy blue woollen jerseys and short corduroy pants, and black boots. They walked to school in ranks, and lined up at school under the direction of the headmaster after school to go home the same way.

We played in a large playground which when I first went was covered in black ash. Consequently when we fell in our games our knees got ingrained with black gravel. Before I left it was covered in tarmac . . . a great improvement. We played games like Sheep, Sheep come over. The words were, "sheep, sheep come over." "We can't, the wolf's about." "Oh no, oh no, the wolf's away and won't be back for many a day, so *come*." And we all ran across the yard, only to find the "Wolf" was not away.

At Christmas we got a new penny and an orange on the last day of term. In the summer we had a trip to Morecambe. We went by train, and when we were on Oxenholme station all the children whose fathers worked on the railway had to be separated from the rest, because they got quarter-fare, so that had to be sorted out by whoever paid the fare. (I never did discover where the money came from for that trip, and the stick of rock we were given when we got home.)

On Ascension Day we brought Spanish Water to school. This was made by putting broken-up hard liquorice in a bottle and filling it with water. This was then shaken until a froth formed at the top, then we could suck the top of the bottle and drink the froth. It was not done to drink the liquid. The shaking of the bottles was the best part, and the shape of the bottle helped or hindered the shaking. I remember acquiring a small flat brandy bottle from somewhere, and this was just right.

There was very good swimming tuition. At about the age of seven we began having "land drill" at school when we were taught the arm and leg movements for breast stroke. Then we went to the baths in Kendal one day a week in summer. We had to walk up to Oxenholme for the bus, and then got the bus back again, but those of us who lived at Oxenholme could go straight home. Most of us got as far as lifesaving before the age of eleven.

Going to school we walked, or cycled, about a mile. If fine we went down the fields; if not fit for the fields, we went by the road, and if we were lucky, and the farmer was in a good mood, we *might* get a lift in his milk float as he trotted home after delivering milk to Oxenholme station. If we were so lucky, we gloated over the others who were further on than we were and missed the lift.'

THE HIGHEST SCHOOL IN ENGLAND

'When I was four years of age I began my education in a school three miles from the source of the South Tyne river, six miles from the summit of Cross Fell and 1,500 feet above sea level – the highest in England for any school. Aptly enough it was called Tyne Head school, and it was built in 1823.

As you can imagine, snow abounded from October to April/May. The 15 scholars, aged from four to 14, walked to school from isolated farms for months at a time when the whole surrounding countryside was lying under between three and five feet of frozen snow. The stone walls were completely lost, footpaths obliterated, and we virtually had to guess the route to school. We all wore clogs, with "hoggars" to keep our legs warm, while in our dinner bags we carried our sandwiches. Snow froze rapidly and many times we walked on top of the snow. The winds swirled, the snow blew, tiny hands were frozen, yet it was only very seldom that scholars missed school because of snow. On arrival at school we were always greeted by a very young and attractive teacher who had also struggled two miles, battling against the elements. School consisted of one room with a large stove at one end and an open fire at the other end. During the winter weather our ancient desks were pulled up to the fire, and here we worked. Our frozen clothing was removed and dried on the fireguard.

Our teacher, Miss Dixon, taught all scholars, bright or otherwise; quite a formidable task. Yet the success rate of minor scholarships and free places to Samuel King's grammar school was much higher than in many of the other primary schools in the area. Amenities were primitive, our playground was the steep, rocky, stony hill on which the school stood. There was no hot water supply, desks were ancient, floorboards were uneven and walls stained with dampness. However, we were a happy band of youngsters and a family atmosphere pervaded the school. In addition, we had what was probably the only water sanitation in the whole area – the loos were built over the running mountain stream and the clear mountain running water did the rest. Happy days which made a lasting impression on our young minds.'

VILLAGE SCHOOLDAYS

'In most village schools in the 1930s, when the school bell or whistle announced the start of the school day, boys and girls congregated in separate yards and hung their coats in separate porches. We were lined up in twos and escorted indoors by the class teacher for registration: "Present Miss/Sir" as our names were called. The classrooms were heated by big black tortoise stoves with an iron fireguard round which sent out plenty of heat if you were fortunate to have a desk near the front – no central heating in those days.

Poorer children got a free third of a pint bottle of milk and I remember being very envious of those who also got a buttered tea cake and digestive biscuits at playtime. We didn't take anything to eat at mid-morning and walked home for dinner (a mile) – no school meals service till after the war.

Boys and girls wore clogs; my sisters and I didn't as we had an uncle in Scotland with a shoe shop and each autumn we got a pair of Clark's lace-up brown shoes and in summer a pair of sandals. Boys mostly wore corduroy or grey flannel short trousers and grey woollen stockings and chapped knees were common – "Snowfire" skin emollient was the cure. Girls wore tweedy skirts or gymslips, hand-knitted jumpers, "locknit" knickers in brown, green or navy with a pocket for a hanky. "Combinations", liberty bodices and long lisle stockings kept us warm in winter. Stockings were held up by suspenders attached to the liberty bodice with rubber buttons. We wore cotton (gingham) dresses in the summer, but not till "May was out" (always debatable as to whether it was the May blossom or the month of May which should be "out").

Each class had its ink monitor responsible for distributing and collecting the ink-wells and, when necessary, making up the ink from powder – a very responsible operation! (Naughty boys stuffed blotting paper in the ink-well and "bombed" the ceiling or their classmates with these pellets using a ruler or catapult). There was always a "teacher's pet" who was asked to do all the extra jobs, like cleaning the blackboard or giving out books.'

MORESBY SCHOOL

'For many decades of the 20th century teachers and pupils at Moresby school came from a very widespread area, with some having to walk many miles, At 8.50 am a pupil would ring the school bell and five minutes later the headmaster would blow his whistle – lessons commenced promptly at 9 am.

Religious education was an important part of school tuition with Moresby pupils doing exceptionally well – maybe because, if successful, they had a half day's holiday.

Reading, writing and arithmetic were also given great emphasis, but around the 1920s lessons became more varied, including recitation, tables, history dates and spelling, and it was an everyday occurrence to test the memory on these subjects.

In 1919, while children were having their playtime, an aeroplane was spotted circling around the village, and eventually landing in a field nearby. In the excitement, some of the boys ran to see it, and were chastised by their headmaster who, however, when he realised what was happening, led the rest of the children up to see the plane. The pilot was a well known fighter pilot, Captain Archie McCudden, who had been forced to seek a landing site when he ran out of petrol. Once a can of fuel had been brought from Whitehaven, he was able to take off again.

Children who had to take lunch to school because of the distance from home, also took their own tea – in bottles. These stood on top of the stove to keep warm but corks had to be removed to stop the bottles from exploding.

On starting school, one of the first sights a child saw was a beautiful rocking horse, only to be told that the only time they could ride on it was on his or her birthday. There was also a doll's house for the girls to play with, but nothing special for the boys.

During the great depression of the early 1930s, poor children were able to take advantage of summer camps at Drigg and Silecroft.'

THE SCHOOL STRIKE

'The school in Waberthwaite was started as a private school early in the 19th century, and was on land adjacent to that occupied by the reading room.

By the beginning of the 20th century, compulsory education had been made obligatory for all children, and pupils came from all the surrounding villages. Numbers continued to grow and although by this time the original school had been replaced by a larger one, the school was still very full.

The syllabus included Land Surveying, Joinery, Arithmetic and Book-keeping for the boys. The girls did not do Joinery or Book-keeping, but had the addition of Needlework. The aim of the school was to train children for the work they were likely to do when they finally had to leave. Also, by this time government grants were available for education – but only on a basis of payment by results!

In 1915 the Rev Percy Parminter became the rector of Waberthwaite and Corney parishes. He took a great interest in the school, and became chairman of the school governors. For the next 15 years or so, very little seems to have been documented about the activities of the school. It does appear, however, that numbers were very high, and during the 1930s the Rev Parminter began campaigning for the building of a new school.

He visited parents to get their support and started a fund to finance the building. He also persuaded craftsmen and others to pledge their practical support to the enterprise without any remuneration. Sir J. Ramsden of Muncaster provided a site at Lane End where the present school now stands. Meanwhile, not all the parents were in favour of this project. Their concern had been aroused by the frail financial backing available and protests began to surface. The Rev Parminter was not to be dissuaded, and he forged ahead with his plan.

At the same time, the Rev Parminter's son John was the manager at the Waberthwaite granite quarry, and by coercion, or cajolery or some such method, was persuaded to supply the granite for the building.

Work went ahead and the school was completed, but the process had involved putting on a slated roof for which professional slaters had to be employed. The Rev Parminter had been unable to persuade the slaters to do the job gratis, and they wanted their money.

It was 1938 and the school was finished, and the Rev Parminter called a meeting of the school governors, which included most of the dissident parents. He informed them that the school was now ready for use, and that the old school must be closed and all the children must go to the new school. The managers refused to take on the new school, saying that it was so heavily saddled with debt that they would be unable to run it successfully.

Nothing daunted, the Rev Parminter sacked the Board of Governors, and convinced some parents that the old school was being closed and that the children should attend the new school. So, some went to the new school and some went to the old school. During the mornings the Rev Parminter would collect his children together and take them over to the other school at break time, and his children would shout "blackleg" and hiss the others when they came out to play. There was virtually a strike in operation, and neither side would give way. Some of the children involved in this strike are still living in Waberthwaite.

A stalemate had been reached at this juncture, and fortunately the diocese of Carlisle stepped into the fray. They took over the school, debts and all, and peace was restored.

The school today is a delightful building, in attractive surroundings, very solidly built of granite. Of the children who attend the school now, many have grandparents, and possibly great grandparents, who were involved in the struggle to open a new village school. Waberthwaite school is a real village school in more ways than one.'

PASSING THE MERIT

'It's 1956, and Standard Three at Bishop Goodwin junior school is keyed up to take the Merit. It was drummed into us at school that passing the Merit was your passport to everything a good education could give. Passing the Merit and going to the city's high school for girls was the ultimate accolade and only a few were able to have this opportunity.

My Mum and Dad had never had the chance to carry on their education even though my father had won a scholarship to the grammar school, and deep down I knew they wanted me to have the chances they never had.

My recollection is that there were three sections to the Merit – English, Arithmetic and Intelligence and we all took the exam on the same day.

My Mum was still in bed enjoying her morning cup of tea and I took the letter upstairs, not realising what it contained. She opened it and suddenly the tears coursed down her face and she jumped

In the schoolroom at Holme St Cuthbert in 1950, and how the clothes have changed since the early years of the century!

out of bed. "You've passed," she said. "You've passed for the high school, just wait till I tell your Dad."

I sat down on the bed slowly, the enormity of the situation engulfing me like a huge wave. I'd passed the Merit and I was going to the high school. "Mam," I said hesitantly," it costs a lot of money to buy the uniform." "Never mind," she said. "You're going and that's that."

I called for my friend. "What did you do?" was the excited cry and joyfully I replied, "High school." "Brainy, eh?" she joked, "I'm going to the secondary modern." This conversation was repeated time and time again as we met our other friends. My heart sank every time. I was the only one. I would have to go on my own, no friends to go with. It got so bad that I hardly dared answer when asked if I'd passed. My pride was quickly turning to despair.

In the classroom our teacher called me and Mary to the front. "These girls have passed for the high school," he said with undoubted pride. Relief rose up in me so hard that I thought I would choke. There was another girl – I wouldn't have to go on my own.

The uniform was bought, at what cost I'll never know but it was several years before Mam had a new coat. The gaberdine was on the long side, "You'll grow into it", and the gymslip had to be the regulation length, touching the floor when you knelt down. Grey knee-socks were held up with garters. Badges were sewn on along with dozens of name tapes. A leather satchel was handed down complete with an Osmiroid pen and Lakeland pencils.

I was ready, but was the high school ready for me – that is another story!'

QUITE AN EXPERIENCE

'In 1957 my aunt died. I was teaching in Hull but as my mother was left on her own I came home at Christmas to get a job near Hawkshead for a while. Canon McLeod Murray, vicar of Sawrey helped me find a job in a country school as this was what I had been trained for.

I was offered a post by Lancashire Education Committee (as it was then) for the post of infants teacher at Colton school near Ulverston. Every day I managed to take my bicycle up the Grizedale Hill, cycling where I could and then down the other side, where the Theatre in the Forest is now. I left my bicycle there and caught the school bus at about 8 am to Colton. We picked up a variety of children on the way. Some went to Colton, others to the secondary school at Backbarrow and some may have gone to the Ulverston grammar school.

It was January when I started, 1958. A cold and frosty morning, as winter was in full swing. Mr Barton, already out with the road men, had cleared the road up the hill before I started out. I was very lucky as the weather kept fairly open all the time. I looked forward to the lovely views of the hills on my return journey each day, spectacular in all their different moods. No trees to block the view!

Travelling through the Rusland Valley there were glimpses of wild life; a cuckoo in the oakwood, a barn owl searching for mice along the hedgerows at dusk, wild flowers in profusion along the banks.

The school on the hill was very small, I suppose there must have been about 20 children. I had seven infants from four to seven years. Miss Snape, the headmistress had about 13 or more. I had a small room at the back, she had the large one.

In the cold winter months a coal fire was lit in each room. Mine was roaring up the chimney when I arrived; I had a bucket of coal ready for replenishing it. There was a large gap under the door so a cold draught cooled down the hot atmosphere. I made an alphabet frieze for the children; I had one or two new children of four and a half years who soon learned their letters. Reading, writing and numbers were done in the morning. As I only had seven children we soon got through our daily routine. In the afternoon we did handwork, music and movement (clumping round in heavy boots!)

and any other practical lessons. In the summer Miss Snape took us all onto the fell and we danced to an old record player. The toilet was outside and we had to brave the elements to go. Dinner was brought by a van in containers. As you can imagine I was ready for mine! I never enjoyed thin stew and red cabbage so much. One little boy, however, refused to eat anything. No cajoling or threats would tempt him: I don't think he knew what a square meal was. He rushed out of school like one demented at the end of the day in order to get home as quickly as he could, presumably for biscuits from a tin.

Mrs Snape was a good headmistress. We would have a cup of tea together by her classroom fire at lunchtime and talk about her life. I think she was delighted when it snowed hard and I had to stay the night with her in her cottage on the hill. I was only there for two terms as I got another job the following September, but I felt really healthy and fit with the day-to-day fresh air and exercise. It was quite an experience.'

THE WORLD OF WORK

Ulverston Hiring Fair

ON THE LAND

It is hardly surprising that over the years it has been work on the land that has sustained so many in Cumbria. While Cumbria's often difficult terrain has ensured that farming has retained a continuity over the generations perhaps not found in every county, farming has of necessity changed with the coming of mechanised machinery and better transport. But we still have fond memories of the old days, when horses provided the only power on the land and haymaking and harvesting, sheepshearing and ploughing, were community activities, highspots in every year.

THE HIRED LADS AND LASSES

'Before the last war every farm had at least one hired lad and lass. Even the smallest farm had someone to help as without the tractor and other modern machinery the field work was done by horses and, of course, the cows were milked by hand.

Most of these lads and lasses "lived in". On bigger farms there was a separate staircase to a bedroom over the kitchen where two or three double beds covered by patchwork quilts were used. The lasses often shared a bedroom with the children of the farm. Most of these lads and lasses started work as soon as they left school at 14, going to the local fair at Martinmas or Whitsun to get hired. Each town had its own special day, Carlisle was Saturday, Cockermouth Monday, Wigton and Penrith Tuesday, Workington Wednesday, Whitehaven Thursday and Maryport Friday.

Most of these lads and lasses were the children of coal and ore miners, who liked their children to work on the farms as times were hard and at least on the farm they would be well fed and have a healthy outdoor life. At 21 many of the lads went back to the industrial towns as they could then command full wages down the pits.

At the hiring fairs a lot of bargaining went on; the fact that the farmer's wife was a good cook often helped him hire good men. A wage for half the year could vary from £6 to £14. Holidays were not as plentiful as today, though they always had a week off at Martinmas and Whit. The farmer gave the lad a shilling and he turned in to work on the Saturday evening.

Most of the lads enjoyed a night out on a Saturday and would get a sub of half a crown from the farmer to pay them into the pictures and get some sweets and chips afterwards.

Not many had a coat to work in but who needed a coat when there were plenty of hessian sacks? A large corn sack was often used, pushed corner into corner over the head and tied with "John Robert" (binder twine).

In each village there was generally a special corner where all the lads met after work and put the world to rights. The highlights of their year were threshing days, clipping days, boon ploughing days and local shows when they had a chance to get together and show off their skills, but even on these special days the cows had to be milked and the stock and horses fed and cared for, making them very long days.

The farmers had a saying: "Cumberland born and Cumberland bred, strong in the arm and thick in the head," meaning a strong lad who didn't ask questions was a better worker. However, the hired lad had a special prayer: " O Lord God, if it be in they power, send a little shower just about fower." This applied to haytime and harvest on a Saturday night!'

'An elderly man told me how he stood in the street at the Kendal hiring fair in 1911. The lads stood at one side of the street and the lasses at the other. A farmer came and asked him how much he wanted for the half year, and he said £8 10s. He was offered £8 but he refused it. He stuck out for his price and the third farmer agreed. At the end of six months, after paying for his clothes and clogs, and repaying his father 25 shillings which he had borrowed to buy a bicycle, he had £3 5s left to put in the bank. He had just a few hours off work on a Sunday, when he would cycle home to see his parents. He was then 17 years of age.

Some of the young men used to get up to pranks. When they heard that someone was going to kill a pig, they would go and paint the pig with ruddle, a kind of red colouring they used for marking sheep. When the farmer found the pig in the morning, he would have to cancel the killing until it could be cleaned. Another prank was to paint white stripes on a black horse. A farmer once lost his horse plough, and it was not found until the autumn, when all the leaves came off the trees. The plough was discovered hung by a strong chain up in the branches. There was not a lot else in the way of entertainment for them.'

'When I left school at 14 in 1933 I fancied farm work and took myself to the "hirings" at Cockermouth. I was terrified but had learnt to milk at one of the village farms. My father went with me and I was duly hired for six months for £7 10s. The farmer gave me a shilling there and then, and bound me to turn up at the farm near Penrith the following Saturday or he would expect his shilling back.

I was met at Penrith station by the farmer and his family with a car. I had expected a horse and trap, as not many farmers had cars then. My bed was a feather mattress and a clean chaff bolster.

There were horsemen, cowmen, labourers and me – "the nipper". I was expected to learn all the jobs, and did. The farmer was a kind man and a good teacher. We got up at half past five and worked till half past six at night, except at harvest and haytime when it was often ten o'clock (no overtime then). I decided to stay on for the winter "term" as it was a "good meat shop" (plenty of good food). I thought the farmer was going to have a fit when I asked for a ten shilling rise – ie £8 for six months' work.'

EIGHTY YEARS OF FARMING

'Mr Bird sat by the fire and recalled over 80 years of farming in the Carlisle and Penrith areas. He has lived on farms all his life, being turned out of their farm near Warcop when it was made into a shooting range and then moving south of Carlisle. When a farm was sold the neighbours joined in ploughing all the arable land on the new farm in February. There were 52 draughts (pairs) of horses required for 75 acres.

On his mixed farm there would be grass for grazing and for hay, corn (not barley) for fodder and for sale, turnips for the sheep in winter and potatoes. The potatoes fetched twopence halfpenny per stone at Daltons. Haymaking was done by hand and the haycocks had to be well made with a fork and capped to protect them from rain. Later, the hay was taken by horse and cart to be stacked and capped. They had three horses. The corn was sown either by hand or with a fiddle, when the corn was put in a sack and run into a mechanism which was worked with a bow drawn backwards and forwards. Later it was harrowed into the land. Neighbours helped one another with the threshing as twelve men might be required. The corn was carried to the barn in sacks on their backs. The Dutch barns were roofed with sheets of zinc, ten feet long and six feet wide. The sheep were grey-faced, black-faced and Cheviot breeds and all lambing took place in the fields. The cows, dairy shorthorns, were milked into open buckets in the byre. It was then put into churns for the milkman to collect. They were paid sixpence halfpenny for a gallon before the Second World War. They had about 20 cows which were hand-milked by three people, usually women, sitting on milking stools. Mr Bird recalled that a farm lad who lived in was paid £5 for six months' labour early in the century.

When animals were sold for slaughter their weight was guessed by feel. There were two slaughterhouses near St Nicholas in Carlisle. The carcases were sent to London and Manchester and the hides to the dealer. The blood and guts from the slaughterhouses were brought back by rail and spread on the fields. Farm sales were held in winter and all stock and implements were offered. The neighbours joined in a party at night for refreshments and card playing.'

A HARD LIFE

'In 1926 the Great Coal Strike spread into other industries and caused havoc and.hardship to all. I was just ten years old but I can remember my school mates bringing their lunch to school – a crust of bread and a tiny bit of cheese or half a hard boiled egg. The poorer working class people practically lived on bread and potatoes. The trout in the local rivers had to be very wary or they did not live very long! The dole money was very little, hardly enough for a bare existence.

Then came the great slump which affected everyone, self-employed and workers alike. Hundreds of farmers went broke. There was no market for anything with prices at rock bottom. I have heard my mother say many times it was poultry that kept them going. The eggs used to pay for the groceries and most of the stock feed as well.

Every Saturday morning the eggs and butter were taken by horse and cart to the village grocer's shop. The grocer always sent a little packet of sweets with the groceries for us kids, we would be lucky if there were two each. They were the only sweets we got. I can just remember that the price of farm butter was tenpence per pound and eggs from ninepence to a shilling a dozen, depending on their size. My father took a good milk cow to Wigton auction and won first prize and it was sold for £25 10s when £10 was usually nearer the mark.

Most of the children went to school in clogs. Only a few better off children had shoes. The teachers used to tell us to march quietly because of the clatter made by the clogs – at least the noise was in time, left-right, left-right. Schooldays passed fairly quietly with most of us just waiting for the day when we would leave and get to work. If we could have foreseen the future we might have put a bit more effort into lessons.

I left school at 14 in the summer of 1930 and went straight into farm work on the family farm. My elder brother was 17 then and he had to leave home and hire out on six monthly terms as the farm wasn't big enough to carry us both. So it was man's work for me from then on. I worked at home until Martinmas 1937 when it was my turn to move on. My younger brother had left school at Easter and had to take my place.

I got married and went to work on a bigger sheep farm at Caldbeck. It was mostly hill sheep and a bit of ploughing and milk was sold from a herd of shorthorn cows – hand milked then. My wife and I had a cottage which went with the job and £1 10s per week – but we could live comfortably on that and save a little as well.

After working on various farms until 1949, I got the tenancy of Adamthwaite Farm at Ravenstonedale and we were really happy; our own farm and our own boss, it was great.

It was a hard struggle for a few years but it was worth it. We had very little capital but that didn't matter. We had our health and a good landlord and the rest was hard work and determination. My wife baked all the bread and cakes. How I wish we could have that bread now and those fruit pies, or pasties as they were called. We grew our own potatoes and vegetables and had our home-cured bacon and ham, eggs and milk.

The farm was very isolated – our nearest neighbours were a mile and a half away – but we never felt lonely. The family was increasing as the years passed and we ended up with eight children and not one too many.

Winter could be a bit trying. There were some bad snow storms; 1963 was the worst when the road to Ravenstonedale was blocked for eleven weeks. However, we had a Land Rover by then so after a lot of hand snow-cuttings we could get out partly on the road and partly on the fell.

We had no tractor until 1963 so all the work was done with horses. The hay meadows were very steep, which made haytime very hard work and a lot of hand work. The kids had to help as soon as they were big enough to handle a handrake. The hay was all taken in on hay sledges as the land was too steep for carts.

The last week in June or first week in July was sheep clipping time. There were clipping days then when about 15 neighbours would come on a set date and clip all the sheep, then we had to go to each other's day and help them. It made a lot of work getting all the sheep in ready – and some big baking days in the house too!

If the weather was wet it was just bad luck, we had to wait for a fine day when there was no other clipping on. It was a great improvement when clipping machines came on the market and everyone started clipping their own and clipping days died out. There was more time to attend to the sheep and not such a rush. That was one piece of mechanical progress that I welcomed.

I am not sure whether it was in 1961 or 1962 when the electricity came, which also was a great help. Then the telephone came shortly after and the three miles of track was tarmacked and made into a good road, which brought us back into civilisation. The telephone came from Ravenstonedale and there were 57 poles and six miles of cable to Adamthwaite, but it spared a lot of going out to contact people.

After we got the tractor, mechanisation crept in and eventually the work horses were sold and more tractor implements were bought. Life was getting more modern, but I doubt if it was any better.'

THE BULL AND THE STALLION

'Usually one farmer in a village kept a bull and all the other farmers availed themselves of this essential commodity. There was no piped water to the byres so the cows at Dean went down to the stream for a drink. When the railways were built, a special arch was made under the railway called a cattle creep, to enable the cows to get to water without going onto the road. The bull was always led by the farmer separately, a long pole hooked through the ring in his nose. The farmer always carried a pitchfork just in case!

Another typical sight in spring was the coming of the stallion. These magnificent animals with mane and tail braided to perfection were walked from farm to farm around the county. The man in charge of the stallion lodged at different farmhouses en route, no doubt finding out by trial and error which were the best lodgings.'

'The principal occupation of the area around Holme St Cuthbert was and still is dairy farming, the rearing of dairy/beef cattle and some sheep, and the growing of associated crops for stock feed. Prior to the 1960s the use of the horse, notably the Clydesdale, for farm work was almost universal. At the beginning of the century, it was said, "they thought more about the horses than the men." Since the loss of a horse was a major disaster for a farmer, foals were much sought after and "men could fall out over horses".'

THE MOLE CATCHER

'In the village of Ullock there was a little old lady who was the mole catcher. She caught the moles by trap and charged threepence per acre.'

MOVING THE SHEEP

'My father had grazing on the island on Grasmere lake and when I was a girl I remember going with him to take sheep there for summer. We went in a rowing boat pulling behind a flat-bottomed sheep boat loaded with sheep. Usually they stood very still although I do remember a lamb standing on its mother's back, then falling into the water; luckily it swam around and we were able to retrieve it quite quickly. We used to take the wandering sheep in the hope of keeping them quiet. Occasionally sheep were known to swim off. Once a sheep swam off to the opposite shore and after much bleating to its lamb left on the island, the lamb also took to the water and swam ashore to its mother.

Early this century my father remembered farmers from the Hawkshead, Out Gate and Satterthwaite areas taking their sheep to Wythburn, where they had stints and fell rights to turn their sheep onto Helvellyn and Wythburn Head for the summer months. In July the sheep were gathered for shearing and the wool taken back to Hawkshead by horse and cart.

If the weather became stormy the sheep could be seen wandering off down Dunmail Raise (which was not fenced in those days) and heading for home. They returned to their respective farms before winter set in. At the same time some farmers also had rights to turn geese onto Wythburn Head; obviously there were not many foxes in those days.

Before the First World War my father told how each autumn when he was a boy, he helped to walk five hogs from Grasmere to Walney Island for wintering. Leaving Grasmere they passed over Red Bank to Skelwith Bridge via the Drunken Duck Inn, Outgate, skirting Hawkshead and travelling down Scarhouse Lane to Colthouse and then on to Sawrey where an overnight stop was made with grandparents. Next day the journey continued along the western side of Windermere lake to Newby Bridge, then on to Ulverston and Barrow and finally over the bridge onto Walney Island. They did the return journey the following spring.'

'When I was a child in the 1920s, I remember sheep being driven through Underbarrow from their winter quarters on Gummer's How (Cartmel Fell) to Hawes. The sheep had to be moved by 5th April and it was arranged for them to pass through Kendal at twelve noon, when traffic would be quiet.

One night the drovers rested their flocks in one of our fields at Fallen Yew Farm. As payment I was given a small black lamb which we named "Mamie". Mamie lived to be almost 14 years old, and produced twin black lambs most years.'

COUNTING THE SHEEP

'Like most areas of Great Britain, Cumbria has its own dialect, which seems like a foreign language to "off comers". A good example of this is to listen to the fell farmers counting their sheep! It would sound something like this (from one to 20):

"Yan, tyan, tethera, methera, pimp, sethera, lethera, hovera, dovera, dick, yan a dick, tyan, tethera, methera, bumfit, yan a bumfit, tyan, tethera, methera, giggot".'

AUCTION DAY

'For many years How Mill had its own auction mart. Farmers walked their sheep and cattle for miles to be sold. After the sale, most animals were sent by rail to various places.

Mrs Gilliland had a hut in the auction field and she sold soup, tatie pot and meat rolls to the farmers. On auction day the village shop had a roaring trade selling sweets, biscuits and cigarettes.

In the school holidays the children loved to go into the selling ring to see the animals sold by Mr Armstrong (the auctioneer). On other days they played in the auction yard.

Then the time came when cattle waggons were getting more popular on the roads, and this meant farmers could send their cattle to larger auctions. So, sadly, How Mill auction closed down and everything was transferred to Longtown, where the auction remains to this day.'

LEAVING THE FARM

'1st May 1925 was the day of my father's farm stock sale at Low Holme – a very sad day for him, leaving the place where he had lived for 40 years, but great excitement for myself, brother and sister. We had never seen so many people at the farm at one time. Apart from auctioneers, clerks and general helpers, there was a candy seller – a great attraction to us!

Refreshments were provided in the large stone-built barn by a willing band of lady helpers, tables having been laid the previous evening ready for the big day. However, on that morning a practical joke was played on my mother, observing the custom of making her a "May Gesling" (gesling is Cumbrian for a young goose). She was told that the hens had got into the barn, and had scratched all the tablecloths and crockery off the tables, she not realising that all the hens had been barred up the previous evening ready for the sale the next day.

To round off the sale day, my father entertained his friends and helpers to a napping party in the parlour, with something to "wet their whistles" as well.

The following day I walked from Low Holme with my father and his collie dog, driving Border Leicester sheep and lambs to Armathwaite station to be put on rail there, travelling via Hornsby, Hornsbygate, Commonholme over the Eden Bridge at Armathwaite and up the steep village street to the station, a round trip of approximately seven miles.'

'My aunt related this interesting account of her move from Lamplugh to Torpenhow in 1919 when transport was vastly different from today. She was living on a small idyllic farm, a quarter of a mile from their nearest neighbours and two miles from the school. They were all well equipped with laced boots, macintoshes and sou'westers for they had no option but to walk everywhere and never missed school.

When she was ten her father decided they would need a larger farm for her brothers, as they grew older, and it was decided that Craft House, Torpenhow would be the new home. With no convenient station at either end or cattle trucks, after much deliberation, the idea of "The Great Trek" was put into operation. So on Candlemas Day, 2nd July 1919, ten year old Sally, a twelve year old sister and a brother of 14 set forth tearfully from their beloved home with a herd of young cows, a flock of sheep and two dogs for the great unknown, starting along the Ennerdale to Cockermouth road.

It was a quiet road and the animals moved peacefully along until a small fracas at Paddle school scattered them to all points of the compass, but they managed to reform again. Then at Cockermouth the children discovered to their dismay it was market day and their animals were soon integrated with other flocks and herds at South Street, which resulted in more sorting out. Eventually, footsore and weary they reached Gate Brow, which to the young travellers seemed like a mini Skiddaw, and then on to Moota. At this point they heard the clatter of hooves and their mother appeared in a horse and trap. It was bursting at the seams with a heavy load plus their mother's maid and the other children. To her mother's dismay, Sally refused to join her and was determined to complete the trek on foot.

At that time all the traffic had to pass through Bothel. They thought the first farm they reached was their resting place but there were curtains at the window. They hopefully turned into several farm yards only to be told they still had two miles to go.

Sally doesn't remember the time of the arrival but remembers that they were very proud of accomplishing what their parents had asked them to do. Soon they were followed by a cavalcade of their neighbouring farmers' carts carrying their implements. It was probably a common sight in those bygone days but today unbelievable.

She remembers that night they all slept on mattresses, which were on the floors in all the rooms, then the farmers had to return home the next day.

Then they had to start their new life with not a little trepidation: new friends and schools, Sunday school and a new vicar.'

FARMING IN THE 1940s

'My childhood memories are of growing up on a large rented farm (400 acres) with two brothers and two sisters. Everyday life revolved round the farm and life followed a similar pattern each year.

We had a large house with cellars and attics and huge rooms in between. There were two flights of stairs – one for the family, the other a very steep, bare wooden scrubbed stairway which led up to the "lads' room". This was a huge room directly over the kitchen and could have been about eight yards square – bare wooden floor with whitewashed walls. There were three large wooden double beds with huge wooden knobs on the bedposts. The men who "lived in" slept in this room – never less than two – and my mother used to have to wash their clothes, their bedding and provide meals. They lived as family. I always vowed I would never be a farmer's wife.

As time went on fewer and fewer men went to farm service and "lived in". The tendency moved towards employing married men who lived in tied cottages attached to the farm.

The beginning of the war brought more activity on the farm. The War Agricultural Executive Committee decided that a certain proportion of each farm had to be ploughed and therefore mechanisation of farms began. I well remember the first tractor arriving at the farm, probably collected from Grange railway station. I can see this dark green Fordson tractor chugging along the A590. Gradually we became more mechanised but we still retained the horses for carting the grain from field to farm. This was one of my jobs as soon as I could lead a horse and cart. I had to "go between" as we had possibly six horses and carts loading grain. As I travel along the A590 today (between Lindale and Greystone filling station) I wonder what the reaction of motorists would be to a constant stream of horses ambling along the road.

Many of the regular farm workers had joined up, although agriculture was a reserved occupation. We had to depend on extra help from all walks of life. We had German and Italian prisoners of war who were brought from their camp each day to help with the harvest and potato picking. The Italians were very loath to work if it was raining. We used to bribe them with a good meal instead of the doorstep sandwiches they brought with them each day. There was also a camp of Manchester grammar school boys nearby. They came regularly to work and some of these boys became great friends, often returning for several years.

In 1944 we came to live at Ulverston, my father having bought a farm (only about 60 acres) on the outskirts of the town. Gone were the days of ploughing huge fields and growing grain. This farm had a milk round attached to it, which was something quite new.

The milk from the farm had previously been delivered by horse and float – possibly twice daily – measuring the milk from the kit into a jug. We now were beginning to deliver milk in bottles. We had to take a turn at bottling the milk, filling the bottles individually with a jug from a kit of milk – a cold job on a winter's morning. In those days we used the wide-necked pint bottles which were sealed with a cardboard disc in which a hole was marked out so that the disc could be removed. The price of milk and a loaf of bread was the same – fourpence halfpenny – and I well remember putting milk up to six pence when we became tuberculin tested.

As a special treat for Christmas we used to separate for cream. This was another manual job which involved standing by the machine and continually turning the handle. We continued to do this for several years but what joy when we finally bought an electric-powered machine – which incidentally we still use today.

In March 1946 I became eligible to learn to drive. My father took me into the field with the car and instructed me what it was all about. I was left to my own devices and told to get on with it. Eventually I ventured on to the road but no competent driver was required to accompany me. For a year I delivered milk in Ulverston and then the government reintroduced the driving test, which had been suspended during the war. My examiner was a stranger to Barrow so after several manoeuvres he told me to take him anywhere I liked for the next 15 minutes. I kept to the quiet roads. I passed my test that day but often think if I had to go again today I would probably fail.'

'Sixty years ago a farm worker's wage did not provide many luxuries. My uncle worked on a farm for £1 per week and six shillings of this went in rent. The remaining 14 shillings provided everything for his wife and daughter. Only 50 years ago a married man with two children working at a farm at Ings earned £2 a week.

During the Second World War my father-in-law had a milk round in Kendal. The town was divided into areas, and the milkmen were told which areas they could supply. In the winter of 1947 he still delivered milk from Crook to Kendal, but had to dig the road out every morning, there was so much snow. There was still snow behind the headriggs in June when the turnip seeds were sown, but because the ground had been warmed by the snow for so long, everything grew very quickly and the turnips were harvested at the usual time of the year. During that harsh winter, farmers at Kentmere knocked their newborn lambs on the head at birth as there was no hope for their survival. Hard times indeed.'

BOON PLOUGHINGS

'Boon ploughings used to be very common around Thornthwaite. All the farmers joined together and did one farm's ploughing, by horse and usually in one day, with a competition to see who could plough the straightest furrow. At night they had a kurn supper provided by that farmer and his wife, and then danced the night away.

All farmers helped each other to move house or farm. As many as 20 horses and carts would gather.

Shepherds' meets were held every two years so that local farmers could bring stray sheep to find their rightful owners. This was of course held at the local pub and some only returned home a day or two later.'

'During the 19th century a boon ploughing was reported at Overthwaite which is a good illustration of this old custom.

"One of the largest boon ploughings that has been seen for many years past took place on Wednesday last, on the large farm at Overthwaite, the property of Mrs Hutton of Beetham. Mr Barrow Bell of Witherslack, having taken the above farm, his friends, willing to lend him an assisting hand on entering upon his new undertaking, readily came forward to give him a day's work. The day being remarkably fine for the occasion drew together a vast concourse of people. There were 85 draughts to be seen busily engaged in turning up the soil, and the work was done in first-rate style, each striving to finish his work better than his neighbour. About four o'clock they finished, when upwards of 200 sat down to an excellent dinner of roast and boiled beef, plum puddings etc, and plenty of real October nut brown, to which ample justice was done. The evening was spent in a convivial manner."'

'Haytime was a tiresome time in the early years, with horse power and very little machinery. Crops weren't as heavy as the present day, as very little artificial fertiliser was used. The cutter bar was used to mow the grass and was drawn by either one or two horses. The grass was mown either early morning or late afternoon, to spare the horses working during the heat of the day. The hedgerows were mown mainly by scythe; the working machines were either a turner or a strewer, only used if the horses weren't tired. Hand tools were used, such as hay rakes for turning, when all the family followed each other around the swaths. When the hay was nearly dry it was usually made into little heaps called cocks – this allowed the hay to season. The best seed-grass hay was always kept for the horses and it was later led into a loft above the stable; the storage for hay was either stone barns or lofts above the byres. Many farms had a field house, a stone building set in a field away from the homestead, which was used for convenience of storage and meant shorter journeys for carting the hay and leading the manure in the spring as young cattle were wintered in the byres there. On the hill farms these buildings were used for the convenience of sheep

Cutting the hay at Knott Houses, Grasmere in August 1902. Horses would remain an essential part of farming life for another 50 years.

farmers. Many of these stone buildings have now been converted into houses.

The hay was led with either a sledge or "boggy". The hay was swept with a "tipling paddy", used if the hay was dry enough without cocking and like an outsized rake with handles. The horses were yoked into this with chains. The hay was left in heaps either for the convenience of leading, making pikes or hay stakes. After the hay was led the fields were raked either with the hand rakes or the "old mare", a large-size rake used by the strongest member of the family. As tractors came some of the old machines were converted by changing the tow poles, and more modern machines were available as the years passed by.

A mechanical mower on a tractor can now do in an hour what it took a horse-drawn mower days to mow. Also a tractor with a hay tedder can soon go through the crop and spread it out, and row it up, at a much faster speed than the horse-operated machinery. A baler can bale a field and in a few hours it can be led away into barns for the winter by mechanical handlers, which is a lot faster than by leading loose hay. Also becoming more popular are the large round silage bales, which can be lifted by a loader and dropped into a feeder, and one bale can last the stock a day or more, whereas with more traditional small oblong bales it would take several to satisfy their needs.

Nowadays there is not as much haymaking done due to the increase of making grass into silage, which is an all-mechanical operation.'

'Harvest time when I was a child was much more of a chore than in these days of combine harvesters. Firstly, the farmer had to cut a swath round the outside of the field with a scythe, bundle the corn into sheaves and tie them with a band of straw; this made a passageway for the reaper (or binder) to be pulled round the field by two horses. When the field was cut the sheaves were placed upright in stooks of six or eight and left to dry for a week or two according to the weather.

Next the sheaves were taken to the farm by horse and cart and forked off into a Dutch barn or into individual stacks. When all was gathered in, the stacks had to be thatched to keep out the rain. When the time came to thresh the corn the threshing machine came round the local farms pulled by a steam engine, which also drove the machine. The farmers helped each other on these days; the grain went into stacks and the straw was once again stacked up for bedding.

Threshing days were busy days for the farmer's wife too. She

A happy group of harvesters taking a tea break in the summer of 1954.

sent out picnic meals at coffee and tea times and at lunchtime all the men trooped in to the farm kitchen for a meal of, perhaps, tatie pot followed by apple dumpling.'

'Gone for ever are the fields of golden stooks of corn that used to be seen in late August and early September followed a few weeks later by the crowning glory of the neat stackyard. Farmers vied with each other for the neatest row of stacks, rapidly followed by threshing days.

Usually two and sometimes three times during the autumn and winter the old steam thresher and later the tractor-drawn machine would arrive in the district. Out would go the rallying call by bush telegraph for all the neighbouring farm hands to turn up by 9 am to make an early start on the threshing of the heads of grain. Bagging the grain and carting the bundles of straw was plenty of work for some ten to a dozen men.

A lot of hard, dirty and dusty work but made lighter by the spirit of camaraderie which existed. There was usually the chasing with the farm terrier of rats which had sought shelter in the stack bottoms.

Dinner time would be around twelve o'clock, eagerly looked forward to by the gang. This meal was taken in the old farm kitchen and was usually a good old Cumberland tatie pot followed by rice pudding. The next feast would be about three o'clock when one or two milk cans of tea and a butter basket of apple platecake or currant cake, rock buns and gingerbread were quickly devoured.

The team would move from farm to farm in rotation and this could take as long as a week, the bigger farms taking more than one day. Today the local agricultural contractor arrives and within a few hours the job which provided employment for so many farm hands for weeks to cover the reaping, binding, stooking, baling, stacking, thatching and threshing is accomplished in one fell swoop.

The price to pay for this progress is the loss of the spirit of comradeship and the drift from the farming community of something like 75% of farm workers.'

'Our busy time at Preston Patrick was when the steam threshing machine came. We went out to see it coming down the lane – chuff, chuff, chuff, with smoke going way up into the sky. The machine went up into the yard ready for use the next day. A supply of coal and water had to be laid on to run the engine. My mother had a big baking day and aunts came to help with the food. The men had tea taken up into the big yard, they had dinner in the house, tea again in the yard, and later again in the house. Quite a few men came from nearby farms to help and then our men went to their farms in return. A man was needed to throw the sheaves from the stack, which had been laid a certain way, heads to middle. Another man cut the string on the sheaves and fed the thresher, and one saw to the sacks of corn. The lad got the dirty job of bagging the chaff. They all used to end up very dirty with dust and sweat. Next day it was someone else's turn to have the threshing machine.'

CLIPPING DAYS

'I remember clipping days of the 1930s and 1940s, as a lad on a fellside farm above Bampton, when everybody joined together to clip their flocks of sheep that roamed the fells. Clipping day was a social occasion in those days, when the women prepared the feast for the menfolk, working for days beforehand preparing food on the old kitchen range.

On the day, all the ladies would arrive from neighbouring farms to help, dressed up in their best clothes. The menfolk would arrive. Some had not seen each other since the last clipping. It was a great time for crack (jokes) and some great tales were told by the real old-timers.

Little had changed since the clipping days of the early 1900s when this photograph was taken at Grasmere in 1963.

After the work was done and the beer and food consumed, away home they would go, perhaps with a few of their own stray sheep. The next clipping day would take place after the next farmer had got his sheep gathered in and sorted.'

'At the sheep clippings in Langdale at the beginning of the century, farmers from many parts came to help and all the sheep got clipped in one day, except for odd ones which escaped the round up. We children helped, one taking bands around to tie the sheep's legs, and another salve, in case any got cut. Some carried fleeces away to be rolled up, and we helped to take all kinds of sandwiches, pasties etc around at lunchtime and hot and cold drinks.

It was usually about 6.30 pm when clipping was over, then the men had a good wash. Then there was a big meal, usually hotpot and plenty of rice pudding and fruit tarts, and dancing in the barn began at about 8.30 pm. This is where we young folks learned to dance. They were the best dances and the jolliest I've ever been to. At midnight refreshments were served and dancing continued to 4 am, when my uncle played "Now the day is over", then we joined hands and sang "Auld Lang Syne".'

IN SERVICE

While most of the lads who went to the hiring fairs were looking for farm work, the lasses who also made their way there were hoping for domestic work of some kind. Many a girl left school and went straight into domestic service, sometimes the only employment open to her. Before the 1940s most middle class families kept at least one servant, to say nothing of the numbers needed at the 'big house'.

MOST GIRLS WENT INTO SERVICE

'Choice of work around Moresby was very limited before the education system was changed, as many children did not even get the opportunity to sit exams for further education, and in most cases parents couldn't afford to keep them at school for many years. Most girls seemed to go into service. Up until the Second World War, a family did not have to be wealthy to have a maid. As long as the man of the house had permanent work (tradesmen and other manual workers did not), the family were able to keep up a good standard of living and many small homes employed maids.

A typical example of earlier times is of the woman who tells of going to the hiring fair at Egremont at the age of 16 years. From there she went into service on a farm for £5 per half year. The work was hard and at harvest time she started at five in the morning, not finishing till eleven at night. Once hired, a person could not change their mind.'

'In the villages of Braithwaite and Thornthwaite in the early years of the century, the girls usually went into service at the big houses, cooking, cleaning etc.

One lady who was a cook told me the female staff would go to a village dance occasionally, but couldn't go until late when all the chores were done. They always had to go to the mistress's room and be inspected first and she always made a point of lifting up their dresses to see what they had on underneath – but she always gave them a dab of perfume.'

A WORKING GIRL

'In 1928, at the age of 14, my mother Mary Ann Slater left school and went into service at a large mansion called Wanless Howe. This later became Cobblestones knitting factory and subsequently the Ambleside Park Hotel. The owner of the house, Mrs McKeever, widow of a shipping owner, employed a cook, housemaid, under housemaid, head parlourmaid, under parlourmaid and kitchenmaid to look after her. Mum earned £3 8s 4d a month and rose to the dizzy heights of head parlourmaid. She worked six and a half days a week and her half day off, between 2 and 9 pm was spent at home helping her mother. The housemaid carried a white cloth which she used to rub along the surfaces throughout the house to check for dust. Despite the hard work my mother enjoyed her job for eight years until her marriage to my father.

Elsie, Mum's younger sister, was less fortunate in her first job. She was in service to two old ladies who ate porridge for two of their daily meals and retired to bed at 8.30 pm prompt. They had a regular routine each night of checking that Elsie was in bed before finally locking up. After suffering the porridge and restrictions for several months, Elsie became desperate. One winter's night she got into bed fully clothed and after being checked and before her bedroom door was locked, she crept down the back stairs and ran all the way home across miles of farmland. The next day her mother sent her to stay at her Auntie Sarah's at Borwick Fold in the village of Crook, until the fuss died down, and she eventually became a cook in a much happier household.'

'It was January 1935 and I was 14 years old and on my way to start work for the first time. My destination was the Sawrey Hotel, Far Sawrey. Feeling very grown up, I was most indignant when the bus conductor asked if I wanted half-fare. Really, couldn't he see I was a working girl?

The job was quite good by the standards of the day. I learned quite a lot, setting tables properly, waitressing and chambermaiding among other things. My wages were eight shillings a week and food, but I had to provide my own uniform – for morning a blue dress, large white apron and a cap; for afternoon a black dress, small fancy apron and a cap.

I made a few friends during my off duty time. Most of them worked on farms. That was when I realised my work was reasonably good against their hard labour.'

LIFE DOWNSTAIRS

'My memories are of life "downstairs" as a 14 year old kitchenmaid earning five shillings a week in 1940 at Dalemain mansion near Ullswater.

Each morning I was awakened by a sharp knock at 5.45. I had to be downstairs at six to light the coke-burning stove, the only method of heating the domestic water supply. This stove was the bane of my life – what trouble I had in getting it to burn.

The large kitchen had a red composition floor which had to be washed every morning before seven. That floor was also polished with Red Cardinal and buffered once a week.

Having lived all my school days at Melmerby this was my first experience of living away from home. I was very homesick and would hide myself in the scullery where I seemed to do nothing but wash up all day and weep into the washing up water. The gardener tried to cheer me up when he came in daily with the vegetables. He would lay them out in a row on the long stone shelf which ran the length of the scullery. It was one of my duties to prepare these vegetables for Cook.

I also had to skin and cook rabbits for the dogs. I got this off to a fine art. If I didn't tear the pelt I got one shilling and sixpence each from a trader at the door. Game was hung in a meat safe on legs situated in the yard and when a pheasant or some such bird was required for dinner "upstairs" I would often find the carcase had been visited by bluebottles and the insides were full of maggots.

A bell was rung at staff mealtimes. The head housemaid, the under housemaid, schoolroom maid, cook and myself were served from the head of the table by the butler. As rationing was in force Cook would put so much sugar in jars with each person's name on for their own personal use. On forgetting to collect my jar en route to the table, I would ask to be excused to get it. The butler's reply was "If you forget it again, you do without." Consequently, I did and realising tea was not so bad, I've done without sugar ever since.

The lady's maid lived in the front end of the house and it was the highlight of the week to be invited to listen to her collection of Richard Tauber records. He was her hero and we would listen with awe to his glorious voice.

On my day off, I would cycle into Penrith to get a ride to Melmerby to spend a few hours at home before hurrying back to be in by 9.30. Once, I was ten minutes late and it was straight to bed with no supper.'

OTHER WAYS WE MADE A LIVING

There were, of course, dozens of other ways in which we made our living in the past, some now part of a world gone forever. Here is just a selection, from mining to shoemaking, the workhouse to the blacksmith.

DOWN THE MINES

'The majority of boys at Moresby went "down the pit", a very arduous and dangerous job. Even if a boy was very reluctant to do so at first, the companionship seemed to make up, in time, for initial disappointment. Occasionally the Co-op or other small stores would require an assistant, and it was a very lucky boy who got that job.

Miners worked very long hours, and sometimes had to walk many miles to the colliery where they were employed because at times there was not enough work at the local Walkmill Colliery.

In the 1920s and particularly the 1930s the economic depression hit the whole area very badly. Very few men were in work and the women had great difficulty in making ends meet. Trousers, pullovers, dresses, stockings and underwear were patched and patched again. Once outgrown, garments, including shoes, were handed down to a younger child. Everyone pulled together. I can remember going home from school and being asked by my mother to take a jug to a neighbour's house and fill it from a set-pot. This contained an appetising stew made from a variety of inexpensive ingredients such as turnips, barley, rabbit meat etc. All those in need availed themselves of it. Miners from the nightshift roamed far and wide during the daylight hours replenishing the pot with whatever they could find.

In time, though, things got better for the miners. With pit-head baths they were able to come home clean, and houses were built that included bathrooms. Of course, coal was desperately needed during the Second World War and it was then and after the war that conditions really improved for them.'

'Both men and women worked in the mines around Thornthwaite. The mines were at Brandelhow, Thornthwaite, Barrow, Force Crag, Stoneycroft Ghyll, Goldscope, Dalehead, Catbells, Yewthwaite,

Ladstock, Rachel Wood and Beckstones. They produced galena, blende, barytes, iron pyrites, stoltzite, malachite, cerussite and silver. At 5.30 each morning the sound of miners' clogs could be heard setting off for the mines.

One day the conveyor belt broke down so five girls walked up-fell to investigate, but on the way they passed the miners' shed, looked in and decided to clean the place up a bit. They cleared it up and washed all the dirty cups and beakers (and were surprised to find that some of the cups had lovely patterns on them), but the miners were annoyed – they couldn't tell which was their mug now.'

'One of my childhood memories is watching the buckets that carried iron ore on overhead lines, from the mine near our house to the railway line near Stainton.

I wondered how these buckets went down one line full and returned on the other line empty. One day I was taken to see what happened. The buckets were emptied into railway waggons and these were pulled off to join the main line to Barrow and go to the ironworks. They were pulled by a little engine known as "Stainton Bobby". This was stopped after a very wet winter in the mid 1930s. The mine became flooded and although there was still a quantity of ore left in the ground, the cost of pumping out the water was not an economic proposition. That meant the closure of the last working iron-ore mine in the Furness area. This was the Woodbine mine, commonly known as "Dickie Pink's", as the workmen all used to go home with their clothes and skin looking very pink.'

'My father was a coalminer so I was brought up in a mining village. We were poor, as wages were very low and there were eight of us. My mother must have been a good manager as we always had one wholesome meal a day.

One of the highlights for us children was when there was a strike. The pit ponies were brought to the surface and children were allowed to feed them.

As my father worked nights, we did not see much of him through the day, but he was always there at bedtime for a prayer and "goodnight and God bless".'

'The iron-ore miners at Lamplugh wore trousers reinforced with patches of leather or moleskin at the knees. Their work clothes needed to be soaked for at least two days, changing the water three or four times before washing to try to get rid of the red dust. Clog makers abounded, even in small villages. Miners wore "duck-neb" clogs.'

THE MILLS

'The school leaving age was 14 when I was a child in Longtown. One source of employment was the bobbin mill. This was at the end of Burn Street on the site now used by Suttons. It was managed by a Mr Robert Dixon who lived with his sister in Bridge Street. In later years the mill was managed by a Longtown man, Jimmy Bell, who lived in Albert Street.

Some of the girls and men of Longtown worked there for most of their lives. The average wage for the girls was twelve shillings per week and for the men 18 shillings per week, both paid fortnightly.

The men made wooden bobbins for the cotton and woollen mills of Lancashire and Yorkshire. These were taken to Longtown station by a horse-drawn cart. The girls decorated the bobbins, painting lovely colours on most of them. In the evening they came home covered in sawdust. They were awakened in the morning for work by a buzzer known as the Too.

Eventually a bus service was started from Longtown to Carlisle, so work was easier to find in the shops and factories there – the bobbin mill became less important to Longtown after that.'

'Although the district was, and still remains, agricultural, there were extensive woollen mills at Hallthwaites, making carpets, rugs and blankets, some of which are still in use in local homes. These mills finally closed in 1930. Several local industries derived their power from the fast flowing Black Beck, including two corn mills, now abandoned.

There was an iron furnace in Duddon Woods, there being an ample supply of charcoal from the surrounding coppice woods. Ore could be brought up the river Duddon in shallow boats, on favourable tides. For many years the buildings were abandoned and derelict, but they are now being preserved.'

BLACKSMITH AND WHEELWRIGHT

'Years ago Urswick, like many other villages, had a smithy. As children we used to go to see the horses being shod.

The inside of the smithy was quite dark, lit only by paraffin lamps and the glow from the fire. The floor was made from earth. The blacksmith was a little man very bent with years of working over an anvil. The horses were brought sometimes to have a full set of worn shoes replaced, or maybe for one shoe that had been lost.

A narrow strip of iron was placed in the fire and while it was getting hot the blacksmith would take the leg of the horse and hold it up between his knees. He would take off the old shoe and take any small stones or dirt out of the foot. With a sharp knife he would trim the foot and prepare it ready for the new shoe.

The iron was taken from the fire with long tongs and put on the anvil and made into the shape of a shoe. To cool the shoe it was put into a stone trough full of cold water, while steam rose everywhere. When the shoe was cool enough to place on the horse's foot it was put on and tried for size and reheated again to soften it to make it a good fit. After cooling in the trough it was put on the horse's foot and hammered on with thick nails. Finally the edges of the shoe were filed smooth.

During this process the farmer held the horse with a halter, the animal being very patient.

The smithy was a warm place to go on winter school holidays. The boys used to brighten the fire by using large bellows. The steam and the smell of the shoe on the horse's foot are things to remember and the blacksmith was kindly and never sent us away.'

'It was Easter 1928 at the Highbridge blacksmith's. "Get that boy out of bed," shouted my father, "I have a lot of work to get through today."

He handed me a broom and I swept the ashes from the hooping plate where the day before he had hooped the wheels of a large cart. I tidied away buckets and watering cans which we had used to cool the metal and seal the hoop onto the wooden cart wheel, and eventually he was satisfied.

The smithy fire was already hot and glowing and the smiddy coals were piled up ready on the hearth. His leather brat stretched over his large frame and his ginger hair shone even redder in the glow of the fire. He worked steadily at the coulter from the ploughshare which had broken on one of the stones which frequently turned up from the Roman encampment on the hill. His hammer rang out on the anvil and the sparks showered high in the air.

Tam, the whipper-in from the local hunt dropped in at the forge and Father quickly trimmed and dressed the feet of his fine bay mare.

Plodding up the lane came the sturdy black Clydesdale of our neighbour Jack Fiddler. He was booked for shoes all round and Father prodded me to work the bellows to bring the fire back to a working temperature. Father soothed the gelding with a stroke and scratch. He rarely had to use the nose twitch and horses instinctively trusted him. He picked up a white feathered hoof and checked for size and selected a half-made plate from the stock he kept ready hanging in the rafters. He heated the shoe, checked it on the hoof, reheated it and when completely satisfied nailed it on with deft hammering while I wrinkled my nose at the smell of acrid burning hoof. Two hours later all four shoes were on and my father painted the hooves with knacker fat which gleamed as he led the horse out.

He then entered eleven shillings in his notebook, which later would be copied out when he made out his bills. Jack was a good payer, not like some and Father often returned home with cheese or other produce which had been given in lieu of money.

Dusk was falling. We had a paraffin vapourising burner which roared like a blow torch and provided a reasonable light, but Father only used this in emergencies, so we were finished for the day, but not before all the tools were greased with some more knacker fat. Father made a mental note to visit the Hunt kennels for some more fat as supplies were running low and he knew they'd had a good supply of fallen stock in the last few weeks and there would be lots of rendered fat to spare.

I didn't like the blacksmith's life and as horses disappeared from the land, trade dropped off until the smithy closed in 1941.'

Blacksmith Jack MacNeil working at Castlerigg Farm, Keswick in 1960.

'The village blacksmith at Troutbeck was Tom Bell, who was also a good bass singer and bell ringer and organ blower at church. We spent many hours watching him making horseshoes. He also made our iron hoops and crooks ("bouly" we called it), costing ninepence.

Village carpenter Tom Grizedale was a real craftsman, a wheelwright and coffin maker. His business was run from the same premises as the blacksmith so it was always a fascinating place for children, but on no account were we allowed to get in the way or misbehave.'

'I loved to watch my grandfather in his workshop. He was a joiner and wheelwright. He would take a large wooden wheel to the blacksmith to have an iron hoop put round it for the cart he had made and then roll it back home. I watched him make coffins and polish them by hand. He would pop his apprentice in to try them for size!'

THE SHOEMAKER

'The first house on entering Parsonby was that of the village shoemaker. The room on the right-hand side of the house could only be entered from the outside and was the shoemaker's "shop". It had a fireplace and opposite, a long wooden bench for customers to sit on. Between the fireplace and the window was a seat with a tray attached, divided into sections for nails, tools, etc. Opposite the window was an open cupboard with partitions for lasts, some bearing the name of customers because they had been adapted to be a perfect fit for that man's foot by building up with layers of leather in certain places, eg for a bunion or dropped instep. There were standard lasts for all sizes, bags of wooden soles for clogs, and caulkers ("corkers") – the metal strips fitting round the soles. Leather uppers which were nailed onto the wooden soles. Hanging from a nail were strips of leather for laces.

If a man came in for a pair of boots the shoemaker would measure his feet and make up a last to fit exactly, and then cut out the leather with a razor-sharp knife. There were three thicknesses of leather, the thickest for the sole, the medium for the upper and a thin one for the lining. They were sewn together with special thread, several strands of which were rolled together to make one, and then a piece of beeswax was rubbed up and down them until they were saturated. At the end of the thread a stiff hog's hair was incorporated which acted as a needle. To sew the boots they were held in a "vice" – two strips of pliable wood joined at one end and shaped like tweezers, the shoemaker holding the thin end between his knees and gripping the boot at the other end. Before each stitch, a hole was made through the leather with an awl and each stitch was a quarter of an inch long. The stitches in the lining were an eighth of an inch long. Two threads would be worked together through the hole and pulled very tight with a jerk. You can imagine what a strong man he was, working with both arms and legs – no wonder he won so many Cumberland wrestling bouts. He made a thick paste of flour and water to rub on the soles when finished. This paste lasted for six months, by which time it smelled foul.

These boots were as watertight as any wellington boot and more comfortable, for the beeswax coating on the thread prevented any water penetrating the boot, and this was essential for farmers tramping over muddy fields.

He also made clogs which were everyday wear for men, women and children, the latter calling in his shop after school to have their clogs caulkered. Clogs would last a long time if they were caulkered, for the wood never touched the ground.

The shoemaker worked from breakfast until suppertime, and men of the village would drop in his shop even though they did not need anything, just to sit on the bench in front of the fire and gossip. The shoemaker was glad of their company but he never stopped working.

He carried on his trade until he retired at 65, and the house and shop were sold, but that was the end of the village shoemaker and villagers then had their shoes mended in the nearby town. Mechanisation had taken over and the craftsman's skills were lost.'

COBBLING

'I always wore the heels down on one side of my shoes because I was a bit knock-kneed which meant that Dad had to put segs onto the bottom of my heels. He put segs on all our shoes but the ones he used on mine were called fairy segs and they were tiny silver crescent moons with nails which stuck into the leather. When Dad was mending shoes he had to get out the last, a little hammer, a card of segs and a tin of little nails. It was hard to get the segs in straight round the heels but he always managed. I liked segs because they made clickety sounds when I danced. Some people took their shoes to a shop cobbler but my Dad could do it himself so we never paid to have our shoes repaired.

First he bought a square of leather. It had a lovely smell and was smooth and pale on one side and dark and rough on the other. Dad would take it onto the backdoor step and tap it all over with the toffee hammer to make it nice and soft. He just turned and tapped, turned and tapped till it was right. Then it was time for cutting, with his very sharp knife that had a broken pointed end. He sat on the floor with the last between his knees, took a shoe, put it upside down over the last, laid the leather on top of the sole, tapped a little nail into the toe end to keep it straight and then he cut. Slice, slice, round and round, like trimming pie pastry. Then out came the nail, off came the leather, a quick slash with the knife and there was a new sole ready for nailing on.

The worst bit was when he put the nails into his mouth. (I tried it once and they tasted like water out of the iron cup on the park drinking fountain.) I never saw him spit them out, he just kept eating them as if he liked them, but he never swallowed one either. Round the sole he'd go. Nail and tap, nail and tap, till it was all fixed. Then it was trimmed again with the sharp knife and it was ready for the heel ball. I was allowed to help with this, holding the coloured wax to the fire to warm it then rolling in my hands to make it soft. Then it was rubbed along the edge of the new sole to make it look dark like the rest of the shoe and it was done. It was nice having newly cobbled shoes but they felt heavy for a few days!'

THE TAILOR

'My husband's aunt was born in 1877 in Hartley Road, Kirkby Stephen. When she was 16 she went to Leeds as an apprentice in a tailoring business; her parents had to pay for her apprenticeship and lodging money. She returned to Kirkby Stephen when she was 21 to start her own business in Hartley Road, renting a cottage next door to her parents. She trained many local girls over the years, who stayed with her until they married, many of them taking up dressmaking in their own homes.

Apprentices in 1932 were paid four shillings and sixpence for 40 hours, one with more experience £1 3s 6d for 41½ hours and fully qualified 29 shillings for 41 hours. Apprentices would thread needles, tack up hems, and oversew inside seams to prevent fraying. They would also pick up pins off the floor with a magnet, and do other menial jobs such as chopping sticks and breaking coke into small pieces to burn in the special iron heating stove. The coke was bought from the Gas House for sixpence a hundredweight in the early days. I was told that the manager himself emptied the penny-in-the-slot gas meters in the houses, and sometimes if the bank was short of change, he would go and empty a few meters to oblige them, putting in a shilling in exchange for twelve pennies. For many years when there was a death a whole family would wear black and need dresses and coats made very quickly. This meant long hours for everyone, and the Nicholson family, Aunt Mary, her sisters and her mother would work through the night to finish the order.

In 1938 she bought a house in North Road when the council demolished her cottage for road improvements, and she carried on business in the attic on her own. She still managed to lift the heavy iron from stove to ironing board and worked till she was over 70. She did not get a pension as she was too old when the law was passed that if you paid sixpence a week you would be entitled to a pension

The stove and irons used by Mary Nicholson in her tailoring business at Kirkby Stephen.

at 60. In the 1950s she charged £1 5s to make a coat fully lined, £1 for a dress, eight and sixpence a blouse, 15 shillings a pleated skirt. She more than repaid her family for paying for her apprenticeship.'

IN THE WORKHOUSE

'From 1941 to 1961 I worked in Eden House (the workhouse) at Kirkby Stephen as an attendant, which involved looking after the sick men and women in the sick wards, as well as bathing and seeing to "Part III (healthy destitute) inmates" as they were then called. I also did washing and ironing, serving meals, making beds, dumming floors. The hours were very long, 15-hour days; every other day 7 to 10 pm, the other days 7 to 6 pm, except Tuesday when I had half a day off and every other Sunday half-day.

The pay was £50 per year and my emoluments were valued at £60 as we were obliged to sleep in. I worked a month on days and a month on nights, 10 pm to 8 am one night, 8 pm to 8 am the next night, no night off. When we finished the month we had off from the Saturday morning until the Tuesday morning.

There were no cleaners employed as all the Part III inmates were made to do all the work – cleaning rooms, washing up, preparing vegetables, gardening, shovelling coal and chopping sticks under supervision. The bedrooms of Part III were very basic with a bed, chair and chamberpot. The toilets were outside except for the sick wards.

Eden House used to take in casuals (tramps) too, but the ward was closed just before I started. When they did come in they were bathed, clothed, fumigated and had to do a day's work, chopping wood, and were let out the following day. We still took in the occasional tramp but they were encouraged to come in permanently.

The food was plain; soups, stews, puddings (rice, sago, semolina), and occasionally they had roasts. They also got an allowance of cigarettes or tobacco and the ladies got sweets each week, but no pocket money. Things changed in 1948 when we got a day off each week, the inmates got a little pocket money and if they did quite a bit of work were allowed extra.

We also had a maternity ward and had a lot of young girls in to have their babies. There was no other support in those days.'

CHARCOAL AND SWILLS

'Charcoal burning, a long slow process of reducing wood to charcoal, was carried out in the Furness area. Swill making was another craft

– a swill being an oval basket about nine inches deep, with a curved bottom, made from thin strips of woven wood, then bound round the top. They had many uses, both on the farms and in the house.'

ON THE ROADS

One of the figures gone for good is the lengthman – responsible for his own section of road and well known to all the locals on his 'patch', especially the children. Watching local men surfacing the road, too, was one of our entertainments!

THE ROADMEN OF DENTDALE

'In the mid 1920s my father obtained work as a roadman under the West Riding County Council, a job which he held until his retirement in 1958. At that time there were four lengthmen and a foreman employed in Dentdale to keep the highways in good order – one responsible for Cowgill and Dent Head, one for Gawthrop and Barbondale, one for Deepdale and Kingsdale (to the summit) and another, my father, responsible for Dent village, Sedbergh Road (as far as Mopas Bridge), Deepdale Road (to West Banks), Hollow Lane (to Hiring Hill), Floods Lane and the Cowgill Road (as far as Cross House).

These lengthmen kept all the roadside verges cut and "skirted" (edges trimmed with a spade), roads swept, drains and gutters open and wall-gaps repaired. My father swept the village streets every Saturday morning and weeded the cobbles when necessary. All this, in the early days, was done with a brush, shovel, spade, wheelbarrow, bill-hook and scythe. Usually the lengthmen worked alone but as the years went by, in the 1940s, it became more common for them to work in pairs or gangs and a local haulage contractor with a lorry and driver was hired to replace much of the "wheelbarrow work".

After heavy overnight rain the lengthman's first duty was to "look his length", to ensure there was no serious damage to the road and that all drains and watercourses were unblocked – a practice which, alas, seems to be so sadly lacking today.

Roads in Dentdale, up to the early 1930s, were of stone and sand and it was during my early youth I witnessed them being "scurrified" (roughened up by large metal spikes attached to the rear of a steam roller), watered by a water cart, rolled and finally topped off with tarmac, the drainage system having been installed during the process.

At the end of each day's work, when this was going on, a nightwatchman would install himself close by the current day's working, in a sentry-box type of cabin with a brazier full of red hot coke at hand to keep him warm. His task was to take care of any equipment and to tend the oil lamps which provided warning lights to the sparse traffic, wheeled or pedestrian.

Many of us village youngsters loved to take potatoes from home to be chipped or baked for us by this genial old man on his glowing fire during the dark evenings.

Eventually the tarmac surface was itself covered with tar and chippings – this tarring process being repeated over the years as certain sections of the road surface became worn and dangerously smooth. When tarring was to take place, during dry weather in the summer months, the roadmen were issued with a special pair of overalls, clogs (with buckle fastenings to prevent hot tar seeping or spilling into them) and gloves. Two black tarpans, under which fires were lit to heat the tar to keep it sufficiently liquid to pour and spread, would arrive, as would coal, barrels of tar and loads of chippings, as well as the inevitable puffing, hissing 16 ton steam roller, towing its driver's mobile home. More roadmen would come from Sedbergh to join the Dent men whenever this type of work was undertaken and the reverse applied if similar operations were carried out in the Sedbergh area.

Each man would have his own particular job in the resurfacing process. My father's job was to keep one of the tarpans operating – feeding the fire and agitating the tar inside the pan, which he did by pumping a handle backwards and forwards on the outside of the pan.

After a period of two weeks or so the "sweeping off" would begin – sweeping up with large stiff brushes and carting away all those surplus loose chippings not compacted into the tar. Another use would be found for them on other roads in the area.

My father, after a day on the tarpan, would return home sporting a light mahogany tan, brought about by a combination of heat, smoke, sun, sweat and fumes from the boiling tar. Each day his tanned complexion would become progressively darker. Outside in the back yard, he removed his overalls and clogs to leave them in the coal-house overnight and, still outside, using a bucket he washed

The road being laid at Tracey Tree Corner in the 1920s. The roadmen and lengthmen were a familiar part of our lives.

off the thickest of the grime from his face and hands before coming inside to the kitchen where he had a thorough wash down. We had no running hot water and no bathroom, of course, in the 1930s. I used to love the aroma of hot tar which seemed to cling to my father on these occasions.

In his later years my grandfather was also employed as a roadman in Dent. When he reached the age of 70 (there was no works pension in those days and no official retiring age) the Highways Department continued to pay him a small amount each week and told him he could carry on doing a bit of work as and when he felt like it, but there was no compulsion! He died in 1929 at the age of 83.

When he worked on the roads the surfaces were all of stone and sand, apart from the cobbled sections. Until the late 1920s many people in the dale, including schoolchildren, used to break limestone into small pieces using special hammers. Payment from the council was nine shillings per cubic yard of broken stone, which was used to repair and maintain the road surface.

One group of young stonebreakers used to work near Church Bridge, collecting large limestones from the river bed and breaking them on their own little "pitches" along the roadside from the bridge

to Floods Lane end. Sometimes brothers and sisters worked together. There was no trespassing nor stealing from someone else's pile. Children who broke stones were paid at intervals by the local foreman, who used to meet them, with his notebook in hand, as they came out of school!'

WAR & PEACE

THE BOER WAR

Fought in the last years of Victoria's long reign, the Boer War may have been far from Cumbria but defeat and victory were as closely followed as in later, more devastating conflicts. Memories still remain of local celebrations.

A GREAT IMPRESSION

'Just before the start of this century, in 1899, Irish volunteers for the Boer War landed at Maryport and marched through the district to embark at Whitehaven docks for South Africa. It made a great impression on local small boys, and for weeks afterwards they played at being soldiers – marching back and forth, making helmets out of brown paper bags, and using sticks for rifles.

After the relief of Mafeking, near the end of the Boer War, villagers at Moresby joined in the celebrations when miners dragged sleepers and tar from the pit and built a bonfire which could be seen for miles.'

'The news of the relief of Ladysmith in February 1900 came by newspaper to Finsthwaite, and there were bonfires at Graythwaite to celebrate the relief of Mafeking in May 1900.'

THE GREAT WAR 1914–1918

Just a few years after those bonfires of celebration had been lit, England was again at war, this time the 'war to end all wars'. Troops and prisoners of war became familiar sights to many youngsters, and many a sock and scarf was knitted for our boys at the Front. Food shortages spurred on early efforts at 'digging for victory' and for the first time the horrors of modern war came closer to those who stayed behind in Cumbria. Celebrations were held in towns and villages across the county when peace finally came, but the times they ushered in were hard for many.

U-BOATS AND ALLOTMENTS

'There are still a few residents of Moresby Parks who remember the years of the First World War. In 1915, a U-boat shelled a factory on the coast at Lowca, and there was a rumour that someone had signalled to it from the window of a house in the old part of Moresby, which is within sight of the sea. Another U-boat was captured in 1918 and put on display in Whitehaven. Parties of children, accompanied by their teachers, were allowed to look round this boat.

The local boys tended allotments at the top of the field which is now the rugby field, the land having been provided by a local farmer who also provided free manure. The produce was sold around the village and the profits shared amongst the boys. A share of five shillings for a year was described as a "king's ransom". The small garden at the front of the school was still planted with flowers, however.

At the end of the war the celebrations included a service at the school, and a sports day held in one of the local farm fields. The children were marched up the road in the afternoon and, after games and competitions, were presented with "Peace Mugs".'

GUNPOWDER AND SOCKS

'During the First World War, we older girls of Langdale knitted socks which were sent to the Red Cross, and our vicar gave us permission to take our knitting to church and knit during the sermon. We had concerts at school to get cash to pay for the wool.

I remember the gunpowder carts on their way to Windermere station each day (from Elterwater), usually twelve, a certain distance apart, in case of accident. The drivers had to walk there, but could ride coming back when the carts were empty. Powder was carted also to many quarries: Kirkby and Low Wood in Furness, Gatebeck and other places below Kendal and Honister. When going to Honister they left Elterwater soon after midnight, when there would be very little other traffic on the roads. On May Day the drivers decorated their horses and the best decorated got a prize. They were paraded around the village, and always stopped outside the school for the children to come and see them.

I was always told that it was the gunpowder works which dammed Stickle Tarn. A platform was put underground leading to two huge brass taps. Each Saturday a man from the works came to turn the taps off and on Sunday he came to turn them on again. Some of us children used to wait at Stickle Force and follow the water down to watch the beck fill up again.

I also remember seeing the huge volumes of smoke that arose when an accident occurred at the gunpowder works, killing four employees.

Sometimes I used to go with several others, including adults, to Stickle Tarn to set night lines. We used to set off at 8 pm on Saturday and set the lines, and return at 4 am on Sunday to collect our catch. We used to take a picnic breakfast of bacon sandwiches and hard boiled eggs, which we always ate sitting beside the tarn. The churchwarden, who was one of the group, was never late for morning service. I've never been interested in legal fishing, but as a child I also learned how to tickle trout!'

SWEETS FROM THE CANADIANS

'I well remember playing in the "big wood" between Barras Lane and Lingey at Dalston, where Canadian foresters worked felling timber to be used as props in the trenches in France. The attraction for this particular jaunt was always the sweets that the men doled out, and the chance to watch their miniature railway that wound its way around the forest and down to the nearby station.'

GERMAN POWs

'There was a German POW camp situated on the Salter road near Kirkland School. My parents used to tell of taking me past in the pram. Sadly, there was a serious outbreak of flu resulting in the

The end of the war in 1918 was greeted with tremendous relief and sadness. Peace celebrations took place all over Cumbria – these children were part of Braithwaite's peace procession.

death of some prisoners and locals. The prisoners were buried in Lamplugh churchyard. The graves were well tended, then a few years ago their remains were removed to another place by the War Office.'

CELEBRATIONS

'The Armistice in 1918 was celebrated at Lakeside Institute when all the villagers from Finsthwaite were invited to a party given by the man who lived at Stock Park Mansion. The children were given their tea first, then watched a Punch and Judy show. Later the adults arrived and there was dancing, and everyone joined in, young and old alike.'

HARD TIMES

'During the war it was very difficult to get help on the farm at Holme St Cuthbert, as most of the able-bodied men were away fighting. I remember we did get one young lad from Cockermouth and paid him a shilling for hiring.

A farmer now in his eighties recalls that farming in the years after the war was in a very poor way – not much worth and very hard work. "Men coming out of the Forces after the war with a little bit of gratuity – many of them ex-farmworkers – would get a smallholding, hoping to settle and make it pay. They didn't last three years – it was very sad. Some who settled at Tarns did succeed, but they had to work really hard to do it."

War casualties lasted long after the cessation of hostilities and I remember there were men on the roads after the Great War who would call at the farm looking for food. I supposed they were men who couldn't settle after such terrible experiences and my mother would give them a bit of food, maybe bread and jam. They carried their own mug for a drink of tea. Sometimes they'd come back if they were in the area again, knowing they would get something – they were never turned away.'

THE SECOND WORLD WAR 1939–1945

Just over 20 years later, Cumbrian families once again said goodbye to their loved ones called up for service, and faced dangers of their own. German planes droned overhead on their way to bomb industrial targets and Cumbria's town dwellers grew used to the sound of the air raid sirens. Prisoners of war again worked on the farms – and often endeared themselves to the local children by their skill in toy making.

THE BOMBING STARTED

'My childhood was spent in Barrow-in-Furness and my first recollection of the imminence of war was being fitted with a gas mask; the smell lingers in my memory to this day. After the declaration of war these masks were carried in a cardboard box with a piece of string attached, later progressing to a smart carrying case.

In May 1941 the bombing started. The Germans were aiming for the shipyard and the docks but most bombs fell on the residential areas. By that time we had an Anderson shelter in the garden which my father had erected. As half the shelter was several feet below ground level this meant that most of the time it was full of water!

However, a single bed was put in the shelter and the springs just cleared the water level. Fortunately in May 1941 the shelter was dry and therefore made it more comfortable for us when the bombing commenced in earnest. The top of the shelter was covered with a layer of sods and at the height of the attack we could hear debris falling on it. If the alert continued after 10 pm schools opened one hour later next day, which pleased us schoolchildren greatly.

The worst night we experienced, I can remember my mother lying on top of us on the shelter bed whilst bombs fell all around us. When the all clear sounded we discovered lumps of clay the size of footballs in the driveway but worse was to come when we entered the house. There was no electricity and so we could not see what we were standing on nor the devastation inside. As soon as it was light we saw that we had been walking on a mixture of glass, soot and plaster. Our two year old house had no windows, no ceilings and we could see the sky from the bedrooms. It was devastating that we could no longer live there. We left the area for a year and lived in cramped conditions with a relative.

On our return we found the ceilings had been partly repaired and the windows covered in black tarpaulin except for one frame in each room which was covered with a white woven canvas to let the light in. As it aged this canvas stretched and flapped noisily whenever the wind blew. Eventually some of the tarpaulins were replaced with very inferior glass.

Our Anderson shelter was replaced by an indoor Morrison type. These were constructed of steel with caged sides and were about seven feet by four feet. As there were five of us in the family we rated the two-tiered version which half filled the sitting room. By this time of course the bombing in our area had ceased and it was never used for the purpose for which it was intended. Nonetheless we children used the space to full advantage, our dolls filled the lower cage and we practised our tap dancing skills on the top.

As someone who has always enjoyed her food I found the shortages rather hard to bear! In 1945 at the whisper that the Co-operative store had bananas, children appeared from all directions, some of whom had never seen one. We attended several street parties to celebrate the end of the war. All available food was pooled and the children sat at trestle tables in the streets enjoying the attention of all the adults.

The shortages of food during the war were nothing compared with those for the next five years when all aid was diverted to the starving in Europe.

Many children went through traumatic experiences during the war and counselling had never been thought of, we just got on with life.'

'I can remember the German bombers coming over Barrow and being awakened by loud explosions and the street lit up by fires when the first incendiary bombs were dropped. There was the awful acrid smoke and my mother would hurriedly get my sister and me into the bath under the stairs for shelter, as this happened before we had an air raid shelter built. One neighbour had his feet burned when a bomb went down the chimney and bounced onto his bed.

I was sleeping at my Nana's once when a land mine whistled over her house and landed on the next street, demolishing six houses on each side. Everyone gathered to watch the dead and injured being carried out of the rubble.'

'I can clearly remember when the first bomb was dropped at Silloth. I was working at Silloth Golf Club, and was on duty that day. All the staff charged down to the coke and coal cellars for safety, emerging later when the all clear was given – shaken and sooty faced! I absolutely refused to take refuge there again, preferring to take my chance in the comfort of the club room.'

TARGET PRACTICE

'As a young girl I lived in a cottage at Southerfield, between Abbey Town and Aspatria. I would watch the RAF at target practice on Southerfield Moss, barely three quarters of a mile from my home. The planes came in low to aim their dummy bombs at large wooden arrows set up on the ground. As the bombs hit the ground, a small column of smoke would be released and RAF personnel in small huts parallel to the line of targets (albeit at a safe distance!) would send the results back to base. All this was greatly exciting for a small girl living in the depths of the countryside where nothing much usually happened.'

GREAT EXCITEMENT

'Having fought for four years in the First World War, my father was recruited as co-ordinator for the ARP in the next war. When the Germans flew on bombing raids to Northern Ireland they passed, very noisily, over Lorton in wave after wave. Receiving an early warning telephone call one evening, my father decided to leave me in my bed instead of seeking shelter and whilst most of the village had been awake all night, I had slept through the noise and wondered what everyone was talking about on the bus the next morning on the way to school.

Many aeroplanes and their crews perished on our fells, but one in particular was a Wellington bomber, which crashed on Red Pike, near Buttermere, above Sour Milk Gill. There was great excitement as the recovery crew were billeted in and around our village and every bit of wreckage had to be carried down the mountainside from an altitude of over 2,000 feet.

Concerts and entertainments were staged on a regular basis in the village hall for the benefit of the airmen, being so far away from "civilisation". We shared our school with a boys school from Newcastle on Tyne, only attending for half a day each. It did not seem to affect our exam results, but it did wonders for our social life!

A land mine which was dropped in Flimby Woods missed its intended target of the armament depot, and the sole casualty was a small red squirrel.'

'Mother would surely have won the prize had there been a competition during the war for the number of ways to cook a rabbit. Father was an excellent shot, and being too old for the army he was a keen member of the Home Guard and spent many nights on watch at Skellghyll. In 1941, a German bomber jettisoned its load of bombs at the head of Troutbeck Valley, a lucky escape for Town Head. Just one sheep and one hare were killed. At Long Green Head Farm the shippon windows were freed by the blast – they hadn't been opened for years!'

THE POWs

'Most of the men not called up for service at Holme St Cuthbert were in the Home Guard. There was a bit of excitement when one of the German prisoners of war escaped from the camp at Moota.

In fact, a number of the prisoners, both German and Italian, helped on the farms. They were brought out in the morning and returned at night to the camp in vans. There was one German who was very friendly and he wanted to stay in England after the war, but he had to go back. We liked him very much and he made us toys – I remember one with pecking hens, and also a puppet acrobat, just made with odd bits of wood.

During the war the low drone of the German planes could be clearly heard as they made their way northwards. There was a bomb dropped at Green Row in Silloth and one dropped at the back of the Tarn which failed to explode. The RAF was stationed at Silloth then and some of the men were billeted at Mawbray.'

'A prisoner of war camp was set up near Elmsfield Bridge (between Holme and Milnthorpe). I recall the first prisoners were Italians, then Germans, followed by displaced persons, and the camp later became an open prison – now it is Riverside School for children with special needs. The Italians spent a long time in tents, even through the winter. They were sent out to work on farms, cycling out in the morning and returning at night. My grandparents farmed at Sedbergh and they had one to live in. I remember he made slippers by plaiting string or twine and forming the soles and then making the uppers.'

LIFE GOES ON

No matter what the war news, life had to go on. Village life changed almost beyond recognition and mothers struggled to bring up their families on short rations and 'make do and mend'. But there were still dances to go to and weddings to plan!

WAR IN OUR VILLAGE

'My most vivid childhood memories are of the war years. We were farmers and lived in the village of Levens, so it was the effect that the war had on us, rather than the fighting that I remember.

The evacuees from the North East held the most memories in the early part of the war – most families had at least one child to stay and some had up to three children with the mother. Some stayed the duration but others drifted back after a few weeks. Our classes at school were bursting at the seams and there were evacuee teachers too. There was gas mask drill each day and woe betide anyone who had forgotten theirs.

Another vivid memory was rationing and how Mother always seemed short of sugar. Two or three elderly people in the village exchanged sugar for tea with her; we children always drank milk so tea was no problem. Sweet rationing – how we looked forward to spending our toffee coupons! We were never short of food and Mother was a great cook. She could almost make a meal from nothing. We always had home-cured bacon and eggs in the pantry, produced on the farm, so we were lucky.

I remember the blackout and how all the windows had to be

literally blacked out and not a chink of light had to escape. The ARP patrolled the village and made sure that everywhere was in darkness. Bicycle lamps had shades over the top to stop the light shining up to the sky and letting enemy aircraft see them – cars also had shaded lights. There was very little transport about as petrol was also rationed and unobtainable without petrol coupons.

I remember the salvage drive that took place – to build Spitfires they said. A lorry came round the village one afternoon and men removed all the iron railings and gates from people's houses for the war effort. One or two people, in the know, removed theirs and hid them! Sometimes there was a film show in the village institute – Mickey Mouse and the like and admission was by one pound of waste paper! How we children hunted for paper; we all managed to find enough.

Many more memories come crowding back – the convoys of troops going over Levens Bridge; the WVS taking cigarettes and other little luxuries to the airmen at Flookburgh; the planes flying over to bomb Barrow, and many more.

VE day eventually came and celebrations took place in the village – a service in church, tea in the village institute and sports. How we enjoyed it all.'

'Within a month of the outbreak of the Second World War evacuees arrived in Patterdale, mainly from the North East. A special committee was formed to deal with the problems that were expected to arise and members of the WI (founded in 1921) were ready. One problem was "knickers for the girls" as they had not been able to bring much with them. The committee decided that their members should make them. A despairing member arose, "Knickers," she wailed, "no self-respecting child would ever be able to wear knickers that I could make!" But they coped.

Another situation arose regarding the custom of the evacuee mothers of going out in the evening for a drink at the "local". Their appearance in the pub was a novelty for the local men but their wives and sweethearts did not agree with "such goings-on" and it was arranged to take over a room at Patterdale Hall with a billiard table and other games.

Our village certainly "did its bit" for the war effort. We had the largest "Gas Warfare" training school in the country with a monthly intake of hundreds of troops. The officer staff were billeted in the Ullswater Hotel and the ATS personnel at Patterdale Hall.

Patterdale Hall – before the ATS arrived – was filled with refugees from Czechoslovakia and we had an Italian prisoner of war camp at the Greenside lead mines. The prisoners used to make "silver" rings to give to us youngsters which, when worn, promptly made your finger go black!

The army camp provided film shows and what I think must have been ENSA variety concerts – if we were lucky we children were allowed in to these shows. The "Leas Schools" from Hoylake (a public school of some repute) was evacuated to the Glenridding Hotel and they too provided excellent entertainment with concerts and plays. We had Scouts, Guides and a thriving youth club. Our tennis courts were the busiest of places during the long summer evenings – double summer time then – even though it was, and still is an awful place for midges!

Football, cricket and rounders were all played in their season, with whist drives and skating on Mill Moss and Lanty Tarn in the winter. It seems as though most of the summer holidays were spent either on the fell or on or in the lake. Our Sunday school outing was a trip on the lake steamer to Howtown where we ate our picnic and played rounders. We had a very good choral and dramatic society under the leadership of Dr and Mrs Bird.

The real war touched us briefly when a German plane (for some unknown reason) released a stick of bombs which fell in a line from Grisedale Valley and part-way up Helvellyn. One landed in a field killing a sheep and we were taken from school on a "nature-walk" to see the crater – great excitement I remember!'

'Our little village of Melmerby is situated in the Eden valley between the Pennines and the Lake District hills. The farmers were busy harvesting when news came of the outbreak of war. Only a few villagers had radios but the news quickly spread.

Our village school had approximately 20 children on roll plus two teachers. However, this number was soon increased as we coped with the arrival of evacuees from the North East industrial towns. I can remember the children arriving with a few belongings – gas masks, bags of clothing and favourite toys. They were gathered in the village school, names checked and then billeted out to various homes in the surrounding area. They had bewildered expressions on their little faces – some cried – others just stared into space. A few parents accompanied their children, but returned home in a few weeks. They missed the attractions of city life! The majority of the children soon adapted to the village way of life and made lots of new friends.

Food was eventually rationed, but living on a farm we were fortunate to have meat, eggs and butter. Farmers were directed to plough out extra land to provide additional food. I remember the occasional "visitors" who obtained farm produce and dealt in the Black Market. Extra rations of food were granted for threshing days, sheep shearing days etc.

Some garden railings were removed to manufacture armaments. Windows and car headlights were "blacked out" – it was all rather gloomy.

The ladies of the village held knitting parties in their homes. Many balaclava helmets and socks were produced for the Armed Forces.

The arrival of refugees, a French school, came early in the war years. They took over a large house known as Melmerby Hall. The local village shopkeeper tried to cope with their requests for rationed sweets.

Later, soldiers of the Royal Tank Corps came to the Hall. Large tanks rumbled along the roads and used the surrounding area for military exercises. My young brother was thrilled to sit inside one of these tanks. The soldiers enjoyed the village dances, whist drives and other social events.

The villagers celebrated the end of the war with a huge bonfire on the village green. A village hall was later built as a reminder of the years when community life was so caring. It was named Melmerby Victory Hall.'

'September 2nd 1939 should have been the day when Lanercost WI held their annual flower and produce show followed by a village dance in the evening, but the whole effort was cancelled because war was imminent.

A few of us in our late teens or early twenties had cycled down to Lanercost for a game of tennis. We tried to be cheerful but there was an air of gloom and sadness as two of the local lads who were in the Territorials had already been called up and some of us were in tears.

Suddenly there was pandemonium as three coachloads of very pregnant ladies arrived from the North East as evacuees and the vicar's wife took on the unenviable task of trying to find billets for them with rather reluctant hosts. The church verger, a very conscientious young man, was in a flat spin waving his arms about and shouting, "Oh deary me, what shall we do? Any minute you know. Any minute," as though babies were about to be born on the parish green!

It must have been a very traumatic experience for the women, some of them placed in farmhouses with an earth privy down the garden, no electricity, and far from city lights and amenities. Most of them only stayed a few days and to put it politely their habits and manners were very different from ours and caused a few upsets. One villager remembers a group of them sitting on a farmhouse wall the day after they arrived anxiously waiting for the coach to take them home to their Tyneside terraces because they couldn't visualise living without a picture house, and fish and chip shop nearby.

Nevertheless the few who stayed were well looked after and the vicar, one of the few people who had a car, did a marvellous job ferrying them to a local convalescent home about five miles away which was taken over as a maternity home for the duration of the war.'

GETTING BY

'During the war it was difficult to find your way in a strange area as all the signposts were removed, as were the nameplates on railway stations. Everyone at Thirlmere was compelled to black out their windows and not let a chink of light show or the ARP would be banging on the door. Ration books and clothing coupons were a headache and quite a lot of bartering took place. When petrol rationing was strict a lot of the delivery vans stopped coming so

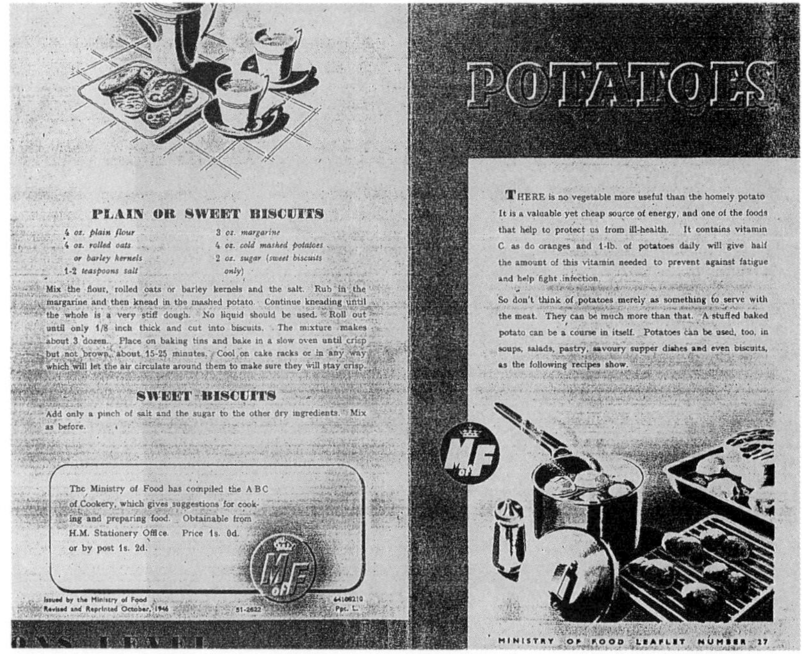

PLAIN OR SWEET BISCUITS

4 oz. plain flour
4 oz. rolled oats or barley kernels
1-2 teaspoons salt
3 oz. margarine
4 oz. cold mashed potatoes
2 oz. sugar (sweet biscuits only)

Mix the flour, rolled oats or barley kernels and the salt. Rub in the margarine and then knead in the mashed potato. Continue kneading until the whole is a very stiff dough. No liquid should be used. Roll out until only 1/8 inch thick and cut into biscuits. The mixture makes about 3 dozen. Place on baking tins and bake in a slow oven until crisp but not brown, about 15-25 minutes. Cool on cake racks or in any way which will let the air circulate around them to make sure they will stay crisp.

SWEET BISCUITS

Add only a pinch of salt and the sugar to the other dry ingredients. Mix as before.

The Ministry of Food has compiled the ABC of Cookery, which gives suggestions for cooking and preparing food. Obtainable from H.M. Stationery Office. Price 1s. 0d. or by post 1s. 2d.

Issued by the Ministry of Food
Revised and Reprinted October, 1946 51-2622 64106210 Ppt. L.

POTATOES

THERE is no vegetable more useful than the homely potato It is a valuable yet cheap source of energy, and one of the foods that help to protect us from ill-health. It contains vitamin C as do oranges and 1-lb. of potatoes daily will give half the amount of this vitamin needed to prevent against fatigue and help fight infection.

So don't think of potatoes merely as something to serve with the meat. They can be much more than that. A stuffed baked potato can be a course in itself. Potatoes can be used, too, in soups, salads, pastry, savoury supper dishes and even biscuits, as the following recipes show.

MINISTRY OF FOOD LEAFLET NUMBER 27

The Ministry of Food bombarded housewives with information and handy hints during the war, and rationing and shortages continued for some years after 1945.

we bought a horse and digby and went shopping twice a week. There were still places to stable horses in some of the hotel yards. The first horse I remember having was an ex-Army part mule. Its number was branded on its hindquarters. She was quite deaf due to heavy gunfire.

Eggs were preserved by putting into a solution called "Water Glass". Butter had extra salt worked into it, then was put into jars and covered with a thick layer of salt. Pot eggs were put into nest boxes to encourage hens to lay there. Fruit was just bottled when sugar was scarce.

There was no refuse collection but plenty of discreet rubbish tips which were cleared in war-time and any metal objects taken for recycling along with everyone's garden railings.

We made hair curlers out of rags and pipe cleaners and occasionally got some metal "Dinkie" curlers, though we also had curling tongs which were heated in the fire.'

'My mother would go off one morning each week to the Village Institute, to the "Jam Centre" run by the WI. Fruit grown locally was bought by the centre, as sugar was rationed and these centres had extra allowances. I cannot remember where the jam went, but the "scum" from the top of the pans was brought home by the jam ladies. We had bread and "jam scum" for tea, and very good it was.

Our family had a serious discussion regarding sugar and butter rationing. My parents, brothers and I voted on whether we wanted sugar in our tea or a piece of cake each day – we took our tea without sugar! If we had butter on our bread we did not have jam, or vice versa.'

IN SPITE OF RATIONING

'Rationing did not hit us too hard in Caldbeck, as most people had a few hens and joined together to fatten a pig, supplementing the ration of pig-meal with household scraps. In our case, my parents did all the work and the other family in the partnership merely enjoyed the sausages and black pudding at butchering time.

We were encouraged to dig for victory and many front lawns became potato and vegetable plots. My uncle got an extra cheese ration because he was a miner working in the barytes mines. We sold milk, so there was butter in abundance. We had an evacuee living with us (we were considered a safe haven for evacuees from Benwell, Newcastle on Tyne) and he and I went home from school for our mid-day meal and Mother always managed to produce something wholesome in spite of rationing. Food was on a "points" system and Mother sometimes had to order tins of syrup and treacle at the end of the month to use them up. There was much black marketeering.

Mother was also a wonderful needlewoman and clothing coupons were often given away to friends who were not so handy at "make do and mend". A friend remembers when her husband came out of the army with his demob suit, which he didn't want. He swapped it with a farmer for a ham, passing the ham through the car window under the nose of the local policeman.

Many village WIs set up jam-making projects utilising locally grown soft fruit. Rose hips were collected in the autumn to make vitamin C-rich syrup for babies. Children were paid threepence a pound collected – and anyone who collected 40 lbs was given a free bottle of syrup!'

SEAGULL EGGS

'Did you ever have pale pink sponge cakes in wartime? You would if you'd made them with seagull eggs!

As one of four land girls employed on the Muncaster Castle Estate, for a fortnight in early summer one of our tasks was to collect eggs from the sand dunes at Ravenglass.

These were mainly sent down to London, but a local baker at Millom also had an allocation, and as we four girls lived in an estate cottage and were self catering, we were very glad to have a few of the cracked eggs.

I must admit we were very dubious about the alleged fishy taste, and only used them in cakes, but they really were a very pretty colour.'

TRAVELLING IN WARTIME

'As a child, I was fortunate in being able to spend my time between two homes – one in the Lancashire countryside and one in Cumberland. Travelling in wartime must have been a nightmare for my poor mother but was a huge adventure to me. Waiting for trains – which were not even guaranteed to be running – on platforms crowded with troops and civilians, all with gas masks and wartime paraphernalia festooned around them, and then watching the huge locomotives hissing and groaning into the station, was desperately exciting to a six year old.

On one occasion in the seething rush to get onto a long awaited train, I became separated from my parents and was obligingly posted through a corridor window into the arms of some soldiers and passed on to my tearful mother. We frequently had to stand in packed corridors all the way to Carlisle, sharing our sweet ration with the troops, and the thrill of hurtling down Shap Fell with two engines attached – one of which had joined the train to help push us up to the summit – is still a vivid memory.

Eventually reaching Carlisle, we had to lug our cases across the city to catch the Wigton bus, which connected with the bus to Mealsgate and Ireby. This was the best bit of all to me, as the buses were what were known as "utility buses" – and lived up to the name. The seats were polished wooden slats and grossly uncomfortable, and unwary passengers, myself included, were inclined to slide off into the aisle when the bus rounded a sharp corner. Of course, the blackout was in force and if we were late arriving in Carlisle, everything was twice as exciting. Torches couldn't be used, and the few cars being driven then had hooded lights which hardly illuminated the road in front of the vehicle, and certainly didn't help us to see where we were going. Travelling in a darkened bus, along black country roads and trying to get off at the right place was an absolute lottery, and frequently passengers would stop the bus, get off, and get back on again, looking sheepish and asking the driver to "carry on a bit further". I always thought the drivers were terribly clever, as there were no signposts to point the way (they had been removed so that invading Germans wouldn't know where they were) but they never got lost and always delivered us safely to our destination.

Usually one of my numerous aunts or uncles met us, and we walked the rest of the way to my grandparents' house, where my grandmother always seemed to be walking across the kitchen carrying freshly baked bread, hot delicious bread. Her loving welcome, the glowing fire and brasses, and the soft light shed by the Aladdin lamps on to the table laid for a meal have been synonymous, in my mind, with the word "home" all my life.'

THOSE FRAGILE MANTLES

'During the war, several regiments of soldiers were billeted in Ulverston. In the run up to Christmas 1944, it was the turn of the Americans to be in town. We were asked to be hospitable to them and invite them into our homes. Dan, who came to our house, was only a young man, having had his 18th birthday on the ship coming over to England. He had never seen a coal fire before and enjoyed sitting beside ours. He had only been used to electric bars at home. We still had gas lighting in our home in those days and Dan was fascinated by this.

One evening we required a new mantle. Not having one in reserve and the shops being closed, I had to ask a local shopkeeper if he would mind opening up to let me purchase one, which he did. Once home with the new mantle, Dan asked if he could please fit it on. Not being familiar with the delicate fabric of the mantle, he proceeded to fit it onto the gas fitting whilst we watched as the mantle slowly disintegrated and fell like snow, with only the ring remaining in place. Dan's face was a picture when he saw that he had actually hung nothing up and so was the shopkeeper's when I returned 20 minutes later to ask if he would mind opening up again for me to have a new mantle!'

GOOD TIMES

'During the war years an unused loft of a big house of Lanercost was used by the young folk as a room to hold sixpenny hops – the proceeds to go to the Red Cross. What an angel's eye view of the blackout was like I do not know, but seen from the farm below, the loft was a monument of darkness against the darkness of the Roman wall. One of the young men had been busy that afternoon putting sacks over the skylights and around the cracks of the door.

We found our way with an electric torch round the farm waggon and up the narrow stairs to the dance floor lighted by oil lamps. There was an air of expectation among the girls, who had not had an outing since the war began.

The dance band was late. Tom, who was home on leave for a week, had left his accordion at camp and was waiting for a borrowed one from the next village. At last they arrived – drums, two accordions and a guitar.

The first dance was a Spanish waltz. There was room for only three sets of eight. The floor supported on wide beams swung up and down to the pressure of their feet. The dance over, the girls gathered on one side of the room, the lads on the other.

There were only three hours to dance before Government regulations sent us home. There was a square eight, an eightsome reel, Drops of Brandy, La Rosa, a valeta, a Boston two-step, a Hulichan (a local form of bumps-a-daisy which was mostly bumps), a Hesitation Waltz, a Bradford barn dance, a Buzz-off foxtrot and a lancers. Members of the band took it in turns to dance.

Tom, his pale, tired face thrown back and eyes closed, stood alone with his accordion. From between his hands the melancholy notes of *Danny Boy* rose and fell. Behind him lay the deserted instruments of the other players. Everyone was dancing the last dance.'

'We weren't able to obtain stockings to wear at St Paul's church dance at Frizington in 1944, but found that rubbing moist sand on our legs produced a lovely shade of tan.

The highlight of the evening was the "Cushion Dance". A cushion was placed in the centre of the room and an eager young man would claim it. He had to kneel on it to kiss the girl he fancied, before dancing with her. She would then kiss the man of her choice, and this carried on until the floor was full of dreamy-eyed young people.'

MY WEDDING DAY

'My supervisor at work lent me her wedding dress, and, in return, my friend later made it into a christening gown for her first baby. Other friends saved up seven clothing coupons for me to buy a wine red going-away coat and a lovely blue angora dress. I had to have a hat as well. It was the rationing that stopped ladies wearing hats whenever they went out – you just had them for special occasions. My hat was grey with a wine ribbon binding and cut-outs round the brim. My mother wore a tan dress and hat.

The wedding took place on 1st December 1943 in Stockdalewath chapel. The Registrar had to be present, as the chapel was not registered for the Solemnisation of Matrimony. I had stayed the last three weeks with the Richardsons at Hempsgillhow to qualify for the residency rule. Raymond and I were both members of the chapel, which was the nearest one to our homes at Ivegill. He was 27, and I was almost 21.

A taxi was hired for the whole day for the wedding party. After the service the bride and groom and the best man and bridesmaid were taken to the photographer's studio in Carlisle. The little bridesmaid, my niece, never turned up – I don't know what happened to her! The guests went straight to Glaister's Cafe where the wedding breakfast was held. The cake had been made by a friend of the family. As it was to be eaten on commercial premises sugar icing was prohibited as part of the rationing laws, so the cake was covered with white paper decorated with horseshoes and slippers. We were only allowed 20 guests. I expect we ate ham and salad.

Our taxi then took us to the train, which was packed with soldiers returning to their depots. I was carrying my bouquet of pink carnations, to be a gift for my aunt who we were to visit on the way to our honeymoon. We were supposed to alight at Carnforth, but to our horror the train steamed on to Lancaster. We had to take the mail train back and, after a long walk, reached my aunt's house at 1 am!'

A CHILD'S WAR

For many children life went on as normal, or nearly so! Schools faced disruption and overcrowding as evacuees from more perilous areas came to live amongst us, some of whom formed lasting relationships with their new families and a life-long love of the countryside – while others couldn't wait to get back to the comforts of home. We learned that there were new dangers to face, and to cope with those awful gas masks and, sadly, we also learned the reality of war.

LIFE WENT ON AS NORMAL

'I started school as the war commenced. In the New Year of 1940 the roads were blocked by snow, making it impossible to attend school. The thaw came very quickly with the result that the roads ran like rivers. I wore waterproof gaiters and overshoes, as there were very few wellingtons in those days. The first wellingtons that I remember were sold by the school, only to those children who lived at least two miles from it. I prayed that there would be some in my size and that my parents could afford them. Refugee Polish soldiers were billeted in the school until their camp was built, and consequently we had an extra-long summer holiday.

Next we were allocated evacuees from Glasgow and our family increased by one girl and two boys. Their parents and parents' friends often visited at weekends. Because food was rationed and city dwellers did not have access to any other source of food, we picked fruit and berries and gave them eggs from our hens. In the summer I was sent to order baskets of tomatoes. Our local market gardener could not get all his produce to market because of petrol restrictions. My father took the menfolk fishing and shooting. He was able to obtain cartridges for shooting as he was paid to shoot crows. This was one of the Ministry of Food's ways of ensuring a high crop yield. We had an influx of Irish labourers to help with the harvest. They brought emergency ration cards with the result that the butchers had not enough meat to supply everyone. When they went home we got double rations.

On the night Clydebank was bombed, my mother got us out of bed when she heard the planes go over. We watched the planes and she explained what was happening. Next day we learned of the devastation caused.

All through this, life went on as normal. We played conkers, hide and seek, rounders and skipped, as children have always done. We went to concerts, fancy dress parades and open-air dances, little realising that the events were held in aid of war charities. Uncles were welcomed home and waved farewell as they went to their postings. The local mansion was turned into a convalescent home for soldiers and the nurses took us rowing on the lake in the grounds.

When tanks and soldiers camped overnight in the farmer's orchard it was great fun, and when soldiers marched past we ran beside them offering apples from that same orchard.

When I look back we must have had a very secure childhood not to feel the menace of war, or are all children so resilient?'

SOMETHING WAS WRONG

'The first indication that something was wrong, was when a number of men dressed in what looked like space suits and carrying "fire torches" came to pinch our garden railings. I ran to tell my mother, who then told me they were taking them to help build planes, as we were at war with the Germans.

The next thing I recall was a great big barrage balloon floating over our house, ready, it seemed, to drop on my home. We had some fun watching the soldiers lowering it and setting it up again, as it was in the field over from our house, by the river. They put up a barrier of old sleepers, but they didn't really deter any of us kids from climbing over and paddling in the river, and watching what was going on. One day I climbed over the fence – which of course I had been warned not to do – and left our back door open. Upon going back some time later, I found my Mam chasing a water-rat down the yard, trying to hit it with a brush. Needless to say she missed the rat, banged the brush head on the ground, this flew off and went through the kitchen window – happy days.

I suppose I was one of the lucky children as my father was in a reserved occupation and was only away at weekends in the Home Guard, so my life wasn't disrupted as much as some. Every morning I was woken up when the "siren" went for Cowan/Sheldons men to go to work. The women who worked in the laundry at the far end of our road went to work in clogs, and I was sure they met in the middle, outside our house – what a noise!

They built air raid shelters just down the road from us – great places to play hide and seek and thankfully they were never used for the purpose they were built, as, luckily for us, the nearest bomb to be dropped was in Scotby.

We were really very fortunate in Carlisle as we had very little disruption from bombs etc, and the seriousness of it all only hit me some years later, when I went on holiday to my grandparents in London and saw the devastation. One night a doodlebug blew the roof off their home and it was only by quick thinking on my grandfather's part that they got under the bed and escaped unharmed, as when they emerged they were open to the sky. My grandparents came to live with us for a while, but they missed their home so much they returned as soon as the new roof was on.

Now that I myself am considerably older, and, I hope, wiser, I can appreciate the very worrying times my parents must have had trying to feed, clothe us and keep us happy.'

LIVES CHANGED

'We as children never realised how lives would be changed. We moved up to the tiny hamlet of Longdale, which I loved, next door to the school. Dad was born at Orton, one of ten children. Mum was born at Coatflat Hall near Orton also one of ten, so our families were all around us.

I spent many happy holidays at Orton with my Gran and aunties. Our little school had 24 pupils, but as the evacuees arrived from Barrow, Sunderland and London the school complement swelled to 84. These unfortunate children were very shy and unhappy when they first came, but soon adapted to our ways, especially Westmorland accents.

We had two teachers from Kirkby Stephen and at play times we would play "hide in the woods". In winter we would take our sledges up the fell and ignore the school whistle, only to suffer later!

Dad got a job on the coal stage at Tebay engine shed, which increased his wages from 38 shillings to £4 a week. We paid six shillings rent and kept a pig each year, which the local farmers butchered. We cured the bacon and made sausages, black puddings, potted meat, and rendered the pig's feet – nothing was wasted!

I recall the clothing coupons which were issued, but Mum couldn't afford to buy many clothes, so we sold our coupons to the school teachers. My clothes were mainly cast-offs from my richer cousins, but I looked forward to the parcels coming. My brothers had three hand-me-downs from oldest, and on down to youngest. Gran knitted all our socks after recycling our old woolly jumpers etc.

As I was eleven years old I could have what was known as a "half day card" to help on a farm, as most of the young men were away at the war. Two and a half days per week for two shillings and sixpence. I went to a farm a mile from home, where the farmer's wife had ill health. I soon learned to run a farmhouse. I did the weekly baking on an oil fired stove with oven. This was our only means of cooking apart from the old-fashioned blackleaded fireplace, with oven, which was stoked up with logs when needed. The Boss used to dry the sticks in it and keep his slippers warm and his cap aired. There were also the water boilers in the fireside which we filled every morning with buckets of cold water, to heat to wash the milk buckets, make the calf gruel and provide hot water for the household needs.

Every fortnight we made butter after separating the cream, leaving the skimmed milk. We had a big wooden churn which had to be turned by hand. It was hard work, taking hours sometimes. When the butter was ready I used to weigh it into pound pieces and then start to shape and pattern it with butter pats. We also made cheese. Some of the butter and cheese was sold to the locals, but most went on the 9 am train to Kirkby market, all packed nicely in big wicker baskets.

Haytime was a busy time, all work done by hand or horses. I used to follow the mowing machine round the field, taking any swathes that fell on to the uncut grass. Most of our meals were taken to the field in baskets, with big cans of tea, so a whole day could be spent outdoors. The hay when ready was loaded onto sledges and pulled by the horses to the barn, a very slow process as we had to fork it off onto the hay mew and repeat this dozens of times. If it was too late to load any more, it was put into pikes – they were long, hard days!'

GETTING INTO TROUBLE

'Living in the heart of the country my sister and I wandered the fells, tarns and intakes often. We were particularly interested in bird-nesting and exploring an area near Barngates which became very familiar to us, and during the war soldiers used to practise there. At that time a public footpath ran through the fields although very few, if any, other people used it and it must have been out of bounds when the soldiers were there though we weren't aware of this.

On the occasion that I remember so vividly, my sister and I went together with two evacuees who were staying on the farm nearby and we wandered through the intakes and found discarded ammunition, – thunderflashes, They resembled large fireworks though were too damp to go off when we pulled the starter tapes. However, we collected them up and when we got home we emptied the powder from them into a newspaper and stood around in a close circle, each holding a corner of the paper, and one of us dropping a lighted match into the powder. There was an almighty yellow flash which brought us all very quickly to our senses. We were all burned on the hands and singed about our faces, eyebrows, eye-lashes and hair. Our horrified parents and guardians informed the police who came and interviewed us and we were told in no uncertain way of our lucky escape.'

THOSE GAS MASKS

'In 1941 I was ten years old and attending Brunswick Road Girls School in Penrith, travelling the five miles from Greystoke by service bus each day. Carrying of gas masks at all times was compulsory and as I arrived at school one morning without this necessary piece of equipment, I was promptly sent home to get it.

I set off to walk the five miles home, and had covered about half the distance when a man offered me a lift in his car. I gladly accepted, told him my tale of woe, and he dropped me off on the outskirts of Greystoke. I ran full pelt across the field, grabbed the gas mask from my astonished mother, ran back to the road and caught the eleven o'clock bus back to Penrith.

Although at the time my parents felt the incident unreasonable, the law had to be obeyed at all times, and they did not think of complaining about the strict discipline. My gas mask was never forgotten again.'

'Every Thursday morning, after play-time, we had to line up with our gas masks. Then, when the handbell was rung, we had to take them out of their containers and put them on. A quick check was made by the teacher, Mrs Mallinson, and Standard One was ready to go with the rest of the school-children into St Mary's church. The infants with Miss Swan and Mrs Pearce went first. They had red gas masks with a red nose-like piece, so that they would think it was fun. Our class was next, and to my shame, I was the only one to still be wearing a red gas mask. Everybody else had proper black ones. We had to go forward in an orderly manner and get under the pew designated, and stay there until we were told to get out. Dark, dusty and in cramped condition we waited patiently for the welcome word that we could get out and stand up straight. We filed back into school, took off our gas masks and carefully replaced them in their containers, which we carried at all times.

It was my personal tragedy that when I was given a proper black gas mask, that was the very week that the war was over and we never had another gas mask practice!'

FILLED TO OVERFLOWING

'The arrival of over 60 evacuees from Tyneside filled the viliage school at Moresby to overflowing, and relations with them were a bit strained at first.

Having to carry a gas mask, and the frequent drills in their use, is an outstanding memory of that time, as are the air raid alerts, when everyone had to dash across the school yard, over the playing field and into the shelter of a group of trees. If there had been a real raid, I am sure we would all have been killed before we reached the trees. Drills with a stirrup pump caused havoc, with lots of wet clothing as a result.'

THE EVACUEES ARE COMING!

'One Friday afternoon Mr Parrott assembled the school for an important announcement. We learned the meaning of a new word "evacuee", and that some of them from Tyneside were coming to Kirkby Stephen to escape the bombing of the shipyards. He was at pains to point out that they were leaving their homes, parents and all familiar things and coming to live in a strange place with strange people. They would be feeling sad enough, and he didn't want any of us at the station tomorrow, staring at them and adding to their distress. So having been given the time and the place, there we /all were, the next day, myself and my nine year old classmates, climbing on the railings as the long train pulled slowly in. We waved at the children, and they waved back, hanging out of every window – all with luggage labels tied in their lapels. Once the train had disappeared into the station we left. The evacuees later appeared in ones and twos in the homes of neighbours and we began to get to know them.

One evacuee, Ronnie Patterson is remembered for the fact that everywhere he went he was followed by a quiet little dog, black and tan, smooth haired and with dachshund predominating in his pedigree. Ronnie stayed on a farm at Hartley, and I never knew whether the dog came with him from Tyneside or whether it had attached itself to him after his arrival, but it followed him like a shadow, to school every day right into the classroom where it would lie down under his desk. It would have taken until morning playtime to take the dog back to Hartley and return, so the dog was put in the playground till home time. But as soon as the door was opened the dog slipped quietly in and by degrees, as successive doors were opened the dog got to our classroom and back under Ronnie's desk, only to be taken outside again. We loved this diversion, but the dog was so well behaved that the teachers yielded to the inevitable and the dog was allowed to stay. Together, Ronnie and the dog achieved wider fame when they both appeared in the school play *Tobias and the Angel* which calls for Tobias to be faithfully followed everywhere by his little dog Toby.

Some teachers came with the evacuees and absolutely nothing in our nine years' placid, rural existence had prepared us for the advent of Miss Elders. She burst into our lives, a plump five feet nothing bundle of energy, and taught us to sing. She would sweep into the classroom wearing high heels, a fur coat loose over her shoulders and often a hat. She would stand at the piano and strike a chord for us to sing "Mee, My, May, Moo, Mo" then a higher one, and on and on up the scale till only the highest trebles were left. She taught us how to stand, and how to breathe, to open our mouths, to put the ends on our words and, horror of horrors, never to slur up or down from one note to another. We had never dreamed that there was so much to something as seemingly simple as singing. But we enjoyed her lessons and sang our folk songs and sea shanties with gusto.

At junior school our usual time-table was sometimes set aside for Mr Parrott, our headmaster, to take us for a lesson. Several of these were memorable. One concerned the R in the middle of words such as library and secretary. We were made to say these and similar words over and over and to write them out. We always had to abbreviate February to Febr. Even now mis-pronounciation of these words jars as much as a fingernail across a blackboard.

The arrival of the evacuees and their eccentric approach to grammar, eg "Give us a lend of your pencil" or even, "Give us a borrow of your pencil," led to a whole lesson learning the correct usage of lend, borrow, loan etc.

One of Mr Parrot's own enthusiasms was astronomy and we took delight on starry nights finding the constellations he had taught us; the Plough and the North Star, Cassiopeia and, our favourite, Orion, the mighty hunter, with his belt and sword.

I think every pupil who passed through the school had his lesson on the Nine Standards. These are nine large stone cairns standing distinctively on the skyline above the town. There are several myths about how they come to be there, our favourite being they were made to look like an army and frighten away the marauding Scots.

Mr Parrott linked these nine standards with St Paul's nine gifts of the Spirit in his letter to the Galatians – Love, Joy, Peace, Patience, Kindness, Goodness, Faithfulness, Gentleness and Self-Control.'

FROM THE NORTH EAST

'In the autumn of 1939 we were told we would have to take some evacuees, and four children and their mother arrived. They were from the North East. My mother sat them all down at the table with the family and the children ate until they were sick. The mother explained that they had never before been told they could eat as much as they wanted. At night when my mother suggested going to bed, they said they usually just turned the table upside down and slept in that.

This family only stayed with us a few months but later on a young boy of seven from Newcastle came to us and he is still a friend today, over 50 years on.'

SHE WENT HOME

'Two girls, Pat and Nancy, were billeted with my family in Brampton. One day Nancy was sent off to Edgers shop for bread. My mother gave her the money and off she went. We waited and waited for her to return. Impatience grew to worry but still she didn't come back. Guess what? She had boarded a bus home to Newcastle and paid her fare with the bread money, and we were left without bread and minus one evacuee. Unfortunately for Nancy, her parents were equally annoyed and put her on the return bus to Brampton, where she stayed for the rest of the war years.'

OUR NEW LIFE WAS SIMPLE

'My earliest memories date from 1940 when I was aged two, the daughter of a city parson. We moved to Ennerdale from the Midlands to escape the bombing.

Our life was simple, a large, cold vicarage heated by a coal range and two oil stoves on top of which sat an oven, also used for cooking. Paraffin lamps and candles were the only form of lighting. It was a rambling, damp house, and all the furniture and furnishings were secondhand. My mother wore an old coat to clean upstairs.

My four year old brother was my only playmate; we played in a sandpit, climbed trees, went birds nesting, and helped to feed the poultry (hens, ducks, geese and guinea fowls so we had plenty of eggs). Once we set fire to the common, playing with matches. I used to play with my mother's Victorian dolls, which were dressed in period clothes and would be worth a fortune today. We also had plasticine, Dinky toys, marbles, Bayko, Minibrix, Kliptico and Meccano. Occasionally we would go for rides in the post van, or amongst the churns on the milk lorry. Public transport was minimal; two buses on market day, and three on Saturdays so that if we didn't walk or cycle (on second-hand bikes), we didn't go anywhere. My parents never went out at night except my father who took the choir practice and ran the village library. In the evenings we listened to the radio or read, my mother usually doing the mending. Clothes were on coupons so were worn until outgrown or worn out; we only had one decent coat each, faded navy gaberdine.

My parents (unwisely) bought a pony and trap. The pony had a wicked temper and was impossible to control and soon was sold. Shopping meant a mile walk to the village Co-op shop; every item was entered up in the shop book by hand, and twice a year the "divi" was calculated. A large loaf of bread cost fourpence ha'penny, and coal was £1 a ton. The Co-op paid a halfpenny for one-pound jam jars and a penny for two-pound jars which my brother and I collected and wheeled to the shop in an old pram. We ate bought marmalade, but bramble, apple, rhubarb and gooseberry jam were home-made. Sweets were rationed so there weren't many of them – none if it was the week of the Keswick Convention; we had no idea what the Keswick Convention was, except that it meant no sweets.

Infants school was a delight; being the vicar's daughter was rather special. I was the Queen of Hearts in the school play, and remember taking an Oxo tin full of jam tarts that my mother had made. After the play, I took them all home again in case I got into trouble for eating any of them or giving them away. Some children stayed away from school because they had no shoes.

When I was six, another baby arrived, together with a home help in the form of an ex-Land Army girl who helped out with the cleaning (no vacuum cleaner, all done by dustpan and brush, Mansion polish and Zebo). Ironing was done with a flat iron heated on one of the oil stoves and tested against the cheek.

After the war, my father took out a 100% mortgage on a wooden bungalow at Colwith (near Ambleside) which was rented out to holiday-makers to pay the mortgage interest. We spent our summer holidays there, and this meant an eight mile bus journey to Whitehaven, a steam train to Coniston via Foxfield and then a bus to the bungalow; this took all day instead of an hour by car today. We were free to go anywhere, there was a good local bus service and we explored the countryside. The biggest thrill was to find Noel, the steam roller man who would give us rides on his smelly steam roller and would share his butties with us. We caught minnows, played hopscotch and jacks (five stones). When older, we helped with the haymaking on a local farm; the farmer had a horse-drawn mowing machine and used a scythe for the more inaccessible areas. The hay was turned and raked into heaps by hand for carting to the barn.

We loved it all, despite the war and hard times; it was an unsophisticated childhood, quite unlike today's world of TV, videos and computer games.'

THIS WAS WAR

'So this was war! I was walking home from church on the 3rd September, my father's fifty-third birthday. The Minister had announced from the pulpit that we were now at war with Germany. I don't know what I expected as a nine year old, but it wasn't this. The Harris tweed of my winter coat still prickled my calves and wrists (winter clothes officially came out on 1st September, regardless of temperature). The elastic holding my velour hat firmly in place still cut viciously under my chin. I furtively eased it into a new position and decided war was vastly overrated. Where were the aeroplanes, tanks and refugee columns so familiar to us from the newsreels? These were the same villagers going solemnly home from church as they did every Sunday. There was Roddy getting a belt from his dad for stone throwing – wasn't he always getting a belt from his dad? No two ways about it – war was boring.

I soon changed my mind as time passed and I became a teenager. There were Free Polish soldiers stationed near the village – were any of them less than handsome? Then the GIs came and seemed even more foreign and exotic than the Poles. They had chewing gum, chocolate, white bread sandwiches and a mysterious something called nylons. These Hanks, Lees and Waynes were very generous with these half-forgotten delights. But best of all were my two older, handsome brothers in their uniforms. Their home leaves, as those of all the local lads, were an excuse for wonderful village celebrations. Yes, the village rallied round and celebrated each leave. They also rallied round and supported us when my father died. I saw my mother cry then for only the second time in my life; the first had been tears of rage when Mr Chamberlain waved his "peace in our time" scrap of paper. This was my first taste of death. I had watched German planes twist and turn, caught in the crossed searchlight beams, only to be caught by anti-aircraft fire along the beams. From the safety of our Anderson shelter we watched the explosion and the slow spiralling down of the doomed plane. We did not think of human beings inside. We cheered.

Then the day arrived when a neighbour came to take me home from the Academy. We drove home – he silent and me speculating on this miraculous reprieve from Latin. The telegram said John had been killed in Italy. Mother cried. I couldn't believe it. John was young – not old and ill like dad. By a macabre wartime fluke we received a letter from him two days later. Was it all a mistake? Mother cried again.

When the telegram came two weeks later telling of Bill's death in the Adriatic, mother had no tears left. Now we were two; five months ago we had been five.

This was war; not boring, not glamorous and exciting. War was terrible, horrific, heartbreaking. It always was.'

DOING OUR BIT

Whether it was joining the ARP or the Home Guard, or signing up with the Women's Land Army or the Timber Corps, many local men and women not in the services were still doing their bit for their country.

OUR HOME GUARD

'Like many villages in wartime, Soulby had its Home Guard contingent, with the local postman as C-in-C. One September night in 1940 they were put on alert with rumours that the Germans were about to land. They were called out at sunset to guard the village with one rifle to every three men. The men posted on the Kirkby Stephen road on this beautiful moonlit night got tired of doing nothing, so one went home and got some deckchairs and cigars, took them back to his colleagues, and they sat and enjoyed themselves in the moonlight.

One member of the Home Guard was stationed in the square in the centre of the village to act as a runner to the outposts. There was fear of invasion, and rumours were circulating that fifth columnists or spies were sometimes disguised as parsons or nuns. Round about midnight a car stopped in the square, and the lone Home Guard

Most villages had their Home Guard contingent eager to do their bit towards the war effort, like these four likely lads from Holme St Cuthbert.

approached it only to discover that its occupants were two men wearing parsons' collars! First thoughts were; "Have the Germans arrived?" Then one of the parsons spoke, asking where the Home Guard had been posted, and the speaker was vaguely recognised as the Vicar of Warcop, a nearby village!

In October 1941 a bomb fell near Soulby and shattered the East window in the church, and also windows at the vicarage and Belsey Gate. Local farmers took a hundred cart-loads of soil to fill in the bomb crater.

One villager remembers that during the war a ham was hidden away in the attic. One night a mouse ate through the string by which it hung, and it fell through the ceiling onto her father lying in bed.'

NOT AFRAID OF HARD WORK

'The war brought a culture shock to Lazonby in the form of about 40 land girls who were billeted in a specially built hostel near the auction market. The girls (one who had lied about her age was only 16 years old) came mostly from large cities and were complete strangers to country life, apart from their one month's training. They were not afraid of hard work though and soon proved their worth as farmhands.

The hostel was an L-shaped wooden hut, with two double bunk beds, a wardrobe and a chest of drawers to each cubicle in the dormitory wing. Winter heating came from two stoves. The ablutions block was a stone-built room with six washbasins and two baths, and there was always a rush to get washed before breakfast. They took packed lunches with them to the farms; lots of bread and jam, a small piece of cake, a biscuit and sometimes their ration of cheese or corned beef. Occasionally a farmer's wife would treat them to something extra.

The work was heavy and hard without modern machinery, especially in the winter cold. Topping and tailing (snagging) turnips from the frozen ground was particularly unpleasant. Hoeing the turnips was better and they had competitions to see who could hoe fastest and neatest. Each morning a large army wagon would pick them up from the hostel and they sang popular choruses as they travelled to work.

Sometimes they held dances and film shows, inviting soldiers from nearby army camps as well as locals. There was a little resentment of them amongst the local girls, and with some cause as quite a few of them later married local boys and settled down here. The uniform consisted of two pairs of fawn dungarees, one pullover, three shirts, one overcoat, one hat, one pair of boots, three pairs of stockings and two pairs of corduroy breeches, and the pay was 22/6d per week. One of the girls did their hair for them, all in the same style, sometimes with the hair wrapped round a bandeau made from an old nylon stocking. The orchard next door to the hostel was sometimes raided for apples and the auction mart and a nearby barn provided popular courting spots.

After the war the hostel was taken over by the local council and converted into small bungalows. Many young Lazonby couples began their married life there, including several of the ex-land girls and their new husbands.'

'WHAT AM I GOING TO DO WITH HER?'

'After enduring the Manchester blitz, I decided to join the Women's Land Army, although this was not quite as easy as I had anticipated. Standing only four feet ten inches tall, and weighing only seven stone three pounds (in those days), I was told that farmers wanted big strong girls. However, I kept trying and was eventually accepted. A group of twelve of us were sent to Hutton Agricultural College for a month's training. They were hard on us. I shall never forget being scared stiff the first time I attempted to milk by hand, for of course there were no milking machines there then. Later however I discovered that milking was one of the easy jobs, and soon began to enjoy the feeling of satisfaction when filling a pail of creamy, frothy milk.

We carted muck into the fields, filling the carts with a fork, then dragged it out with a muck rake, and spread it out with a fork at a later date. We snagged and carted turnips, loaded silage with a fork and trampled it in silos by foot. I had never known what it was like to work so hard. At the end of the month we could back out but only one did.

I was sent to Broughton Beck near Ulverston. My first view of the mountains remains with me yet, I thought it was wonderful. The farmer met me at the station, and I guess he received quite a shock. In later years he told me that his reaction had been, "What on earth am I going to do with her?"

At the farm I got my first taste of home cured ham – I really thought that it was bad at first. The food on the farm was quite different to anything I had been used to at home, but after a while I got used to it and began to enjoy everything; bacon, sausages, black puddings, even the home cured ham, lovely grub.

I was disappointed to learn that there was a milk round as I had expected just to work outdoors. Nevertheless it soon became part of the daily routine. They called it tippling milk in those days. We used a can and measure and customers would leave a jug on the doorstep with a saucer on top with a note, sometimes a gill or a pint. Quite often we would be given a bit of warm pasty on our round. When it was snowy we would go with the pony and trap, the rest of the time we took the old Austin with a board on the back to hold the large kit. Very few bottles were used in those days.

Back home all had to be washed and sterilising was done by immersing everything in the old wash boiler. At the farm all water was from a pump in the kitchen. No electric, no taps or bathrooms. Only the earth closet down the back – you got very wet getting there if it was raining. The milk was carried in pails up from the shippons and put through a cooler, all the water being pumped by hand.

Haytime was a favourite time for me. The only machine used was called a side delivery which put hay into rows ready for forking onto the carts. I can remember eight of us in one field turning hay with hand rakes. It was supposed to make a better job than those new fangled machines. If it looked at all like rain we would put the hay up into foot cocks and leave it until it looked safe enough to spread it out again. They were lovely times when I look back.

At turnip thinning time we tied sacks round our knees and crawled up the rows thinning them out. We planted potatoes out of sacks tied round our waists and gathered them in buckets and swills.

I thoroughly enjoyed all this work, and never regretted joining the Land Army. No doubt things are easier now on all farms with modern machinery, but I don't think it would tempt me so much.'

WORKING ON THE THRESHER

'Shortly after war was declared I volunteered for the Women's Land Army. My uniform, of which I was very proud, consisted of riding breeches, blouse, pullover, knee length socks, shoes, hat, and a beautifully warm overcoat. My working outfit was dungarees, boots and wellingtons.

I was sent for two years, in charge of a gang of four, to work a threshing machine. Being "in charge" meant working out time and wage sheets at the end of each week.

The gang travelled from farm to farm spending about three days at each. A mechanic came with us to maintain the thresher.

The thresher was a big base on wheels, about 15 feet long, six feet wide and eight feet high. It was driven by a tractor which stood a few yards from the thresher. A large belt was fitted round a wheel on the tractor, and a wheel on the thresher. When the engine of the tractor was motivated this belt revolved and set the mechanics of the thresher in motion.

The thresher contained many wheels, beaters, and riddles, and the noise and dust created was tremendous. On top of the thresher was a hole into which the sheaves of corn, peas, beans or barley were thrown. These went into the workings of the machine which separated the corn from the straw etc.

We land girls had four jobs, and took turns in doing these as some were more pleasant than others. One land girl threw the sheaves from the cornstock to another girl standing on top of the thresher. This girl cut the string binding the sheaf and dropped the sheaf into the hole, holding on to the string so as not to clog the machine. The third girl had to continually take away the chaff which came out of one side of the thresher. At one end of the thresher was a large revolving fork-like arrangement which tied the bales of straw and ejected them for the fourth girl to throw up to the farmhands to build a straw stack.

At the other end of the thresher some farmhands collected the corn in sacks, weighed them, and tied them up ready for use.

We often found mice, rats or pests in the cornstack, often with babies. The cornstack was fenced in with wire nettings, and when we heaved the bottom the farmhands let in some dogs to kill the rats as they ran out of the stack.

Threshing was hard, working outdoors, in all weathers, in very noisy and dusty conditions, but finally producing the grain was very rewarding. The good companionship in the gang meant we often sang, even though we could scarcely be heard above the thresher's noise.

At the end of two years I was allowed to choose what I wanted to do. I chose dairywork and loved it.'

IN THE TIMBER CORPS

'Several of my friends had joined the Women's Land Army so after a week's walking holiday in Cumberland where I saw land girls working in the woods, I decided I would try to get into forestry (later known as the Women's Timber Corps).

On 18th April 1941 I left Manchester and my destination was Broughton in Furness. I was now WLA 41491.

There were six girls, none of us knew each other. We had to leave the train at Preston to collect our uniforms, then get on a later train. The uniform consisted of green pullover, corduroy breeches, dungarees, woollen knee stockings, strong shoes and wellington boots. Also a fawn felt hat which was later replaced by a green beret for the Timber Corps. There were two of us sent to one house and four to another. We were told we were to work in Forge Woods to peel alder but could not do it until the sap had risen in the trees. This was a few weeks later. There was no labour saving machinery at that time. We used Bushman hand saws to cut pit props which were later loaded by us on to a lorry which went to the railway station where we unloaded them and stacked them into trucks. The trees (which had been felled) were pulled (snigged) down the wood by a Clydesdale horse. It was coppice wood; ash, oak, beech etc.

In the middle of the wood was an old cottage where we sheltered when it rained; the two wood fellers stayed there from Monday to

The Women's Timber Corps trained girls to work alongside local foresters.

Saturday. They brought food to last the week. I especially remember a huge roasting tin full of hotpot. There was an old black range in the cottage and they soon got the oven hot with a wood fire. The bark which we had peeled from the logs, when dry, made good kindling wood. There was of course no electricity (or gas) in the cottage.

At times there were plagues of midges which nearly drove us mad. During the dinner hour we often went for a swim in the river Duddon which was only a few yards away.

At the time when we first started, everywhere was fresh and green and there were wild daffodils, primroses, and bluebells. It was almost too good to be true, after working in a busy office for five years.

We were billeted at the gamekeeper's house, and we were fed like lords; fresh trout from the river, rabbits, once or twice venison, fresh eggs, home-made bread, and we got onions which at that time were unobtainable at home. There was no electricity, the food was cooked in an oil stove but it was some of the best we had ever had.

When the sap had risen we peeled the bark from the alder and this stained our hands a tan colour. The pit props were mostly two foot six inches and went for charcoal.

My friend and I were asked to take a can and get milk from the farm half a mile away. When the young man came to the door he eyed us over; I said what nice blue eyes he had. Two years later he married me, and we went to a farm, so I did not have to return to the city.

My mother had been very reluctant to let her only daughter go away from home in the war but I assured her there could not be a prettier place and I was very fortunate to be there.'

'When I was 20 I had to register for service, so I joined the Women's Timber Corps. I enjoyed every minute of my six and a half years, working in the woods and sawmills, measuring timber and loading waggons. We would go with the lorry and despatch the timber off at Haverthwaite station. We worked at Grizedale most of the time, where No 1 German prisoner of war camp was.'

IT'S OVER!

At last it was over, news which was greeted with joy and dancing in the streets – though that didn't cut much ice with one ten year old! Villages clubbed together to give their returning sons and daughters an unforgettable welcome home. And, in one village church, there is a lasting memorial to the friendships which could be forged in such difficult circumstances.

WHAT A LOAD OF RUBBISH!

'I was in bed one night in 1945, when I was ten, and my mam came up the stairs and pulled my sister and me out of bed. "Come along," she kept saying, "the war is over, it's all over!" We had to dress quickly and go down the stairs and out into the streets. Everyone was out there, shouting and laughing and dancing. I thought to myself, "What a load of rubbish," and quietly sneaked back to bed.

But there was a good friend of mine whose father had been captured at Dunkirk at the beginning of the war and had been in a POW camp. When her Dad came home on the train to Harrington, friends and neighbours got together and decorated the station, with a big banner saying, "Welcome home Gerry". That was quite unforgettable.'

WELCOME HOME

'We had great celebrations for the forces at Ravenstonedale when they were welcomed home. It was held in a field at Park House with a penny mile, races, tug of war football etc.

To fund this, a sale of work was held in Newbiggin on Lune village hall in the form of an auction. Collectors went round the parish for suitable items. I came home from school one day and Dad said he was going to give a sheep, and Mam some groceries. "What are you giving?" Dad asked. "Two goats," I said. I had had a nanny goat for my birthday and it was in kid so now I had two (whatever tree I tied them to they got away and into someone else's field and the farmers were always after me; the next year I saw them on the fell at Scarsykes fostering lambs).

This was the notice, in Cumbrian dialect, put up in the village for the "do" –

Luksta
Thoo'll hetta bide
I' Russendale a
Satada
Dunt
Ga ta t'dances
Or ta t'pictures
Cum ta Park 'oose
An'dee a summat fer
Oor lasses and lads in
T'Forces.'

A SIGHT WE'LL NEVER FORGET

'When the war was drawing to a close, the headmaster of Holme school, Mr Frank Lowis, collected us all together one night and we went to the summit of Farleton Knott. Here we built a bonfire. The wood was collected from the base of the Knott and dragged up the screes. VE Day arrived and that night we went to the summit of the Knott and lit the bonfire. Looking round we could see all the other bonfires burning on the surrounding hills. This was a sight I don't think any of us will ever forget.'

The war is over but not forgotten. The Patterdale Civil Defence and WVS take part in an exercise to construct a kitchen from scratch in the early 1950s.

HOPE FOR THE FUTURE

'During the war the German prisoners of war in Beela camp at Holme in the parish of Beetham were befriended by the vicar of Beetham, the Hon Rev A Macleod-Murray. Amongst other gestures of friendship, he invited those who wished to attend the 8 am Holy Communion services at Holme and Beetham churches. In gratitude, the prisoners made a beautiful crib which they presented to St Michael and All Angels church at Beetham in 1946. Every Christmas since, that crib has formed the central focus in the church's worship.

"We German prisoners of war from Beela River Camp are giving this stable and figures of the Nativity story, which have been made by Bruno Banmann and his assistant Gabriel Fabian, as a gift to the parish of Beetham. By doing so we will express our gratefulness for having been able to realise the real spirit of Christian brotherhood which has been proved to us by the Hon Rev A. Macleod-Murray and the congregation of Beetham. We are praying with you to the Child of Bethlehem. Christmas 1946."'

HIGHDAYS & HOLIDAYS

WE MADE OUR OWN ENTERTAINMENT

In the days before television, and even before radio, we made our own entertainment – and what a wealth of talent there was in even the smallest village. Musical evenings, amateur dramatics, dances and whist drives were enthusiastically supported, the heart of the village often being its village hall or dance room. Sports such as wrestling and hound trailing were our open air entertainment, while radio and early films brought a new dimension to our lives.

SOMETHING FOR EVERYONE

'In the years up to the First World War, there was very little outside entertainment in Moresby parish and villagers made their own, often in the form of musical evenings. These were very popular and well attended with the children giving performances. Proceeds went to provide prizes at school for good attendance, good work etc.

In later years, people still made their own entertainment, centred largely round the churches. There were Guides, Brownies, Mothers Union, Sunday school and the Women's Institute. The local dance hall had the finest sprung floor in the area. Dances were held weekly and were lively affairs, people coming from all around on a Saturday night. Concerts were held about once a month, and there was an abundance of local talent – people played all sorts of instruments. Music halls were very popular and people would walk into town to see a show.

The Miners' Welfare Club was opened in Moresby Parks, and there was a bowling green and tennis court. At Parton there were two billiard tables in the parish rooms.'

'Most families had someone who could play the fiddle or piano, and horn gramophones were popular, so there would be music in the evenings. There was an emphasis on family-centred amusements, with card games, ludo and draughts.

Eskdale had a drama club, certainly for the first half of the century, which rehearsed and performed in the school. There were also concerts at Stanley Ghyll, the holiday centre, which were open to all, and for many years there was a film show on Thursday nights in the Eskdale church hall.

Holidays were rare, so outings are keenly remembered. Until the Sunday school died out in the 1950s there was that outing, and there used to be a school trip to Morecambe. The Eskdale Show was always on the last Friday in September at Boot, and the Ratty had its last run of the year on that day. The other big event was on New Year's Eve, when the British Legion used to organise a fancy dress party, with tea and games, followed by a whist drive and ending with a dance. So there was something for all the family.'

'I lived on Walney Island from the age of six to 29. The old trolley trams used to go from Biggar Bank to Furness Abbey but as children, we were only allowed to use them on rare treats.

Ice-cream carts on Biggar Bank were horse-drawn and we used to go midnight bathing in gangs at 14 and 15 years. There was a miniature golf course, swimming baths and paddling pool, and the beach was always packed at weekends. Not many people could afford holidays but I won one for a week at Southport when I was 14, through the Co-operative Junior Circle. You got ten shillings pocket money for the week and *King Kong*, I remember, was the current film.

There were 14 cinemas in Barrow, mostly owned by Mr James Brennan, who I worked for at 15. I never paid at a cinema, receiving complimentary tickets. I was at the opening of the Ritz Cinema (now the Astra) and also at the Ulverston Roxy. When I went to work in Ulverston at 17, there were three cinemas in the town.

Dances at the Coronation Hall were one shilling and sixpence, or two and sixpence when the big bands, such as Joe Loss and Victor Sylvester, came. They started at 8 pm and went on until 3 am. The Drill Hall was sixpence and finished at midnight on a Saturday night. My boyfriend, later to become my husband, used to drive Jimmy Oliver's band (a local one) to the village dances and so I was able to go to places like the Malt Kiln at Bardsea or the village hall at Greenodd. Otherwise it was walk or hope to meet someone with a motorbike! Evening dress was worn at the Ulverston Grammar School Old Scholars and Conservative Balls – all great nights out.'

'Social life at Finsthwaite was mainly centred round the church prior to the war years. One of the highlights of the year was the annual choir trip, held in summertime, usually to either Morecambe or Blackpool. Each member of the choir was given sixpence to spend at the amusement park. Originally they all went on the train, until the coming of the charabanc. There was also the annual supper party

Dalston football team – the 'Black-Reds' – pose proudly for the camera in 1913.

at the vicarage when they were treated to a dinner with a round of beef, vegetables, plum pudding and mince pies.

Every two years when General Sneyd was tenant of Finsthwaite House he would give a sumptuous party for the children. There would be a tree almost touching the ceiling and one year snowballs made of cotton wool were thrown; one girl who caught one found a beautiful ring inside.

Early in the century there was an annual concert held at the Lakeside Institute, all local talent. Everyone thought it was marvellous. The gentry went in evening dress and were seated on the front three rows of chairs for one shilling and sixpence each, the next section was forms for one shilling and standing room at the back was sixpence. It was always full. One man sang a song called *When we get the ladies into Parliament* which brought the house down because people thought it so impossible and funny. The accompanist was a lady who always insisted on a rehearsal in case there was anything "not quite nice" and she usually opened the programme with a piano solo and then accompanied the songs and duets, such as *Pretty little Polly Perkins*.

For many years were held what were known as "The Demonstrations". The MPs would attend and there would be political speeches until about the middle of the afternoon. Various sideshows and running races were going on but the great event of the day was the Fell Race. The competitors started off in the middle of the field, ran to the edge of the lake, sprang into a boat and if they were lucky a supporter would give them a good push off, rowed to the other side, leapt out and, whilst someone looked after the boat, ran up Gummer's How, round a man at the top and down again. Then it was back in the boat and back across the lake to Buck Yeats. They could do it in 20 minutes. It was very exciting.

There were also interesting election meetings. At one time there were two families of different political persuasion – one staunch Conservative, the other equally staunch Liberal. One night unbeknown to each other, they put their posters of support on the other's house so when they woke up the next morning they were both showing the opposition poster. Voting was not held at the local school but in Haverthwaite so people sometimes gave each other lifts in their carriages and one time a voter went in the train from Lakeside!

In 1920 the village had its first and last Rose Queen. She was elected by her peers and rode from the school to Finsthwaite House on a pony and was enthroned in the grounds there. The rest of the children danced around the maypole but the Queen was disappointed – she just had to watch.'

MUSIC AND DANCING

'Pop John was a fiddle player in Dentdale. On Sunday afternoons he used to play his fiddle while his sister played the piano. The window would be opened and people stood around listening. He played the fiddle at dances and sang; possibly he got his name because he sang "Pop goes the weasel". He was a good singer, by trade a joiner. His sister wore a poke bonnet. When she died Pop John was very upset. He used to wander about at night saying he saw "imps" in his bedroom.

Between the wars they used to have supper dances at Cowgill. They cost one shilling and sixpence, including supper. This was usually ham with pickled onion and beetroot, HP sauce, bread and butter, tea and cakes. Trifle made with sherry and fresh cream was three pence extra. The dance usually went on until two or three in the morning.

Josee Mason, the joiner, delighted in telling tales to visitors. He always emphatically denied that Dent must be quiet in winter time. "What," he would exclaim in disgust, "quiet! Why, we have toffee nights in winter. We aw' club together an' git sugar an' butter an' mak' toffee. Then we twine it into long strings, an' a lass starts eatin' it yan end an' a lad at t'other end till they git t'ert middle." He paused roguishly until his audience, waiting, asked, "Then what?" "Aye," said old Josee, "an' then what?"'

'The dance hall opposite the Patterdale Hotel was reputed to be "the finest dance hall in the North of England" and was very popular. It possessed a handsome crystal centre light and mirrored walls with floodlights creating dazzling reflections. People used to come from as far away as Newcastle by charabanc to enjoy a wonderful outing and refreshments.

One night during the war a vivid glow lit the sky, and folk in Glenridding a mile away heard what seemed to be rifle shots, arousing fears that it was the expected German invasion. It was the sound of glass cracking from the heat of the blazing building. Sadly it was destroyed and no one knew what caused the blaze.'

'Each village in Deandale had a hunt ball after the fox hunt. Usually the music was by Billy Bowman's band with his sister Florrie playing the piano. They used to travel round the villages on a motorbike and sidecar.'

'One elderly man recalled the days of his summer holidays staying at the King's Arms on the A6 at Beetham. The locals would dance the lancers up and down the A6 on summer evenings.'

Cumberland wrestling could take place anywhere and was an essential ingredient in every local fair or sports day. The two gentlemen kneeling are the umpires for this bout at Dean in 1918.

'Entertainment at Far Sawrey before the First World War was mostly do it yourself. We had a very good mixed choir who were not afraid to let their hair down and also a dramatic society. A good supper always followed any entertainment. Dances after the end of the war were great fun. We thought nothing of biking five or ten miles to a dance, but if the weather was bad we had to stay at home. Hunt balls were the best. We wore long dresses and on our bikes we had to pin them up to our waists, with our gloves and dancing shoes in our pockets. We just got home in time to change and go to work.'

'In the 1920s a certain Mr Tom Cannon travelled the area around Troutbeck giving dancing lessons and his classes were very popular. He was accompanied by a violinist. My parents met at one of his classes and their love of dancing lasted all their lives.

We would dance the lancers, eightsome reel and many others, including one that was performed by an elderly farmer and his wife called the Lava Sophiana, a lively dance and I think very similar to the Italian Lavolta, a popular dance in Elizabethan times. Dances were often preceded by several games of whist and a supper of good farm fare, served in the billiard room. In fact many people came for the supper only, but the whole evening cost just half a crown.'

'In late spring, before the barn was filled with hay, we held a barn dance with all the local people taking part. We girls could not afford shoes so we scrubbed our clogs and painted them silver. It was quite an occasion.'

'My earliest memory is of my grandfather playing a concertina. It was after a harvest supper at Croglin, which was then called a "churn". Everyone had contributed to the supper and the barn had been swept and everyone danced on the uneven flag floor.

During the 1940s there were regular dances in the village hall, and an annual sports day which attracted many from all over the county to the hound trail, wrestling and a sheep show along with all the usual sports. In the summer hired hands from local farms would gather in the village, one would play a harmonica and the villagers would dance in the open air.'

'The Mill Room, then the warehouse of the mill, was the centre of social life in Broughton Beck and surrounding villages. Swept out and cleaned it was the venue of parties, dances and dancing classes. Boys and girls learned a wide range of dances. Periodically fancy dress balls were held in Ulverston, ending at about four in the morning. With a three mile walk home after that, Mother said it was often a case of out of the dance clothes and straight into working clothes, especially if the boys had had to see home girls from distant villages.'

'Dances were held at the reading room, Soulby, with soapflakes on the floor to make it easier for dancing – and more slippery! Many remember the Peaslands Band, a local farming family who played the piano, drums and accordion at local dances.'

GROWING UP

'I don't remember ever being called a teenager. We left school at the age of 14 and felt very grown up. The boys had their hair cut in a grown-up style; they went into long trousers (the word would be passed around that a certain boy was now in "lang uns").

The girls changed their dress style and "put up" their hair (we didn't have our hair cut – there weren't any ladies' hairdressers). Perhaps one mother or a friend would trim our hair by putting a basin on our heads and cutting round the edges. When the First World War broke out we had many girls who came to work in the munitions factory at Black Bank and stayed in Longtown; they brought many new ideas for dress and hair. I can well remember the "earphones" fashion, when the hair was centre-parted and put in rolls over each ear – it looked very grown up.

For entertainment in the summer we went for long walks and to the places we could meet with our friends. The Scaur was a very popular place where we would chat and flirt with the local boys; it was usually crowded on a Sunday afternoon. We would meet up again at church in the evening. When the dark nights arrived and we hadn't much pocket money we went to Benson's pictures (silent) where we enjoyed watching Pearl White, Charlie Chaplin, Norma Talmage, etc. We all had our favourite actors and as the films were silent we were kept excited and happy by the music of a local trio – Helen Benson (piano), Jimmy Bell (cornet) and Matt Barnfather (violin).

Then there were the annual balls – these were grand affairs held at first in the picture hall and later (when it had been built) in the Memorial Hall. The girls in the village would be very busy choosing a nice ballgown; some were home-made. These balls were an annual affair, the tickets costing two shillings and sixpence. We also had a girls club in the "Rec", now the Longtown industrial estate. The building was a wooden hut and was run by a lady called Miss James who lived in Netherby Street. We would meet once a week to talk, take some refreshments and listen to a guest speaker. Sometimes we had a "social" and could invite a boy!'

THE HEART OF THE VILLAGE

'Lazonby has an imposing village hall, but in the 1930s a large debt of £1,800 was causing great concern, so every week a social function was held to raise funds. This might be a whist drive or a village hop on a Saturday night (one shilling or one and sixpence) with local men playing piano, violin and accordion. Some weeks there was a Friday night dance with supper (two shillings or two and sixpence). One unusual event was a "living whist" game with each person in fancy dress with a huge playing card attached to their front. A big circle was formed and as the suit and number were called out, the card person walked into the middle of the ring. This event was held in a field, giving a lovely outdoor occasion. Further funds were raised by the village ladies holding sewing sessions in the hall. The village was divided into sections, Uppies, Middles and Downies, with groups meeting on regular nights each week. They made garments to order, mostly nightdresses and underclothes but also some dresses. Profits from their giving their time played a large part in paying off the debt.

The exceptional floor of the hall brought such important social events as the Police Ball and the Farmers' Ball. Tickets for these cost five shillings and had a programme on the back so partners could reserve dances, the lancers and the Circassian circle being very popular. The knife and fork suppers were served in relays with the girls usually invited by a male partner. The larger bands came from Penrith or further afield. Before the Second World War a lot of the older men wore dinner dress and the ladies wore ankle-length gowns.

Concerts were also very popular. "An Edwardian Village Wedding" was rather special having local people entertaining with old fashioned songs and dances, including a comical pan-lid dance by two of the cast. The beautiful genuine period dresses, mostly hand-sewn, were loaned by local people. For a few years musical operettas were performed. They were held for three nights following a winter of rehearsals, which were a part of village social life bringing all ages together. Audiences from all over the area filled the hall at each performance.'

CLUB DAY

'The Lamplugh Club appears to have been an early Friendly Society or Mutual Aid Society, flourishing as far back as 1808, which supported workers and their families who came upon hard times.

Their annual gathering took place on the second Friday in June and was last held in 1939 when the procession assembled as usual at Lamplugh Cross carrying a banner and led by a brass band. They walked to the rectory and then on to the church for a service. They returned to the Cross for a meal, held in a marquee in later years, followed by dancing and sports. This may well have been the only "holiday" for some people so they made the most of it. The story goes that one local character started celebrating the night before and was so inebriated that he fell asleep in the dyke. He awoke the next morning to hear the band striking up for the Walk. He told his friends that he "thowt he had deed and gone to heaven!".'

RADIO AND CINEMA

'Before anyone in Hallbankgate ever had a wireless, a Mr Stobbart from Aspatria brought one to the village hall and set it up. The place was packed at sixpence a head to hear this wonderful invention and everyone waited expectantly. It was switched on, and then all we heard was a "squeak".'

'I recall, in 1921, as a small girl, listening to our home-built wireless set. The accumulator stood on a shelf underneath (this required recharging at intervals). The aerial was across two tall poles, one of which was quite a way from the house. We listened in on earphones, and only one person could listen at a time.

At the Christmas season there was more excitement as we listened to our village church bells and then went in and heard the bells from London. In those days you had to obtain two references in order to get a wireless receiving licence, costing ten shillings.'

'I used to go with my Grandad into Ulverston on the bus to pick up a charged battery for our wireless. We always had one in the wireless, one ready to go into it, and one at the shop being charged up. I remember getting holes in my navy blue interlock knickers from sitting on the battery waiting ready-charged for use, and getting my ears boxed when my mother realised why all my knickers had holes in them.'

'I remember hearing my first wireless, as we called it then. A man called Joe Smith who lived at Parks Road, Arlecdon, built his own crystal set. He allowed us to listen to this wonderful thing through earphones. All kinds of noises came through, then came this voice, to us children it was magic!

Perhaps by today's standards we enjoyed very simple things. There was Biddal's Picture House at Frizington. Saturday matinee was one penny and we walked there and back. Not everyone could afford one penny every week. They were silent films and someone played the piano at the front, changing the tune to match the action in the picture.'

'I remember in the days of silent films watching the young girl being courted by the handsome villain. A regular Longtown viewer used to shout out a warning to the pretty actress, "Hev nought te dow wud him, lass. Yon gadgee'll just git thee into trouble!" Even the pianist would be laughing. "Div as a tell thee, me lass. Gan heem till thee mother!"'

HOUND TRAILING

'Hound trailing is a leisure occupation which can only be carried out in extensive areas of isolated country, and Cumbria exactly fits this criterion. Waberthwaite had its share of trail hound enthusiasts, and the beginnings of it go back to beyond the First World War.

Anyone could run a trail hound, providing you had a good enough dog to do so. The name trail hound is self explanatory. A trail is set for the dogs to follow, and the method for doing this has been in operation since the sport started.

The trail is roughly circular, and covers a distance of about 23 miles. The dogs start and finish at about the same place. Those who lay the trail start at a point known as the split, equidistant from the beginning, and each man covers about twelve miles travelling in an opposite direction from his companion. They drag bags behind them filled with rags doused with aniseed lure.

There was great competition over these dogs and the deserted fells were alive with people at special vantage points when the races were being run. The officials involved in this were starters, timekeepers, judges and catchers. The catchers were posted at the finish to get the winning dogs as they came in.

The enthusiasm of course would not be maintained unless there was some reward, and this was catered for by betting on the dogs. There were bookmakers on the field, and the excitement was felt over the whole field.

Pedigrees and performances of dogs were avidly discussed and interest rivalled the horse racing of the day. It provided an all-engrossing leisure occupation in addition to time expended on the care and breeding of the dogs by the owners.

Today the sport still thrives, and travelling along Cumbrian roads on the west coast one can often come across groups of cars in odd places, with numerous men sporting binoculars, and looking at what appears to be nothing on the fells. They are actually watching the dogs to see which one is likely to come in first.

The dogs did not necessarily have to be owned by one person, but two or three or more could get together and form a syndicate for running the dog. As could be expected, anyone owning a dog with a winning streak would immediately find that he could get a high price for the progeny, so prices for desirable dogs produced a business in that direction.

Young dogs were initiated into the sport by having special races arranged for them. Occasionally a dog would go astray on the fells, and then there would be no more racing in that particular area until the dog had been found.'

OFF TO THE SEASIDE

Holidays were few and far between for most people, even a day's outing being a real red-letter day. One of the popular destinations for holidaymakers was the coastal resort of Silloth – 'Carlisle by the Sea'.

SO MANY HOLIDAYMAKERS

'Many people at Causewayhead remember the trains bringing holidaymakers from Carlisle to Silloth. A favourite pastime was to watch the trains discharging their passengers – not just hundreds but thousands would arrive. In fact, the first people to leave the train had arrived on Silloth's West Beach before the end of the crocodile had left the station. The fare from Carlisle to Silloth before the Second World War was one shilling and sixpence return.

A particular visitor to Silloth was a lady by the name of Sister Lily. She brought parties of 30 to 40 poor and needy children from Carlisle to the beach for weekend holidays. She had her own holiday hut on the West Beach with swings and see-saws at the rear on which the children played.'

'The steam hissed from between the large steel wheels and the smoke blew gently from the funnel of the black steam engine which waited in Carlisle station to take us to Silloth for August Bank Holiday in 1958.

Jam sandwiches were ready in greaseproof paper and carried in Dad's ex-army rucksack along with our ruched bathing costumes and towels. The train clickety clacked along and Dad let down the leather strap to look out the window as the train stopped at Kirkandrews and got a cinder in his eye.

An hour later we were walking along the green at Silloth deciding what to do first. We each had one shilling and sixpence to spend so a ride on Johnny Gray's donkeys was first stop and we followed this with a swing on the swing boats. The amusement arcade was a great attraction and the halfpenny slot machines swallowed up our money as we vainly tried to get the little metal balls into a winning slot. We looked longingly at the "grab for presents" machine but that was threepence and too expensive.

The paddling pool was very busy so Mam and Dad decided we should go to West Silloth to swim and as we made our way along the golf course path we were promised an ice cream at Longcakes shop. A bottle of pop was purchased and once we got to the sand dunes we enjoyed our sandwiches while Mam and Dad had their tea from a flask.

After a lovely paddle we walked along the West Beach to the pier and then had a look at the railway carriages which were used as holiday accommodation, and eventually came to the docks. It was very daring to cross the dock gates to the lifeboat station and watch the fishermen catching flounders.

The long concrete promenade curved along to the lighthouse at Skinburness and we scampered up and down the steps and threw stones in the sea as Mam and Dad strolled along. We found a ball and promptly lost it again as the tide took it away. Dad rolled up his trousers to try to get it but even he couldn't catch it and it slowly bobbed away out of his reach.

We went into the summerhouse to eat our tea then spent the threepence we got back on the lemonade bottle at the funfair. The Mission Man was on the green and we joined in the gospel songs, so we were first in the queue when it was time to catch the sweets. Soon it was time to make our way back to the station for the last train. Everyone else had the same idea and the platform was full to capacity with families. Somehow we all got on the train with three or four families to each individual compartment and it was a very tired set of twins who finally arrived back at Carlisle. A super day for ten shillings for us all.'

THE SILLOTH PIERROTS

'Before air-conditioning, many London and provincial theatres closed down during the summer months, and so lots of entertainers then joined pierrots at the seaside.

Silloth Pierrots was usually a very good concert party, run by a well-known local baritone, David Fuller. The show was at the seafront, with seats outside, if fine. The stage and dressing rooms were all under cover.

Usually, the uniform costume was a white jumpsuit, with black pom-poms down the front, a big white frill round the neck and a cone-shaped hat, again with black pom-poms up the centre front.

The company started the concert with a jolly song with actions, which fitted the subject and the timing. The comedian then took over, with his "feed", in good Morecambe and Wise fashion. The next "turn" would perhaps be a buxom lady rendering songs of the day, and so on, through a varied programme.

No charge was made, but a collector came round for expected contributions. Usually all the children sat at the front and adults behind on deck chairs – a real family show, with quite a lot of back-chat between performers and audience. Words of a typical song were:

"Weeee . . . watched the train come in,
  Hearing the porter shout,
We sat and held each other's hand,
  As only lovers understand.
We watched the trains come in,
  Hearing the porter shout
And when we'd watched all the trains come in –
  We watched all the trains go out!"

And all Silloth would be singing and whistling that song for days!

So many families went to Silloth for their summer holidays. One strong memory is of paddling out across the sand, in *very* shallow water when the tide was out, to a channel where we bought flounders from the fishing boats. We would get two large carrier bags full for sixpence – all live and wriggling.'

ALLONBY

'Allonby straddles the road between Maryport and Silloth, on the shores of the Solway Firth, and has been known by thousands as a holiday resort. Very little has changed in the past 40 years.

Going back to the 1950s, the population in winter was but a fraction of that in the summer months, with several caravan sites at both ends of the village. During the summer there was an influx of visitors from Carlisle during Race Week. Another week Glaswegians, the Boy's Brigade would camp here, another week "Geordies". It is worth remembering that compared with the present day there were few private cars on the road, but then there was the railway line from Carlisle to Silloth and a regular bus service from Silloth to Allonby.

On a Sunday afternoon the "charas" descended on Allonby from every town and village in the west of Cumberland, and of course, pre-yellow line, they parked the buses where they could and chaos reigned. The fair came to the green for two weeks in summer, a few swings and a roundabout. On a Saturday in August there was the carnival – the fancy dress parade through the village, then the judging followed by the sports. We had our own fortune teller, Madame Sereta. The putting green earned its keep, a few pence being the charge for a round.

The tide going out so far left plenty of sand for every design of sand castle, and sometimes it was warm enough to bathe! From the shore the view then as now is of the Lakeland hills to the east and the Scottish hills in the west, and many a glorious sunset must be etched in the memories of those visitors who came year after year for a holiday at Allonby.'

SPECIAL OCCASIONS

Royal jubilees and coronations were enthusiastically supported in towns and villages across Cumbria, with even the smallest community coming together for sports and celebrations. There were other special occasions too, such as the day we saw our first aeroplane, and how many remember the Wordsworth Centenary and all those wonderful daffodils!

ROYAL CELEBRATIONS

'In 1897, for the Diamond Jubilee of Queen Victoria, all the children at Finsthwaite were given a medal and a service was held in the church. Running races were held at Stock Park Mansion.

Everyone wore black on the day of the funeral of Queen Victoria in 1901 and a church service was held at the same time as the service of burial at Frogmore.

It was thought that celebrations arranged for the coronation of Edward VII in June 1902 would have to be postponed until August as the King had needed an operation for appendicitis, but the country villages were told to carry on regardless so they had the usual running races down at Stock Park Mansion.'

'When George V was crowned in 1911, sports were held in the top meadow at Elterwater. It was a lovely day and I found the hidden treasure, a silver thimble, which I still have.'

'There was one day which was, for the people of Egremont, extra-special, 29th June 1927. The Prince of Wales was coming to visit the town. I was a four year old pupil at Bookwell infants school and I remember cutting up coloured paper to make a flag to wave as the procession came up the street. This was to be followed by a tea party in school – a very rare occasion and so exciting. We were allowed to go home at dinner time to put on our Sunday special dresses. We marched from school and lined up along the street. I'm sure most of the infants were more excited about the party. This Prince of Wales chap didn't mean much to a four year old, but I did love Egremont brass band.

The cheering started so we knew the procession was getting nearer, when suddenly some big boys ran behind us. One of them fell and pushed me off the pavement edge in front of one of the motor cycles leading the procession. I didn't know who picked me up. My mother told me I was taken into the doctor's surgery suffering a broken collarbone. Everything was very quiet when I was finally brought outside, the cheers had died down and the children had gone to the tea party in school to receive a special mug with the Prince of Wales' photograph on it. My next trip was to Bransty, part of Whitehaven, in Mr "Shiggy" Ratcliffe's taxi to visit a bone setter – evidently no casualty department then at Whitehaven Hospital which we passed on the way. What a disaster on the day that was to have been so special.

Everybody was so sorry I hadn't seen the Prince of Wales; as for me, my mother always told me the real disappointment was missing the party and the mug. A nice surprise the following day when the headmistress came to see me and bring me my mug, which still has pride of place in the cabinet, and a bag of special "goodies" from the party. When I got back to school there were pictures and stories of me on the classroom walls done by my classmates and probably a story in the *Whitehaven News*. If one has to be pushed into a motor cycle why not a Royal one – it doesn't happen very often.'

'It was the year 1935 and the month of May when the village of Matterdale kept the special day for the Silver Jubilee of George V.

It was a lovely sunny day and it started with a thanksgiving service in the church. Nearly everyone in the village seemed to be there. Lady Lawson planted two trees in the new churchyard. Then everyone went to the hall and we had a cold meal of ham, cakes etc with tea. The water for the tea was boiled in an urn on the open fire.

The afternoon was spent in a field with games and sports for the children, then more tea and food. A concert, games and dancing followed. Anyone who could sing or recite had to do their bit, with dances in between – the lancers and other old dances.

Then all who could climb went to the top of the fell where a bonfire had been built. At 10 pm it was lit. All over England, on the hills, bonfires were lit at the same time. It was possible to see many of them from the fell top and was an unforgettable sight on a beautiful starlit night.

I remember the following week – there was an inch of snow!'

A royal occasion celebrated in style at Edmond Castle, Hayton in the early 1900s.

'Two days stand out vividly during my schooldays. The first was the Silver Jubilee in May 1935 when King George V and Queen Mary celebrated 25 years of their reign. Every child in the school at Distington took part in a carnival. We were "Children of the Empire" – apple girls from Canada, Zulus from Africa, tea pickers from India. Some dressed as Scots, others from Ireland and Wales. I was an English milkmaid, complete with stool and milk pail. Some of us were to be chosen to ride on lorries; who would be the lucky ones? Miss Downes, the teacher called out the names – gosh, my name came first. I was going to get a ride on a lorry. I still have a photograph among my treasured possessions. Off we went round the village, the sun shining and everybody happy, joining in the fun, then back to school for tea, every child receiving a bag containing a bun and a cake. Mr Wilson from the council presented us with commemorative beakers; he lived two doors away from me. I remember him telling me to look after it and I would still have it when I was an old lady, which I have.

The second day was also a Royal occasion, this being the Coronation of King George VI and Queen Elizabeth in 1937. This time we didn't have a carnival, but we did have a dancing display by the girls and the boys did a physical training display on the cricket field, where the flat-topped houses were built in the 1940s, now Glebe Road. I remember wearing a white dress bought for me from a new shop in Workington called Marks and Spencer – nothing sold over five shillings! My eldest sister embroidered french knots round the collar in red and blue to make it more patriotic. Tea was again served, yes, another bag, a bun and a cake. Then we had sports, but before we were halfway through the heavens opened and our lovely white dresses were soaked. We were told to go home. Next day at school we were all given a mug.'

'My joyous memory of the coronation in 1953 is of watching it on black and white television at my aunt and uncle's house. They were among the few people in the village to have a television and the whole street were in and out at some point during the day. Many and varied children sat in full splendour on the front row, sandwiches, cakes, pop and tea appearing at intervals. A magical experience.'

'In 1953 at Scotby we had maypole dancing on the village green. When the pageant was held at Bitts Park, Carlisle around the same date, some Scotby young people were dressed up for the Gretna Green scene and we travelled each day by pony and flat cart to Carlisle. The coronation was the first time I remember seeing the television. There were only a handful of sets in Scotby but where a household had a TV others were invited. We took some food and it was pooled and we had a wonderful day with all our friends.'

'Coronation Day 1953 – what a day that was! The village of Hayton was agog. Money had been collected, plans laid, and no household was immune from something of the spirit of the occasion.

There was a children's fancy dress parade, leading to sports for all at Hayton House – which had latterly served as a boarding school for boys, but which was soon to be demolished. We remember with a tinge of sadness and nostalgia this last use of it for a village celebration when, after the judging of the fancy dress and the excitement of the sports, all the adults sat down there for a splendid "knife and fork" tea, such as is only produced by country folk doing their best. The children were happily catered for by good carers with a picnic-in-a-bag meal at the school, while a present of tea-time food and tins of tea were delivered to all the housebound.

A short lull in the early evening saw tired children put contentedly to bed and eager parents get ready in full evening dress to join in at the glorious Coronation Ball with its real Border variety of dancing and catering held in a lavishly decorated WI hall. What a memory!'

EARLY AEROPLANES

'I don't recall the exact date but it was in the late 1920s. Women had got the vote and the newest thing was aviation. We did not see many planes in the north west of England, but on one particular day four of us were kept home from school. Dad took us to the old Roman camp, the highest point in the area. We had a grandstand view of the Round Britain Air Race. The small planes hedge-hopped down the Solway coast to their relay point at St Bees Head. The pilots put their heads out of the little bi-planes to wave to the five of us. Better than school!'

'Occasionally, prior to the Second World War, single-engined aeroplanes of wood and canvas construction would come to Soulby for a few days in May or June and land in a flat field down the Musgrave road. This served as a base from which they would give joy-rides to anyone paying five shillings for a flight.'

EARL GREY OF FALLODON

'A special occasion I remember happened in the 1933–34 period. I was a maid working for Lady Camilla Lawson who lived in Matterdale. A new stone bridge, spanning the lower fall at Aira

Force, near Ullswater, had just been erected to the memory of Sir Cecil Spring-Rice of Old Church, Ullswater, one of two great American Ambassadors which the district had given to the world, Lord Howard of Penrith being the other. The stone bridge over the main fall was also erected to Mr Stephen Spring-Rice, brother of Sir Cecil. Sir Cecil Spring-Rice wrote the hymn *I vow to thee my country*.

The bridge was opened by Earl Grey of Fallodon, who was a statesman in the First World War. He was a frail gentleman and was nearly blind.

Lord and Lady Howard were residing at Lyulph's Tower near Aira Force. They gave a lunch there for the guests who were at the opening – Lady Mabel Howard, Lady Lawson and about twelve or more titled people.

Lady Lawson sent me and her cook to help the staff at Lyulph's Tower with lunch. I remember waiting at table and serving Earl Grey with cherry tart, which was the sweet course, hoping I would not drop anything. We were allowed to walk to the waterfall to be present at the opening.'

THE WORDSWORTH CENTENARY

'To celebrate William Wordsworth's centenary in Cockermouth in 1950, all the schoolchildren had to plant daffodil bulbs along the riverbanks and entrances to the town. We walked from Wordsworth House to Harris Park carrying bunches of daffodils, which we laid around the base of the Dorothy Wordsworth fountain. A wonderful sight never to be forgotten.'

THROUGH THE YEAR

Every season of the year brought its own celebrations and festivals, eagerly anticipated as a break in the working routine. Some still delight us, but others have gone forever, such as Empire Day, once celebrated by every schoolchild – if only for the half day holiday from school!

EASTER TIME

'How delighted we were as girls in the early years of the century to have a complete new outfit bought for us at Easter, mostly fine materials which were such a change from our winter clothes of boots, knitted stockings and warm underwear. I was always especially pleased with a new straw hat, trimmed with ribbons and flowers (always bought from Coffee Robbies in Longtown). On Easter Sunday we dressed up and went out to visit, to show off our clothes – we were usually given an egg (boiled and dyed) and an orange by the people we visited; our clothes were looked over and commented upon. As I had a lot of relatives in Longtown I usually did very well. We also walked to some of the outlying farms. I remember walking to Byers and Coulthards farms at Hallburn in my new shoes. Of course, we had to change our clothes when we came home; they had to last until next Easter.

We were usually quite subdued on Good Friday, very quiet in the house. When I was very young I attended Arthuret Sunday school (teacher Miss May Little who lived at Eskbank). We had an annual prizegiving and the prizes were presented by Lady Cynthia Graham of Netherby Hall; the girls would curtsey and the boys would bow from the waist. On Good Friday afternoon I always expected the weather to be different – thunderstorms and complete darkness from twelve o'clock to three o'clock. I was rather afraid.'

'People now in their eighties remember a rhyme taught them in school to help them remember the Sundays in Lent:

Kid, Mid, Misere (Mothering Sunday)
Carlin, Palm, Pace Egg Day
We shall have a holiday
Bonny frocks on Easter Day.'

PASCHE EGGING

'On Easter Day I was at last allowed to wear my new dress, shoes and Easter bonnet, which every year was bought specially as part of our Easter celebrations. My three brothers, my elder sister and I set off proudly on our walk to Sunday school at the village chapel. After the morning teachings and singing of a few songs we were all presented with our annual orange and pasche egg. This was a hardboiled egg which had been dyed using onion skins, flower petals and sometimes pieces of patterned cloth. Easter was always a time when children were sure to get plenty of vitamin C! The oranges had been donated to the village schoolchildren by the local landowner.

After leaving the Sunday school we then set out on our favourite part of the day, calling on all the houses in the village to show off our new outfits and receive yet more pasche eggs and oranges. Sometimes after being told how smart we looked we would be given a little pinch and told "that's a nip for new!"

Each year when we called on one particular villager, with whom one of my brothers was a great favourite, we would offer our thanks for our pasche eggs while watching with envy as he received a small chocolate egg. How I would have loved that chocolate egg, as if there is one thing I have always detested, it is a hardboiled egg!'

'Just as children go from door to door carol singing at Christmas, at Easter they would go pasche egging in Flookburgh, and many other places. "Pasche" is pronounced "pace" in local dialect.

Faces were blackened with a piece of burnt cork and children would dress up as one of the characters in the Easter play and go to each house hoping to get a few coppers or an egg or two. The eggs would be dyed with onion skins, with celandine, cow parsley and primroses etc arranged on them to make a pattern. They were rubbed with a butter paper while still hot to make them shine.

On Easter Monday the children made their way to a steep hill called Robin How, where the eggs were rolled against each other or rolled down the hill to see who had the egg with the hardest shell. The one that did not crack was the winner. This custom seemed to die out in the early 1930s.'

'In the 1930s I remember my grandmother at Milnthorpe, Mrs Hyde, training boys to act out the Easter play. It was a revised version of a story written over a hundred years before. The characters were Toss Pot, King George, Lord Nelson, Doctor, Jack Tar, Bessie Brown Bags and Molly Masket. The song included in the play went like this:

"Here's two or three Jolly Boys all in one mind,
We've come a pasche egging
And hope you'll prove kind.
We hope you prove kind,
With your eggs and strong beer
We'll come no more nigh you
Until the next year.

Fol the ray, fol the ray, fol the riddle di dum day (chorus)

The first to come in is Lord Nelson you see
He has a bunch of blue ribbons
Tied down to his knee.
He has a star on his breast
Like diamonds do shine.
We hope you remember
It's Pasche Egging time.

The next that comes in is our jovial Jack Tar
Who fought for Lord Nelson
All during last war.
He fought for his king and his country so good
He fought for Lord Nelson
While he shed his blood.

The next that comes in is old Toss Pot you see.
He's a valiant old fellow
In every degree.
He has a hump on his back
And he wears a pig tail,
And all his delight is in drinking mulled ale.

The next to come in is old Bessie Brown Bags.
For fear of her money
She goes in old rags.
She has plenty of money
And plenty in store,
But she comes along with us
In hopes to get more.

Now ladies and gentlemen that sit by the fire
Put your hands in your pockets, that's all we desire.
Put your hands in your pockets
And pull out your purse
And give us a trifle
You'll not feel much worse."'

MAY DAY

'In Keswick for many years, up to the beginning of the Second World War, a May Day was held on the first Wednesday in May. All the Bands of Hope, which were attached to the Sunday schools, took part.

The weekend before the May Day we gathered bluebells and primroses to make the Queen's crown, staffs for the attendants and to fill flower baskets for all the other children. These were all made in the Sunday school room.

When the great day came all the girls were dressed in white dresses and socks and new sandals (if we could have white sandals, joy indeed, but usually they were brown, much more serviceable for school afterwards). Grandma would get out the curling tongs and our hair was "curled", and usually our ears got burned because we wouldn't sit still.

Off we went to Sunday school to collect our sashes (purple for the Wesleyan Sunday school on Southey Street) and our flower baskets, and followed the Queen, who rode on a white pony, round the town to the park, or the Pavilion if wet, where we had tea and entertainment after the speeches etc.'

'Memories of May Days at Egremont in the 1920s – the maypoles and the Queen with her mother's lace curtain on her head and a garland of paper flowers, the train bearers, the footballer, the cricketer, carrying his bat and ball, the rest festooned in paper flowers and daisychains. We only walked around Smithfield, collecting as we walked. The highlight of the day was tea; iced buns and sweets. Not forgetting the shareout of the money, about threepence each. What a great day.'

'On the first Saturday in May at Cleator, children picked a May Queen and they all dressed up and walked along the street. Afterwards, mothers made tea and sandwiches, cakes etc.'

'In the picturesque village of Nether Wasdale the tradition of dancing round the maypole has gone on for over 100 years. The present maypole was erected in front of the church on the green to celebrate Queen Victoria's 60 year reign. This event used to be held on the first Friday in May but in later years has been on the first Saturday, still a very popular get-together. The maypole dances were great but we were always careful not to get the coloured ribbons messed up. The music was from a gramophone and records. The button-hole competition was very popular and, of course, they were made from fresh flowers. Next was the sports, egg and spoon, sack races etc, all great fun. The afternoon ended with tea at the Strands Hotel, then owned and run by Miss Smith, whose family had been there over 100 years. In their large dining room were big dark oak sideboards which seemed to hold many secrets. On top of these were large glass display cases. To a child these were so eye-like, that we all sat still whilst eating tea.

Thankfully, this age-old tradition still carries on because of the dedication of a few.'

EMPIRE DAY

'I was so sorry when Empire Day celebrations came to an end in school events – the Commonwealth came into being and the Empire ended. The 24th May was a day of great celebration when the whole infants school took part in a display before parents in the school yard. It always seemed to be a lovely day, for I cannot remember it ever to be in the school hall.

We gave plays, sang songs, danced and recited, but all to do with the different countries or people of the British Empire.

The girls wore red, white and blue ribbons in their hair, or on their frocks; bunches of daisies too. The night before, almost everybody went to the park to pick the daisies. I remember the recitation:

"See my bunch of daisies,
Pretty English flowers,
Picked from grassy meadows
In this land of ours.

See the flag I'm waving,
Red and white and blue
Union Jack is British
I am British too!"

St George and the Dragon were usually there too – the dragon made of ten little boys covered with a very long green tablecloth and a fearsome cardboard head fixed on the front.

The happy day ended with a half-day holiday, enjoyed by all!'

OAK APPLE DAY

'The walk to school that morning of 29th May 1938 was still unfamiliar. My family had just moved from the town to live in a country village on the fell bottom, and I walked alone, not yet having friends.

I turned the corner for the last hundred yards. Ahead stood the school, a sturdy red sandstone building, the single bell in its bell-cote not yet sounding, five minutes more before prayers would begin.

Usually the pupils were taking advantage of the last moments of freedom, running about on the earth playground or chattering in groups. Today it was different. A small crowd of older children was outside the gate and, as I approached, they turned to face me. The boys were all wearing gloves and holding bunches of long nettles! I moved forward with a sense of incomprehension. Then I was surrounded and the nettles were being flourished around my bare legs.

"Where's your oak leaves?"

"You're not wearing an oak-apple," they shouted.

Sure enough, the nettles were not the only foliage to be seen. All were sporting sprigs of oak, and some wore oak-apples too, pinned to clothes and pulled through buttonholes.

"We're goin' to nettle you because y're not wearin' any oak leaves" – and the nettles were flourished more fiercely.

The connection between nettles and oak leaves escaped me entirely. It wasn't fair, should I be punished for ignorance?

"It's for t' King, King Charles."

"'e hid in t' oak tree."

"It's Oak-apple Day."

"'e hid from t' Roundheeds," explained the girls, as the teasing boys moved off. I was amazed at their loyalty to a king long dead.

Was it my innocence that saved me, or the fact that I was "t' skeul-maister's dowter"?'

'Oak Bob Day was the day when all children at Holme wore an oak leaf, and if you didn't your hair was pulled. The rhyme was:

Oak Bob Day the 29th May
If you don't give us a holiday
We will all run away
Where will you run?
Down Moss Lane
And over the hills and back again.'

THE SPORTS

'A typical conversation which could be overheard in any village:

"He was felled with a swinging hype."

"No lad, it was a cross buttock."

Obviously they had witnessed a bout of Cumberland & Westmorland-style wrestling – quite unique to this county for the last hundred years, and a tradition still continuing at local shows. A sport which required no equipment, just two sporting young men prepared to throw each other to the ground by a series of skilful moves. Ideal activity when they congregated on the village green after a hard day's work.

In competitions at local shows two judges and a referee are required, a roped off ring, on grass, and two young men who will wrestle the best of three falls. A fall is given when any part of your opponent's body touches the ground. Expressions like tekkin hod, blown out, swinging hypes, cross buttock, hank and twist, and dog fall are used to describe the moves.

Contenders will be advised, "Traditional costume will be worn," ie leggings which fit tightly to the leg (long johns), a singlet vest, a centrepiece elasticated garment (over-pants) in velvet which will have been embroidered, and socks (shoes are not worn).

The costumes may well be judged by a lady, usually the wife of a local celebrity, generating much interest among the lady embroiderers.

On the 3rd Thursday in August all roads lead to Grasmere for the popular Grasmere Sports. Since 1852 this has been the venue for all Cumbrian sportsmen to compete in Cumberland and Westmorland wrestling, foot races and mountain guide racing, as well as hound dogs following an aniseed trail up the fellside.'

'Braystones lies about a mile from the village of Beckermet. A tower still stands on the side of the river and at one time there was a bridge across to it.

The tower was built in 1897 to commemorate Queen Victoria's Diamond Jubilee, with steps inside leading to the top and it housed local historical finds. On Empire Day, 24th May, it became a tradition to gather by the tower and sing hymns. People were allowed to climb the tower on that day.

Later the hymn singing was followed by sports, a children's event interspersed with a men's event such as wrestling. Mr Tyson Cook recalls that he was the last wrestling champion. The cup with which he was presented is now held at the Midland Bank in Egremont, while he has a smaller replica.

The nearby farm provided a good tea for three shillings and sixpence which was appreciated. There were hound trails too but when the war came in 1939 the Braystones Sports stopped.'

'My husband Willie was a keen Cumberland and Westmorland-style wrestler and was a member of the Gilsland Academy, wrestling indoors in the winter and outdoors in the summer. Grasmere Sports was the big annual event, held on the third Thursday in August. There were different weight categories for the wrestlers: nine and a half stone, eleven stone, and "allweights" or heavyweights. Willie won the nine and a half stone championships in 1936 – the prize was a silver teapot and £13. At the time, £2 or so was considered a good weekly wage.'

'The great social event of the year was the Pooley Sports, held in the field below our house in the early 1920s. We would wait by the road to see Lord Lonsdale ("The Yellow Earl") driving past in a carriage with black horses and postillions wearing, if I remember correctly, cream silk top hats. The Earl had a pavilion in the ring on the sports field, with his personal flag flying over it. He would start the fell race and the hound trail. Cumberland and Westmorland-style wrestling was a feature of the Sports, the wrestlers correctly attired in the traditional colourful kit.'

'Braithwaite Sports Day, though now discontinued, once rivalled Grasmere Sports. There was running, wrestling, pole jumping and hound trailing. The village had its own greyhound racing track – someone had to pedal a bike wheel to drag the rabbit skin around the course.'

'When we were young the sports at Woodland which we always attended were known as "Rasthwaite Sports". The tea was served in the barn above the cow byre. Long trestles were set up for the tables, and forms alongside for seating. Four stable oil lamps hung from the high beams, a lovely soft light. After tea everyone walked to the field where the sports took place. A dance followed at night, also held in the barn. How everyone enjoyed it, humble though it was.'

RUSHBEARING

'The ancient tradition of rushbearing has taken place in the Lake District for many generations; at present the best known ones are Ambleside, Grasmere, Warcop and Urswick.

In the Grasmere church records, the festival was mentioned as early as 1680. The number of bearings fluctuated from year to year. In 1834 there were only seven children with rushbearings and, worried by the decline in numbers, it was decided that each child that brought a bearing should be given the gift of a sixpence. By 1839 the numbers had increased to 115.

It was reported in 1827 that the poet, William Wordsworth, his wife, sister and daughter were in attendance.

The ceremony is to commemorate the strewing of rushes over the earthen floor of the church, which was necessary for warmth and cleanliness before it was paved in 1840.

In early times the festival at Grasmere took place in July or early August but, since 1885, it has been held on the Saturday nearest to St Oswald's Day. In Urswick the ceremony was revived in 1905 and is held on the Sunday nearest to St Michael's Day (29th September). The children gather and sit on the churchyard wall with their bearings; these are usually baskets, crosses or crooks, covered with moss and rushes and decorated with flowers. The babies' prams are also decorated with rushes and flowers. While they wait the children receive a new penny and a ticket for gingerbread.

A brass band provides the music for the march round the village and plays a selection of marches and rushbearing hymns.

Leading the procession, members of the choir carry the gold cross of St Oswald and other large bearings and rush staves. Very prominent at the front is the large banner of St Oswald. Six local schoolgirls carry the rush sheet; they are dressed in the traditional green smocked skirts and white blouses, with garlands of rushes and

The rushbearing ceremony at Grasmere in 1946, a tradition still going strong today.

flowers in their hair. The double crown is carried by an adult and the six streamers are held by small children from the village. Then follow the rest of the bearings, first the large ones, including the serpent and St Oswald's hand, and the children carrying their smaller bearings at the rear of the procession.

On returning from the march, the bearings are placed in the church. The service commences, during which the rushbearing hymns are sung. The words of the St Oswald's Day hymn were written by Canon Rawnsley.

After the service the children go to the school for their gingerbread.

The following Monday, the children collect their bearings from the church and then go to the school to take part in the sports, which include a fell race, Cumberland and Westmorland wrestling and other races.'

FAIRS AND CARNIVALS

'When I was a child living in Egremont, Crab Fair Day was very special. An open bus came down the Main Street with six men throwing out quantities of crab apples for the children to catch. At the fair, men and boys tried to scramble up a very greasy pole to grab a leg of mutton at the top – not many succeeded but it was very amusing to watch them, especially when they could only climb a few yards and slipped down to the ground.'

'Great excitement! The Carnival Queen was to be chosen from our school. All the girls from the age of eleven to 14 were eligible.

A concert was arranged in the village hall. At the interval we had all to line up on stage in our best frocks. We were each given an envelope containing a number; I cannot remember who drew the winning envelope. Number six was the winner. Greatly excited I opened mine, no luck, I had number nine. The girl who won was perhaps not the prettiest, but the committee thought that was the fairest way to choose the Queen. I was chosen to be one of the eight maids-of-honour. We had lots of rehearsals, learning how to curtsy and carry the Queen's blue velvet robe. The great day arrived, a glorious sunny day. We rode on a decorated lorry with the uncrowned Queen on a throne around the town of Whitehaven then onto a field where we formed a procession to where the Queen was to be crowned. We all got a small present and the Carnival Queen got a gold watch. Another treasured memory of that wonderful day was Lord Lonsdale's yellow shooting-brake which contained a shooting party. Two of my uncles were part of this with their guns and game-dogs.'

The Band of Hope picnic at Dent was a great local occasion and took place until the Second World War. Here, the children receive their prizes before the food and fun of a picnic in the 1890s.

'Billy Middleton's shop was always busy at Dent fair time. You could buy everything you needed, even a coat and hat. We bought our dresses for the fair there and maybe for the dance at night too. It was busy on fair day. People came from all over to visit their families and meet old friends. There was horse racing, foot racing, a wheelbarrow race, a slow bicycle race and a sack race. There were always plenty of bookies.

Before the First World War the horse trotting took place on the road between Church Bridge and Scotchergill Bridge and a large variety of stalls selling pottery, toys, knick-knacks etc were erected right through the town on either side of the street. Dances were held during the week in the lodge rooms of the three public houses. Fiddles provided the music and a charge of a halfpenny per dance was paid by the gentleman after he had taken a partner and before they started to dance. The gipsy encampment was in Billy Middleton's wood yard and they provided "all the fun of the fair" in the field opposite the school with donkey rides up and down the road, and sometimes a boat-shaped waggonette provided rides between the school and the Hippins. Unlike the present time, the fair lasted about a week and, as the servants were on holiday with half a year's wages in their pockets, they were bent on having a good time and, needless to say, alcoholic drink contributed greatly to the joviality!

Later, when I was a girl in the 1950s, Dent fair was still the highlight of the year. Inside and outside, everyone cleaned their houses from top to bottom. Outside walls were whitewashed, doors and windows painted and gardens planted. We all had new clothes and shoes for the fair and friends and relatives came from far and wide. When I was first married we always had between 20 and 30 for tea and some stayed overnight. Dent fair dance was always packed with as many spectators outside as inside, watching for drunks and fighting . . . also to see who went home with who! Everybody had a girl or boy friend on Dent fair night and on the Monday night following, the church organised another dance . . . . a sort of "follow-up". Many of the couples met again that night and it was very often the beginning of a lasting courtship. Many marriages stemmed from Dent fair.

The Band of Hope picnic was another great occasion earlier this century. The band used to play through the street and children followed after, and anyone else that wanted, down to the field by the river. There were all sorts of races, a bran tub and coconut shies. No alcoholic drinks! There was a big tent where ladies made the tea. The Band of Hope had their own named cups (there are still ones on the go).

On 5th November late in the evening, the young lads of the village would light a bonfire by the fountain . . . the fire got so hot it would crack people's windows! Tar barrels which had been used for dipping sheep were thrown on the fire. Once an old chap who used to sit by his front door came out to see his chair on top of the fire.'

BONFIRE NIGHT

'A few days before Bonfire Night at Clifton the boys used to go round collecting a few pence to buy fireworks, singing –

> Remember, remember, the 5th of November
> Gunpowder, treason and plot
> We know no reason why gunpowder treason
> Should ever be forgot.
> Ladies and gentlemen, sitting by the fire
> Two pence or three pence is all we desire
> Put your hands in your pockets and pull out your purse
> And give us a trifle, it will make you no worse.'

'For Mawbray children, 5th November was a great day. They would start to collect wood in September, going round farms and houses to get together anything which would burn. Everything was carefully stored in an outhouse with a loft. We collected sackful after sackful and used barrows. The guy wasn't essential and sometimes we didn't have one – it was the fire that was important. We'd even walk the tideline and manhandle huge baulks of timber up to the fire, it was a wonder we didn't injure ourselves. It was a constant worry that we weren't going to have enough. Then just as we were despairing, up would drive a farmer with a great load of hedge cuttings to save the day. The bangers were let off around the fire which would be on Mawbray banks, but the pretty, colourful fireworks were saved for back in the village where there were no lights.'

ARMISTICE DAY

'Armistice Day was not, of course, a celebration day, but it was a very important part of our year, particularly the ones I remember between the wars. It was commemorated every year by the two minutes' silence. This was very impressive, particularly in towns, when at the stroke of eleven o'clock all traffic came to a standstill, and all the children stood silent in the schoolyard in memory of those who died in the Great War. Even those of us who were far too young to remember the war were touched by this act of reverence.'

CHRISTMAS

'As children in Longtown many years ago, before the First World War, we looked forward to the Christmas period for quite a while beforehand. At school we talked about it and prepared for it and were told the Christmas story many times. We made paper chains, learned and practised carols and rehearsed for the annual church concert which was held in the Mechanics Hall in English Street. By the time we broke up for our Christmas holidays we were quite excited and talked a lot about what Father Christmas would bring us.

In the dark evenings we would sometimes gather around the shop windows which were all beautifully decorated and filled with all sorts of games and toys. Perhaps we might find a toy shop or post office, or even a doll, in our stockings. There were no mountain bikes or videos for us then and we didn't do much buying of presents. A Longtown lady who owned a shop always gave me a box of hankies; I was thought to be very much favoured.

The local shops sometimes had what was known as a half-penny dip. This was a barrel filled with sawdust and containing small packets of sweets, toys and novelties. We used some of our spending money (one penny a week usually) to buy these delights.

What made Christmas so different for us children in Longtown was the different atmosphere, at school, at home and in the village. In the dark evenings we watched the lamplighter light the gas street lamps. The country children were sent home early from school if the weather was bad. Going to church with my friends, singing with gusto the familiar carols, hoping that it would snow. The Christmas dinner with all the family, the gathering at the cross with friends to hear the Longtown brass band. Memories of my stocking hanging on the bed rail filled with all kinds of things – apples, oranges, sweets, toys and a small sum of money. Magic!'

'Our main Christmas present would cost no more than two shillings and sixpence and was always appreciated. I still have a marmalade jar which I bought my mother in the 1930s – sixpence for the jar and threepence for the lid. Woolworth's sold nothing over sixpence in value then.'

'Every New Year's morning many years ago, the children of Grasmere used to gather, usually accompanied by their mothers, at the front of the Rothay Hotel. They were given a mince pie, an orange and a new sixpence by Mr Taylor of Helm Side. The Managing Director of Mather & Platts Engineering Company in Manchester, he was also a property and land owner in the valley.'

THE MILNTHORPE SHOUTERS

'Older Milnthorpians recall the Shouters who operated in the early hours of each New Year's Day until the end of the Second World War. This custom probably derived from the night watch which patrolled the streets before the days of a regular police force. Throughout the night the watchman called out the time and the state of the weather and by so doing informed residents (who were bound to pay for his services) that he was doing his job. A lasting reminder of this custom is the name of the Watch Night service held as the New Year breaks. At Milnthorpe as worshippers went to church the passing bell was tolled to bid farewell to the old year while a merry marriage peal greeted the New Year.

Following the service a group of men and boys (never any women or girls) gathered in Milnthorpe Square. In later years most of the Shouters came from the Arkwright, Ashburner or Wilson families who discouraged any alternative bands and restricted the number to eight or a dozen in order to safeguard the perks. They also went round together and did not break up into smaller groups to cover the village more quickly. The first house to be visited was Dallam Tower, beyond the village boundary but the home of Milnthorpe's squire. Here after performing they received hospitality and, with luck, generous tips from the house party.

If Dallam was unoccupied another large house was visited instead. In the 1920s this was sometimes Mallow House, the home of Mr Hadwin Allen. Well lubricated, the Shouters then visited each house in turn, which were never entered even if the lights were on. Every front door was shouted at, even if they were side by side as in Carr's Yard or Church Street. Following "A Happy New Year to ye all" each occupant was greeted by name including visitors and new babies who, depending on social class and the hopes of a good tip, were addressed formally as, eg: Miss Pamela and Master Roger. How everybody was named was always something of a mystery but research was conducted a day or two earlier with the help of newspaper and errand boys who abounded at that time. Even if it was pouring down, the weather was always proclaimed as being fine. No reward was expected at the time but in the following days one of the Shouters would appear outside each house and hang around until someone came out with some small change, or failing that a mince pie or slice of Christmas cake.'

LIST OF CONTRIBUTING WIs

CUMBRIA WESTMORLAND

Allithwaite
Ambleside
Appleby
Arnside
Bampton
Barbon
Bardsea
Beetham
Bowness
Brathay
Broughton Mills and Woodland
Cliburn
Clifton
Coniston
Crook
Crosby Garrett
Crosthwaite and Lyth
Dentdale
Dufton
Finsthwaite and Staveley
Foxfield
Grasmere
Grayrigg
Hawkshead
Heversham
Holme
Kentmere
Kendal Castle
Kendale Strickland
Kirby Stephen

Langdale
Lower Holker
Lowther
Maulds Meaburn
Milnthorpe
Natland and Oxenholme
New Hutton
Osmotherley and Mansriggs
Pennington and Swarthmoor
Pooley Bridge
Preston Patrick and Preston Richard
Rampside
Ravenstondale and Newbiggin-on-Lune
Rusland and Satterthwaite
Scales
Shap
Soulby
Stainmore
Staveley
Tebay
Torver
Troutbeck
Urswick
Warcop
Windermere

CUMBRIA CUMBERLAND

Addingham
Allonby
Alston
Armathwaite
Bassenthwaite
Beckermet
Bewcastle Bailey
Bothel and Kirkland
Brampton

Bromfield
Burgh by Sands
Caldbeck and District
Castle Carrock
Causewayhead
Cleator
Croglin
Crosby and District
Cumdivock
Dacre
Dalston
Dean
Distington
Dovenby
Drumburgh and Glasson
Eskdale and Boot
Fletchertown and District
Frizington
Gilsland
Greystoke
Hallbankgate
Hayton
Heads Nook
Hesket in the Forest
Holme St Cuthbert
Houghton
Irthington
Ivegill
Kirkoswald
Lamplugh
Lanercost
Langwathby and Edenhall
Lazonby
Linstock
Longtown
Lorton
Melmerby

Moresby
Newton Arlosh
Patterdale
Plumbland
Portinscale
Raughtonhead and District
Ravenglass
Rosley
Santon Bridge
Seascale
Seaton
Sebergham
Silecroft
Silloth
St Bees
Stainton
Thornthwaite-cum-Braithwaite
Thwaites
Waberthwaite
Warwick Bridge
Welton
Woodend and District
Wreay

Index